Lone Star Lady

LINDA KENNEDY

Published in the United States of America
ISBN 978-1-970703-08-5 (SC)
ISBN 978-1-970703-09-2 (HC)
ISBN 978-1-970703-14-6 (Ebook)

For Book Rights Adaption and other Rights Permission.
Call us at toll-free **601-914-6178**.

DEDICATION

To my grandmother's: Virgie Rose Vinsel Dennis, Myrtice Ette Williams Kennedy and their mother's and grandmother's who birthed, raised and buried their children in Texas except for a few who wondered into New Mexico by accident, I am sure. These woman survived rattlesnakes, droughts, and tornadoes. Your Kennedy grandchildren thanks you for our lives, they have been good ones.

Linda Gail Kennedy

Dona Jean Kennedy

Donald Glen Kennedy

Melvin Douglas Kennedy

Myrtice Rose Kennedy

TABLE OF CONTENTS

CHAPTER 1

Running Knife looked out at the sunrise over those red hills for the last time and headed to the wagons. She walked past the graves and the village and didn't even look at it again. She had seen enough of it yesterday.

She helped one of the women into the wagon, and a soldier asked, "Is she the woman who killed the man on the black horse?"

The other man who had led these men into their camp looked at her and just nodded.

"But she is a white woman. How could she kill a white man? We were trying to help her."

"She isn't white anymore. She is just a squaw now. She won't ever be white again. We should have just killed the lot of them."

Running Knife didn't say a word, even though she understood every word he had said. He had no idea what he was talking about. She watched him. From then on, he could be the man she needed to get home if he thought that way about her; at least he would leave her alone.

Running Knife had tried to tell White Cloud since he had brought her here that she needed to go. She had even tried to run a couple of times in the almost three years since she had been here. She had always tried to blend in, but she looked out of place. The men hunting her would have been able to pick her out of the other women if they were looking hard enough. And these men were looking hard for her and had been for a long time.

She just tried to do her chores and stay inside the village and not stray too far outside, but lately, Red Wolf wanted to be alone with her, and he kept taking her outside the village. When they were alone outside the village, she was too easy to identify as a white woman. She had to figure a way out of here. She wasn't going to marry Red Wolf. She didn't love him. White Cloud just wouldn't listen to her.

Then two weeks ago, when she was gathering wood, she had seen a child fall into the creek; and she went after her. She had saved her and got the child back to the bank. When the men got to her, she turned and looked behind her and saw two men on the hill, and she knew she had been found. White Cloud couldn't believe that anyone would kill to get her back, and she couldn't convince him otherwise.

Now look at what had happened. Everyone was dead, and she was to blame. Running Knife kept telling him to increase the guard, and he wouldn't. She could feel someone watching her. The hairs on the back of her neck were standing up, and she just knew. White Cloud had sent out scouts to look for the men and didn't find anything but tracks. White Cloud was sure they were gone. She wasn't.

When the soldiers had come this morning, Red Wolf was the first out of the tepee, and that man shot him before he was hardly outside, and then White Cloud went out. He told her to stay, but she knew these men would come in after her, so she quickly changed out of her night clothes and got into a dress. The first one she had grabbed was the wedding dress. White Cloud had insisted she make it to marry Red Wolf. She hadn't intended to wear it. She was going to disappear. She was going to find Miles. She wasn't going to marry a man she didn't love, and she didn't love Red Wolf.

When they shot White Cloud, he turned for a moment and looked at her, and then he knew she had been right all along. They would come after her. She had tried to warn him. He collapsed in front of her, and a man came after her with a knife, and she protected herself.

He slashed at her and got her left arm good, but he was careless and thought she was unarmed. White Cloud had handed her his knife before he died, and she used it on him. She thrust it into his gut and pulled up. She watched as the life drained out of him. She had blood all over her, and the man was leaning on her as she said, "Was it worth all the money you will never see?" Then she pulled the knife out of his belly and wiped it on his shirt as he slid down her dress.

She turned around and got ready for whoever was next and saw Trey staring at her. He pulled a gun, and he would have shot her if the colonel hadn't shown up about then and told him to holster the gun.

"I think this is the woman we have come after, and we need her, so put up the gun."

The man with the gun didn't care either way. He had just wanted to kill the woman he was looking at. She was dangerous. He had no idea just how dangerous she really was.

"They all need to be killed. These women are filthy Indian trash."

Morgan looked at him and then down at White Cloud and Red Wolf. They had killed everybody to get to her, and this man called her trash. Would Miles think of her that way too?

She dragged the man she had killed out of the way and sat down and pulled White Cloud's body into her lap. He was looking up at her, and she gently closed his eyes, then she cradled his head in her lap.

"I told you they would come after me, and you just wouldn't believe me." She placed his arms across his chest and just looked at his face. This was her fault, but there wasn't anything to do about it now.

She was bleeding all over her dress. Her arm needed to be bandaged. One of the soldiers came to help her up, and she brushed his hand away. She didn't want any of them touching her; she could get up by herself. As she went inside the tepee, she found some cloth to bind the wound with till she could do a better job tonight.

The soldiers were gathering up the bodies to bury tomorrow, so she went back inside. She took care of White Cloud and Red Wolf herself; she didn't want these men touching them. She wrapped each one in a blanket for burial and laid them beside the others.

She found a needle and some white thread, and after she had built a fire inside, she stitched up her arm. She didn't even feel it. She didn't feel anything right now, and she was numb to everything. The blankets were still where they were this morning. That seemed like such a long time ago. She needed to rest. She had a long way to go, and she needed to be sharp. Ramon would still be after her when he found out she was still alive.

Two Wings was standing outside her tent, and she pulled her inside and asked about her family, and she just turned and said, "They are all gone. They killed them all." That meant her son, daughter, and husband were dead, and she was all alone, and these men were responsible.

Once she was inside the tepee, she laid her down and covered her up, and she went to sleep. She just lay down next to her and went to sleep as well. Morning would be here soon, and she would start again.

She didn't say a word. She just kept quiet. She helped the other women with their children the next day and with burying the dead. The women who were left buried their families, and the soldiers just watched. The men were no help at all, even though they had done this. They had even asked, "Why were they bothering?" She could hear them talking, but they didn't think she could understand them.

The colonel was impatient to leave and kept telling the women who were left to hurry up. She was really getting mad, but she kept her mouth shut.

When everything was done, she gathered up what she had and put everything in a bag. She looked for White Cloud's rifle, but the soldiers had gathered all the guns and put them in one of the wagons. She would have to retrieve it later. She helped the women get in a wagon, and they started to leave. As they left, she looked at all the destruction and death, and she couldn't leave the village like this. They deserved better.

Running Knife got back out of a wagon, grabbed a torch, went back to the village, and started to light her tepee on fire; and one by one, the other women came behind her and burned theirs as well. Before they were done, everything was gone. They watched them burn, and she said to the women so the soldiers couldn't hear, "Don't worry. When we get to the white man's fort, I will see to it they pay. I am worth a lot of money to one white man, and I am going to make him sorry he did this to us."

The women just looked at her and went back to the wagons. Nobody ever helped an Indian woman, especially a captured white one. They didn't know about this one and how mad she was at this colonel and just how much power she really had, but they were going to find out.

They rode in the backs of the wagons for two days and stopped only at night for rest and to eat. She took care of the women and the children, and Trey heard her talk to them in Comanche, and he began to watch her. She wasn't like the rest. She even looked different from the first day. When they had stopped the day before at a river, she had seen to getting some of the women and children cleaned up before the colonel had them get back into the wagons and leave. She had blood all over her white leather dress, and he knew why.

She kept watching him, and she made him uncomfortable. He was tall and blond and very good looking, but from the way he looked at her, Morgan knew he hated her, and she didn't know why, but he would have shot her that first morning and not thought anything about it.

One of the men who had come with Trey had attacked her tepee and killed the men inside and went after her, and she killed him. He had seemed intent on killing her; the men were just in the way. He had asked the major if she was in the camp. That was why they had attacked that particular camp—to rescue her. But when Trey had seen her, Marcus was trying to kill her, and she was fighting for her life. Now he wondered why he was really there. This group of Indians had not been raiding, and they weren't hurting anyone.

That night, they settled down, and one of the soldiers was wounded in the leg. The doctor had been killed in a raid a couple of weeks ago, but they still had his bag, and they were looking through it. One of the other men was trying to take care of the wound when Trey went to look at it and told the man, "It still has the bullet in it, and it needs to come out. I guess I can try and take it out."

"Move out of my way."

Behind them stood the woman he had been watching for the past few days, and she was talking to them.

"Didn't you hear me? Get out of my way."

They did, and she got down on the ground and looked at the boy's leg, and then she pulled out a knife longer than the man's hand out of her boot and cut his pants open. One of the men reached for her, and she just said,

"Don't touch me. If I had wanted to hurt one of you, I could have done it before now. Open that bag, and let me see what is inside."

When he opened it, all the instruments were covered with blood.

"Did he ever clean them? I am going to need a pot full of water to boil them in and a bowl of clean water and some clean towels. Well, get to it. We don't have all night."

They were still looking at her because she was speaking English, but they gathered the things she needed.

The colonel showed up about this time, and he was yelling about the squaw giving orders as she washed her hands. She finally turned around and looked up at him and told him, "Stop screaming at me."

"How dare you talk to me that way? Who do you think you are?"

She looked at him and asked, "Why did you raid that Indian camp?"

He puffed out his chest and said, "We were bringing back the white women that had been captured so they could be taken back to their families."

She just looked at him and then back at the soldier she was working on as she cut open his pants some more and answered him, "No, you weren't. You were after the reward that was offered for Morganna McKinney Calderon. What is it this time? Five hundred dollars? Or has he offered more?"

The colonel looked at her and asked, "How did you know about the reward for the girl?"

She looked and him and kind of smirked. "Because I am her, and you killed a lot of people for nothing because I am going to see to it you never see a dime of that money. The reward was for me dead."

Trey looked at her. That was why Marcus was trying so hard to kill her.

Morgan looked at him and said, "This woman doesn't die that easy, and I am going to see to it you pay for killing those people. They may not go after you for killing those Indians, but they will for trying to kill me, and I am going to have your head in a noose before I am through." Then she went back to looking after the boy in front of her.

Inside the bag was a bottle of laudanum, and she gave the soldier a small bit of it as she worked on his leg. After the instruments were washed and then boiled, she took one out. "There is still material from your pants in there, and I am going to have to get that out as well, so I am going to have your friends here hold you so I can get it cleaned out. I need your boots and pants off so I can clean this up better. I am going to turn around so they can help you undress and cover you with a blanket, all right?"

The boy asked her, "Do you know what you are doing?"

She smiled at him and then said, "Actually, I do. I was the medicine woman for that tribe back there, and my white father was a doctor, so I have knowledge of both worlds."

About this time, the major intervened and said, "She could kill you too."

Morgan turned to the soldier and told him, "He is right, but if I don't do something right now, you will either be dead from the infection, or you will lose that leg by the time we get to the fort, so it is your choice."

The young man looked at her and then at his commanding officer and figured he had more of a chance with her.

"Do what you need to do. I don't want to lose my leg."

She turned around as they undressed him, and she got things ready. When she turned back around, she was drawing a crowd. She had a cup of warm coffee with laudanum and some herbs she had taken from her medicine bag, and she told him to drink it. He took it, and she looked at him and then told him, "The herbs are for the fever you already have, and the laudanum is for the pain, unless you think you want to try this without it."

He kind of looked at her funny. He didn't want the others to think he was a coward until she said, "They aren't down here with me, digging a bullet out of their legs. Drink the coffee."

She smiled at him, and he drank the coffee.

She started cleaning two days' worth of blood off his leg while the painkiller went to work, and she could see material coming out of the wound. If she was lucky, maybe the bullet wasn't too deep.

"This is a small-caliber rifle shot. Who shot you? He must have been some distance away."

The soldier kind of sheepishly looked down. "One of the little boys in the wagon over there. I really wasn't going to hurt them. I wasn't even sure why we were there. He was protecting his mother, and it was from a pretty good distance. Someone taught him pretty good. I would like to know who. Most of those men knew how to shoot quite well, and I didn't even recognize some of those rifles."

She went to work on his leg, then she got the material out and then went after the bullet, and it wasn't too deep. She got the wound cleaned up and bandaged, and the boy settled down. He was resting, and she went back to the women.

The men were told she would be back in a little while to check on him. Trey stopped her before she got back to the wagons and asked her, "Who did teach them to shoot all those rifles? There are some I have never seen before."

She turned around and looked him in the eye. "I did, the ruined squaw, the one you are so afraid of."

He grabbed her arm. "The woman I am afraid of is the one who killed that man in front of the tepee that morning."

"Then I suggest you don't make me mad. She only shows up when I am really mad. Now you can let go of me."

She spent all night with the boy, taking care of him; and by morning, the leg was much better. The boy and the men who had helped her were now on her side, and the colonel didn't like that at all. Colonel Martin stayed far away from her. He knew he shouldn't have attacked that Indian village. He had been talked into it by Marcus for the reward. Now he suspected he was going to be in trouble, and he was trying to figure out a way out of it.

Before the night was over, she had taken care of several other wounds and ailments, some of them not even too bad, just ignored by an incompetent doctor. The men began to help her with the women more, and after Trey had told them she was the one who had taught the men and that little boy how to shoot, they had even more respect for her.

She went back to the wagons, and they proceeded to the fort. She still kept to herself. The others were too scared and too grief stricken to even care and she was trying to keep everybody together. She had some sort of plan, and Trey didn't know what yet, but there was something going on in her mind.

One evening, she couldn't find one of the women, and she was frantic. She finally asked him for his help to look for her. They found Two Wings under a tree. She had gone out there and cut her wrists open and sat down to die. Morganna talked to her as she wrapped her wrists and told her it was going to be all right; she had a plan, and all the women were going with her. Two Wings listened and looked at her and begged her to stop. She couldn't take any more. Morgan pleaded with her, but she still refused, so Morgan finally stopped arguing and untied the bandages. He listened and watched as she held this woman in her arms as she died. Now the dress was covered with more blood. She was afraid this was going to happen. She had just given up. She saw it in her eyes, and she just couldn't stop her.

"No more people are going to die because of me. It stops here and now. Will you help me get these women to safety and take back what is mine? I will pay you whatever you want. I can make you a rich man, but it may be dangerous. I know what you think of me. I am Indian trash, a white woman used, and I should be thrown away, right?"

He just nodded. Whatever he thought of this woman, she was a formidable adversary. He had seen that the other morning. He went back to the camp and got a shovel, and they buried her friend under the tree where she had died.

He finally said, "You can't save them all."

She turned toward him. "Her children and husband are buried back there. You took everything from her, trying to get to me. Was it worth it?" She turned to walk away.

"What did I take from you?" He walked up behind her and grabbed her arm.

"A man I called my father after he saved my life and a man who wanted to be my husband. I would have stayed away, and my stepfather could have had it all, but no, he had to make sure I was dead, so he killed everything and everybody. Now I've stopped running, and I fight back. If he wants me dead so bad, he is going to have to do it himself. You know nothing about me or these women and what we have had to do just to stay alive. Until you do, maybe you shouldn't judge."

As she walked away, he finally figured out what the white dress and boots were. It was wedding attire, the Indian version, only this one was covered in blood. She had tried to protect her family and had almost gotten herself killed in the process, and he had brought those men into her life. He should have never taken this job.

The next day, they got to the fort. They unloaded the women like cattle into empty barracks, and she was furious. So much for trying to protect them and return them to their families. They were nothing to these people.

She started out of the door and was stopped by a guard. She stayed there for about three hours without any firewood or any food for these women and children until she had had enough. She overheard one of the guards say they were going to be moved to a reservation tomorrow for everyone's safety. Colonel Martin was covering his backside. Well, that wasn't going to work. Not in her lifetime.

She started banging on the door until a guard finally opened it to tell her to shut up, only to have a knife shoved into the middle of his belly, and all she said was "I want to see your garrison commander now."

He started walking toward the commander's office. When he got to the door, she didn't even knock. She just walked in, and she surprised Colonel Martin, who was sitting down in a chair across the commander, chatting.

The commander stood and asked her, "What exactly do you think you are doing, young lady? This is my office, the last time I looked."

She took the knife out of the young man's back and told him to go, and then she shut the door. "There are women and children across the way, freezing and starving because no one has had the decency to bring firewood or food to them after your men raided our village and killed most of the sleeping men. This man has a lot to answer for, and I want to see that he does just exactly that."

Commander Williams of the garrison stood and turned to this woman and said, "That is not the way Colonel Martin is telling the story. He says they were attacked by the Indians."

She looked at him and grinned. "Really? He attacked because he was after a reward on my head, and he thought he could collect, but I am going to see that doesn't happen, and you can ask Trey Walker what happened as well. I have hired him to guard me on my way home. He attacked a sleeping village and killed almost every living thing there. He should be court-martialed. Why don't you ask the wounded men I have been treating for several days just what happened?"

The commanding officer looked at Colonel Martin and said, "He had them all sent to town as soon as he arrived to be checked out by a proper doctor since they hadn't been treated by one on the way here. The women were supposed to be a threat, so they were to be sent to a reservation tomorrow."

"Well, isn't that convenient? As for the women, if you had bothered to go check on them yourself, you would see women broken by sorrow and grief and starving children in a freezing building, and that, sir, is unforgivable on your part."

Morgan took a seat in a chair by the door. The colonel was getting very uncomfortable.

"Why was he after you?"

"There is a reward for me. I am Morganna McKinney Calderon."

"I thought you were dead."

"Not yet. My stepfather wants me to be so he can inherit my land and horses, so the reward gets bigger every year. Ask your Colonel Martin how much it is this year. The last I knew, it was five hundred."

Commander Williams looked at Colonel Martin and said, "If any of this is true, she is right. You are in serious trouble."

He didn't even answer, and Commander Williams called for a guard to escort him out of the room. "What do your women need? I will have it brought to them immediately."

"Blankets, food, and firewood. It is freezing in there, and I need to get to a telegraph. I need to send a message to Dallas. I need to get some clothes for these women, and I need Trey here to help me organize this."

"He went to town. I don't know when he will be back or if he is coming back."

Well, maybe he was lying about helping her.

After she had things under control in the barracks, Trey was back with a horse for her to ride so they could go to town. "I figured you would need some things, and Commander Williams said you needed to use a telegraph."

"Thank you. I will repay you."

She pulled herself up on the back of the horse, and they headed to town. As they rode through town, she was getting a lot of looks and not for the better.

"Let's go to the telegraph and start getting some money sent this way. We are going to need it. Do you have any money we can use to pay for wire transfers that I can repay you?"

He nodded, so they went into the office, and she was promptly told to get out.

"I need to send a wire to the law offices of Burk and McKinney in Dallas, Texas."

She was again told to get out and that they didn't wait on squaws. Trey stood up at the counter and grabbed the man by the collar and told him the lady asked nicely and that he would send her wire. "Now get to it."

The man sent the wire, and it said,

Gary Lee Burk. This is Morganna McKinney. I am alive, and I need money. Lots of it. Get back to me soon. I am waiting. STOP

They sent the wire, and she sat down and waited. If they were in the office, she would be hearing soon. Somebody would be breaking a leg to get to the telegraph office to see if it was really her.

Sure enough, somebody was in the office. It wasn't but about ten minutes before they were on the line. The operator on this end was ready to throw them out when the machine started to click.

Morgan, is it really you? Prove it. Gary Lee. STOP
"Thank God. It's Gary Lee. Send this message back to him."

You have a three-inch scar on your butt that you got in Palo Duro Canyon with me when we were ten years old. My dad stitched it up. STOP
Where the hell are you, how much money do you need, and when are you coming home? STOP

"Where are we, and do you have a bank?"
"You are in Denver, Colorado."
"Can you give him the information when we are through?"
He nodded again.

This man will give you the information you need. Send me five thousand for now, and I am heading home. Don't tell anyone who doesn't need to know. STOP

He is still looking for you. Please be careful. STOP
Is my ranch still mine? STOP
Is now that I know you are alive. STOP
Sending women to it. Have grandpa waiting for them. STOP
Will take care of it. Virgie and Miles are in Steamboat Springs, Colorado. Love, Gary. STOP

The man at the counter asked for a name to end the conversation with, and she just answered him, "He knows. How long will it take before the money is in the bank?"

"I can have a letter of credit ready pretty quickly. If you want to go to the bank, I will meet you there."

"Want to go see if we can get thrown out of a bank?"

She smiled at him. It was the first time she had ever smiled at him. She was starting to enjoy this.

As they walked across town, she was getting looks from everybody, and she turned back and asked him, "If you want to walk a little further behind, you can. I can do this by myself. It won't be the first time."

He started to wonder just how many times she had to do things by herself if she had that much money on her head as a reward.

She walked into the bank, and sure enough, men were meeting her at the door, and several other men were trying to show her out when the man from the telegraph came in and talked to the banker. His eyes lit up instantly, and he showed her to a chair—a wood one, of course. They could wash that one when she left. She could hardly blame him. She looked like death warmed over.

Now he was all peaches and cream. He made her sick, but this was how the game was played, and she was going to have to learn how to play again. He told her she could have some of the money now and the rest later when it was verified in Dallas.

She said she needed to buy some clothes and things right now, so she needed about fifteen hundred dollars. The man almost had a stroke. He couldn't imagine what a woman who looked like she did now could use that much money for, and she didn't intend to tell him. He gave her the money, and she walked outside and counted out five hundred and gave it to Trey. "Is this satisfactory for now, for the horses, and for a down payment for your services? If it isn't, tell me now."

"It is more than enough for the whole job."

"It won't be. I will owe you more before we are through."

Then she walked toward the general store and went inside. The owner was starting to object, but she was ignoring him as she picked out what she needed. She bought several dresses and small clothes for the children then shoes, blankets, and hairbrushes. Then she bought pants, a vest, a shirt, and a long coat for herself. When she was through, she told them to get it all together and she would be back for it.

She told Trey to go buy a covered wagon and put everything in it and get some horses to pull it. She would be back in a little while to pay for them. She told him to get anything he would need and plenty of ammunition. "I will pick out a pistol and rifle when I get back. They don't have a very good selection, but I will find something."

She went over to the hotel and went inside and asked for a room and a bath. Out came the manager.

"We don't let squaws sleep here."

"First of all, I am not a squaw, and second of all, I don't want to sleep here. It is a dump. All I want is a bath, and I am willing to pay twice the usual rate for a hot bath."

His eyes bugged out at that.

"Good move, and I want hot, clean water, and I want it now."

She went upstairs and had her first hot bath in a long time, and when she was through, she dressed, brushed her long hair, put on her clean shirt and tight vest, and looked in the mirror. She carefully folded the white leather dress and carried it under her arm, and then she went downstairs. She wasn't the same woman who had gone up those stairs. Now she was Morganna McKinney.

She walked to the counter and asked the man there, "Do you have a bag I can put this in?"

He just looked at her, stunned. He didn't realize it was the same woman. "Yes, ma'am. I have one right here."

He handed her the bag. She put the dress inside, and she walked out the door and down the steps.

Trey was waiting for her with the wagon, and he didn't recognize her either. This wasn't the Indian woman of this morning. This was Morganna McKinney Calderon. No wonder she hid.

"We need to get started. He will know soon that I am alive, and he will send men after me again. I want to get the women on the way home to my ranch in Amarillo with some men you can trust, and we will go a different way. They will be safer if we aren't with them. I have to write some letters and get them sent to my grandfather and my cousin and get them in the mail so they will know what to do when these women get there. Also, I need to set up an account for my grandfather with money for the ranch in case I don't arrive alive."

He looked at her and realized she had been running for so long, she didn't know any other way to live. She was right. He didn't know what she or any of these women had done to stay alive.

When they got back to the fort, she saw Colonel Martin was in Commander William's office, and she went there after she had left the things she had bought at the barracks. When she walked in, he looked at her with such hate in his eyes. She smiled. He was in a great deal of trouble, and she was the cause.

Commander Williams asked her then, "Will you press charges against him for the attack against you and the others?"

"Yes, I will. I know the army won't take issue with him killing Indians, but they will with him trying to kill me, won't they? Especially for a reward?"

He just nodded, and she knew she had him. She walked over to him and quietly told him. "Maybe I will watch you hang before this is over."

And she smiled as he was escorted out in handcuffs. She knew he probably wouldn't ever see any justice because she would have to testify, and she probably wouldn't live that long. He would sweat a while anyway, and that was something.

"I am going to take the women as soon as they can travel in the next few days, and we are heading to Texas."

The commander looked at her and at Trey and said to them both, "I found out some things after you left today. Your stepfather is still looking for you, and there is still a reward out on your head. Now the price is twelve hundred dollars, and there are men who will hunt you down for less than that. Don't you want to stay here? You will be safe."

"I haven't been safe anywhere for four years now, and I won't be until I settle this with him. The women will travel a different route than us, and maybe I can get home this time. Thanks for the warning."

The commander looked over her head at Trey and wondered about how safe she was with this man. He knew how he felt about women who had been captured. Maybe he should tell her.

She sent Trey out to get the wagon, and he caught her before she left and asked if he could talk to her.

"What would you like to talk to me about, commander?"

He couldn't look her in the eye, and she knew she was making him very uncomfortable. "I don't know how much you know about the man you have going with you, but maybe you should rethink your choice."

She looked at him and said, "Maybe you should explain."

"His younger sister was taken by the Apaches and was kept for two years, and when he got her back, she wasn't right. He didn't find out until later that she had had a baby by one of the braves and wanted to go back, and he wouldn't let her. She finally escaped and got back to her child, and he never forgave her for wanting to live with him instead of wanting to be a white woman again."

"Where is she now? Is she still with her child and husband?"

He looked down at the floor, and when he looked up at her again, she already knew. "She was with Geronimo's tribe, and most of them had starved when he made his run into Mexico, but she wouldn't leave her baby and husband, and she died with them."

So now she knew why he wanted them all dead, to him they already were.

"The way we are treated by most white men after we are with Indian men—we might as well stay with our Indian husbands because we will never be accepted into white society again."

He just had to ask, "Did you have an Indian husband?"

"No, but he has never asked. He just assumes I am ruined in his mind."

"Why don't you tell him? It would make things easier for you."

She smiled at him. "No, it would make things easier for him. He has to make up his own mind about me one way or the other. I want to see if he can see beyond his own prejudice and guilt."

Trey walked back into the room, and he could see they had been talking. She was smiling at Commander Williams, and then she said goodbye. She walked by him and out the door, and the older man told him, "Take care of her, Trey."

He turned his head and looked back at her and said, "She seems to take pretty good care of herself." Then he followed her outside.

She still wore the Indian boots she had worn from the first day. He wondered why she hadn't bought new boots at the store, and she said she liked the ones she had on. Well, you never could change their minds once they were set on something. They were of pretty white leather, and they went all the way up her legs to her knees with silver Conchos down the side. She tucked her pants down inside them, and you could see her coming down the street. She didn't care if the attention she was getting was bad or not let them look.

They left the next day. Trey had found three men he could trust to take the women to Amarillo to her ranch, and she had gotten the rest of her money and paid them. They had money for supplies and ammunition. She had sent the letters to her grandfather with instructions for repairs and for purchasing livestock. He would know what to do. She also sent one to Gary in Dallas, telling him she would be coming home and would contact him again soon and a few other things no one else needed to know but him.

They headed in another direction toward New Mexico, away from the wagon, a little farther around with a bit more cover. They rode, almost never talking. He didn't want to know any more about her than he needed to.

They camped out on the trail at night. She stayed on one side of the camp, and he stayed on the other. He was doing his best to ignore her, but it wasn't working. She would catch him watching her, and sometimes she would wake and find him staring at her. She would roll over and go back to sleep and let him wonder.

He awoke one night to find her gone, and he went looking for her. She was not far off at a small bend in the creek, washing, and he stood very still and just watched her. He told himself it was to protect her, but he knew he was lying.

When she was through, she dressed, sat down, and put her head on her knees, and he could hear her softly crying. She wiped her eyes, stood up, turned around, walked back to the camp, and went to bed, and then she said. "Good night, Trey."

He rose up and looked at her. She had known he was there all the time and never said a word. He lay back down and went to sleep. He didn't acknowledge that she said anything.

The next day, they came to a town of decent size, and she suggested they stay at the hotel for the night. He just nodded—at least he could get a shave and a bath—and as they went by a certain house, he thought he could get some female companionship. Morgan noticed this as well. Obviously, she wasn't considered decent enough for a companion. She was still a used squaw. She didn't really care. He wasn't who she wanted, but she had hoped the man she wanted still wanted her. Guess she was fixing to find out.

They walked into the general store and started to pick up a few items and supplies when a beautiful, older, dark-haired woman walked in. Morgan wasn't paying much attention, but Trey was, and he said to the man next to him. "She must own the house down the street."

The man answered with a smile on his face. "Yes, sir, she has the best girls in this part of the state."

About that time, Morgan smelled the lady's perfume, and she turned and looked at the woman behind her. Gary had told her Virgie was here, and she had found her.

The man at the counter was making it obvious he was not waiting on her first, but at the back of his store, he was proudly displaying a Confederate flag. He came over to Morgan and asked if he could help her, making sure the other woman was bypassed.

"The other lady was in front of me."

Then the man said to Morgan, "She is no lady. She runs the bordello. She can wait."

Morgan walked over to the lady and stood in front of her and just smiled at her and said, "I love the smell of your perfume. A friend of mine used to wear the same kind."

The lady looked at her and smiled as she stood there and began to cry. "It was made special for me in Paris." Tears were falling down her face as she looked at Morgan.

"My friend said the same thing. She told me she would get me some the next time she went to Paris, but the war came, and she didn't get to go back. My friend had a large plantation outside of New Orleans. My mother and I would go to visit her, and then we would go to Natchez and buy dresses. We always had the best time."

By now, Morgan was leaning against the counter. Everybody was listening to this story, and the woman was still smiling at Morgan. It was obvious they knew each other. The woman watched Morgan. She looked at her like she was looking at a ghost as tears streamed down her face.

"This plantation was one of the biggest around, and some of General Sherman's men came down and told her they were confiscating the house and all the cotton. This woman said after they left, she would burn it before she let him have it. The night before General Sherman was to come and claim it, she freed all the slaves, told them to take anything they wanted, and then gave them each a torch. She threw the first one into the house, and they watched it burn. They said it took two days, and you could see the fire from New Orleans. She burned the cotton, the barns, and everything she had to the ground. General Sherman was furious. He wanted her hanged, and he put a reward on her head, but they didn't find her. You lost it all. Was it worth it, Virgie?"

The woman was still smiling at her. "It took three days to burn out, and the only thing better would have been if Sherman himself was sitting in the parlor. Where have you been, my sweet Morgan?"

As the two women embraced, Morgan turned and told the man behind the counter, "You think so much of that flag? Look at a lady who gave up her whole world for the damn thing."

She turned back around and hugged her friend again and whispered in her ear, "Can I come see you tonight? I will come by the back door. I need to ask you something. Is Miles here?"

Virgie looked at her and the man with her and nodded.

"Is he married?"

"Lord, no, girl. He is still waiting for a fifteen-year-old girl from Texas to come back to him."

Before she left, she turned around and told the man behind the counter, "Now wait on this *lady*. She gave up more than you ever did for your precious Confederate Army." She looked at Virgie again. "Don't tell him. I want it to be a surprise. I will see you tonight."

Trey just watched as she walked away. He would never understand this woman.

Morgan got her supplies and left to go to the hotel. She got two adjoining rooms and went to hers and called for a bath. Trey came up behind her and came to her room. He looked at her funny. He was seeing a different woman every time he looked at her lately. Sometimes it was all he could do to keep his hands off her.

"Will you be all right tonight? I thought I would go out for a while."

She just nodded. She was going out too, and she figured it was to the same place, though not for the same reason. "Do you need money, or do you have enough? Virgie's is probably expensive."

He looked at her strangely; she always seemed to know what he was going to do most of the time before he did.

"How did you know where I was going?"

"I am aware I am not good enough for you. Virgie's is the next best thing, isn't it?"

"I should have plenty of money for tonight."

He turned to go, and she slammed the door as he left. She was mad, and she didn't even know why, but she just was.

After she had bathed and dressed, she went downstairs. She had picked up a new blouse and pants that fit like a glove with a silver Concho belt and a bustier that cinched in her waist, and she hadn't bothered to button very many buttons tonight. Her hair was brushed and hanging down her back, just like he always liked it. She even put on a little lipstick, just a little. Miles didn't like it when she wore a lot, so she just wore a little soft pink. She had on her white leather boots with the conchos up the sides. They were her Indian boots. She knew Miles wouldn't mind, and she knew she looked good in them.

The looks she was getting from the men in the hotel told her she looked good even in the boots and pants. Two of the men in the downstairs parlor even got up and asked if she would join them for dinner. She told them,

"Thank you, but no, I have other plans for tonight."

As she walked down the street, she turned a few more heads until she went behind Virgie's house, where she couldn't be seen anymore. She was way too easy a target on the street. She wanted to see Miles, and she wanted to look good, not like the fifteen-year- old girl he had left in Amarillo, Texas. That girl was long gone. She had died somewhere along the way just trying to survive. She wasn't even sure Miles would want this woman anymore. She was going to find out tonight.

When she got to Virgie's back door, she knocked, and it was opened by a small black girl she didn't recognize.

"Mama Ruby, there is some gal here. Want me to tell her we ain't hiring?"

Another voice from inside yelled, "Ivy, tell her go away. We can't feed no more. We got enough."

"But, Mama Ruby, I don't eat much. I promise I won't."

All she could hear was breaking glass and running feet, and the next thing she knew, an old black woman was at the door, and she was crying.

"It is you. I would know that voice when I am cold in my grave. Virgie said you were here. I thought for sure Ramon had killed you."

"Not yet, Mama, not yet, but he is still trying to."

She walked up the steps and was almost crushed by the old woman. She held her in her arms, even though she was almost a head taller than the old woman was. Then she took her face in her hands and told her, "Still the same good-looking woman. Mama, you will never get older."

The older woman hugged her again. She didn't want to let her go. Morgan just held her to her chest. It was so good to see her again.

"We heard so many times that you were dead, and we didn't know what to believe, but you are here, and you are safe. Gary Lee got hold of us and told us they had found you but not where you were."

"He told me where y'all were, so I came to you. That way, not so many people can find me. I am here, Mama, and I am safe for a while. Can I go out front? Is Miles here, Mama?" She looked at her.

"After today in the store, you can do whatever you want. They treat Virgie like she is royalty now, you little devil. He is here. He almost died when they said you were dead. She didn't tell him you were here. She said you would want to."

The younger woman Ivy said, "He told the men he was going to quit early tonight and go riding. He may already be gone."

Morgan looked at the older woman, and she looked almost broken. "Oh no, Mama, he can't be gone. Not tonight. I have waited too long."

"Go check, girl, quick, and come back and tell us."

Morgan was in a panic, but Ivy came back and said he was still playing.

"Mama, take him a glass of the bourbon he likes, and ask him to have the guys play the song I used to sing, and we will surprise him."

"He hasn't let them play that song since they said you were dead. He won't let them play it tonight."

"He will for you, Mama, and I will sing if you can get them to play it. Please, Mama."

The old woman quickly poured the glass half full of the bourbon he liked, and she took it out to Miles personally but not before Morgan took a sip. As Morgan watched, she talked to him. Mama was practically begging, with him shaking his head.

Morgan walked out of the kitchen to the end of the stairs, and a man was walking down and stopped in front of her and looked her up and down. "I don't know what you get for a night, but I will double it."

She looked at him and then answered, "You don't have that much money." And then she walked right past him as she looked around the room.

There were women sitting and lounging in chairs and on couches, and there were men—always men. She saw Trey with a woman on his lap across the room, but he didn't see her. It was Sheri; she always did like blond men.

Miles was at the piano. Lord, he was as handsome as ever, tall and dark-haired, and she could still see those dark blue eyes. She still dreamed of those eyes. He finally smiled at Mama Ruby and told the band to play the song she had requested. He didn't want to, but Mama talked him into it.

Morgan leaned against the wall behind a sheer curtain, and then she started to sing softly at first, and the place began to get quiet as they heard her singing. He continued with his drink as he looked around to see who was singing, and most of the other people in the room were looking at her. The room got quieter as she sang, and the man at the stairs stopped and turned around and just watched her. Her voice was beautiful, and the song was one he had never let them play anymore because they had only played it for Morgan.

He looked up at Mama Ruby, and she was holding a cloth over her mouth and crying. He turned and looked up the stairs at Virgie, and she was crying too. He looked at Mama again, and she just nodded. The woman at the store they were all talking about today. Then he noticed the pink lipstick on his glass. Nobody ever touched his glass but Morganna. She was here somewhere.

He started looking around the room, and then he saw the Indian boots and started walking over to the woman standing behind the curtain. When he saw her, she started to stop singing, and he shook his head. She stood there and finished the song, standing in front of him with the whole room watching and most of the upstairs area as well. He had put his arms on both sides of her shoulders on the wall and was just standing there till she finished. It was dead quiet in the room.

"Hello, cowboy, it is good to see you. I didn't know if I ever would again."

He was still staring at her like she wasn't real. "My god, little girl, you are no little girl anymore. You came back to me? I have wanted to do this since you were fifteen years old."

He put his arms around her, and he kissed her like she had never been kissed before, like a man kisses a woman he wants. He could taste the bourbon in her mouth.

"Your mama hated it when you sipped out of my glass. Do you still remember how to dance?"

She smiled at him and answered, "I haven't danced with anyone since the night you left the ranch."

He pulled her out on the floor, and the people moved aside to give them some room, and he pulled her left arm behind her and nodded to the band. They knew which song to play.

She put her other arm around his back, and he put his hand in her hair and laid her head on his shoulder. They started to two steps slowly around the room.

He whispered to her, "You know the words. Sing to me."

And she did quietly sing the song. They both knew the lyrics. They were for lovers, and she had sung them for him before he left the last time, and he wanted to hear them now. He held her so close, you couldn't see in between them as he took her around the room.

As she sang, she started to cry. She had been so alone for so long, and now she was falling apart. Virgie was watching at the rail above, and she could see what Miles couldn't.

Finally, Morgan asked him, "Please get me out of here. No more."

He finally realized she was crying, and he took her hand and headed to the staircase. As many of the people in the room clapped, she just hid her face and followed him.

Trey couldn't believe this was the same woman he had watched kill a man in the village that morning. This beautiful woman couldn't be the same woman. She even looked different.

Miles looked at her again and said, "I am sorry. Come with me. This is much too public for what I want to say to you."

A man they passed said, "I will give you a thousand for the night."

Miles laughed and looked down at her. "How much are you worth now? Fifty times that or more?"

She shrugged at him. "Probably more than that. I don't even know." As she looked at the man standing in front of her, she replied, "I really don't need your money or you."

As she walked upstairs, Trey watched another man grab her and ask her how much for the night, and he reached to kiss her as well.

Trey was there this time and pulled him off her. "She doesn't need your money. Leave her alone. She is not one of the house girl's."

Trey walked with them upstairs and asked her how long she was going to be and she told him probably a long time. "You might as well go back to the hotel or whatever."

He told her he would wait downstairs for her. She figured he would find Sheri and entertain himself.

Virgie was watching, and when she got to her room, she asked her, "Who is he?"

"My bodyguard when he isn't insulting me. He barely knows I am alive. He thinks I am a ruined squaw, and that's when he is nice to me."

"I think he knows you are alive now as well as most of the other men here. He doesn't know you are a virgin, does he?"

She just looked at her. "How do you know?"

"My dear that is my business besides, I have known you since you were eight years old. You still shine from the inside out, and he should be able to see that. Everybody else can. Why do you think that man offered you all that money tonight? Even he knew. While you two were dancing, he came up here to me. He was furious. Miles was even touching you, much less kissing you. He offered me a fortune for you. Keep that man of yours close. He still wants you."

Miles was listening to this conversation, and he wasn't happy about the fact that the other man wanted her so badly. Justin Winters was not nice to some of the women here. He figured he could always buy what he wanted. So far, he always had. He had been around her only a few minutes, and he still felt the same way he did years ago, and she had been a child then. He hoped she felt the same about him, but they couldn't talk now. Maybe later he knew he didn't want anybody but him to ever touch her again.

"I need something from you, Virgie. Maybe you have it maybe not. Remember the dress you and Mama had made in Natchez years ago? The emerald green dress with the ruffles in the front?"

Virgie looked at her and smiled. "The one she wore to the ball at my house right after she married your stepfather."

"Yes. He had her portrait painted in it, and it was at the top of the stairs when I was taken. I am hoping it is still there. You had one made that looked a lot like it, didn't you?"

"Yes, they were almost identical. Why?"

"When I go back, I would like to wear it down those stairs in front of that portrait and dare him to say I am not her daughter. Do you still have the dress?"

Virgie grinned and went to the closet and started pulling out clothes, and then out came an emerald green dress. She laid it on the bed. "It is a little outdated, but I think with a little altering, we can make it work. Where are you staying?"

"I am at the local hotel down the block."

"Miles take her man and go get their things and bring it over here. This will take some time, and I want her here where nobody can get at her. If her man doesn't want to come, he can stay there. They are still hunting you, aren't they?"

She just nodded. Miles left the room and went to find her man who he had found out was named Trey. He had been with Sheri but was now just watching the upstairs rooms.

"We need to go get Morgan's things and yours as well from the hotel. Virgie wants her here until she finishes what she has to do here."

Trey looked at him and then back at the rooms and kind of smirked and asked, "How long are we going to be here? Are there that many men she needs to bed?"

Miles wanted to take his head off. If this was what he thought of Morgan, why did she have him around her at all? "If you would rather stay at the hotel, I can take care of Morganna myself. She would probably be safer with me anyway."

Trey looked at him and remembered how he had kissed her. She had probably already slept with him too. He was drunk and nasty, and he was pushing the wrong man tonight. Miles wouldn't put up with his mouth when it came to Morgan.

"No, I have been paid to watch over her. I am still on the payroll."

He said it with a smirk on his face. God how he wanted to hit this man. Everything that came out of his mouth about Morgan was an insult.

They went out the door and down the street to the hotel and up to the rooms. Miles packed in Morgan's room, but when he came to the bag with the leather dress in it, he pulled it out and looked at it. It was a beautiful dress. He had seen enough ceremonial dresses in his time with his wife to know a wedding dress when he saw one, but this one was covered with blood. She was going to wed someone in a Comanche wedding dress, and he assumed she hadn't. He would ask her later.

Trey came in about then and told him, "You had better put that back. She is very proud of it. She was going to marry an Indian, but he got killed. I think she was lucky. She has a different idea on the subject. I don't know why she would want to be someone's squaw."

He walked out of the room. He didn't know how lucky he was. Miles was ready to cut his throat right then and there. His wife had been Comanche, and white men had killed her and left him for dead.

They walked back in silence, and it was all Miles could do not to kill this man. When they got back inside, he went straight to Virgie's room and took Morgan aside. He still had the bag in his hand, and his knuckles were white. He was holding it so tight. He just lifted it up and handed it to her.

She sat down on the bed and pulled the dress out. "Beautiful, isn't it? I made it with my own hands. It took me weeks to make. It only took me a few minutes to ruin it."

Miles put his hand under her chin and looked at her. "Tell me."

She took a deep breath and then started to tell him what happened. "Ramon sold me to the Comancheros, and they were supposed to kill me and leave my body behind so Ramon could inherit my land and money. My supposed kidnapping was nothing more than a job for Ramon. He left the ranch unguarded and took the girls so they could raid it and take me.

"Their leader didn't kill me though. He thought he could get more money for me in Mexico in a brothel because he suspected I was a virgin. Then he decided he wanted me for himself. About a week later, we met up with a bunch of Comanche warriors who they had a gun deal with. When they met up with the Comancheros, they had a disagreement over guns, and the chief wanted more guns for his money. Instead, he took me for payment. When I tried to run, he realized I was not just a little white girl who gave up on anything. I was a fighter, and he kept me for his son and kept the other men away from me."

She looked at him and turned the dress over in her hands. "When his son Red Wolf saw me, he wanted me for a bride, not just a slave, so we were to wed. I didn't want to marry him, so I kept stalling, but Chief White Cloud finally made me make the dress. Trey and the soldiers came and killed everybody in the camp except some of the women and me. One of the men Ramon hired came after me. I was in my dress, and I got his blood all over it. Red Wolf tried to help, but he shot him first and then White Cloud."

Miles looked at her. "You killed him."

She pulled a large knife out of her boot that he hadn't seen before and showed it to him. "I gutted him after he cut me." She said it with such calm; it scared him.

"Where did he cut you?"

She pointed to a spot on her arm. He unbuttoned her shirt and pulled down the sleeve then took off the shirt she had on. He took off the bandage on her arm. Someone had flayed open her arm and it had been stitched up, but it was still bleeding in spots.

"Who stitched it up, Morgan?" he asked, even though he knew the answer.

"I did later that day after we buried the dead."

Virgie was at the door and had heard most of what was said. "I will get clean water, and we will rebind her arm." Then she turned and left.

Miles pulled the shirt up over her shoulder and laid her head on his shoulder and just let her breathe. The tears were all long gone, so he just held her. He knew right then and there she wasn't going home alone. He was going with her. He had wanted her since she was fifteen years old, and after that kiss, he was going to try and convince her she needed him as well.

Virgie came back in with the water, and they cleaned up the arm. It was infected in a spot or two, so they put some salve Virgie had on it.

He couldn't imagine how she had stitched it closed herself with no painkiller, but she had done a fair job.

"No one was there to help you?" he finally asked as he rewrapped the arm.

"Everybody was just trying to cope with all the deaths around them and take care of the children. I was the least of their problems." She just watched as he finished the bandage, and he watched her. The stitching was done with white thread, so she had used the same thread she had used on her dress. She had on a bustier under her shirt like the women here wore under theirs, and he didn't like it. He didn't want her to look or act like the women here. She wasn't like them. He would get her some other undergarments tomorrow at the general store.

Virgie came back in with a nightgown and told Miles she could sleep in here, and she needed to get some sleep. Virgie helped her dress and then said to her, "He loves you and has loved you since you were a child. You know that, don't you? When we heard you were dead, I thought he was going to go and kill your stepfather himself. He even contacted your cousin Gary Lee in Dallas, trying to get information on you. He never gave up hope you were alive. Do you have any feelings for him?"

She turned and looked at Virgie and told her, "I haven't had time in my life to love anyone. I am not sure I know how. I just knew I needed to try and get back to you and him, even if it was just for a little while."

"You know how. You just have to let someone in." She kissed her on the head and walked out the room, and Morgan went to bed and slept for the first time in a long time without her knife under her head.

Hours later, she woke, quietly opened the door, walked to the end of the hall, and looked out the window at the sun starting to rise.

Miles had heard her door and came up behind her and put his arms around her. She tensed up to run at first then remembered where she was and relaxed and leaned back against him.

"It's early. What are you doing up?"

She didn't say anything and just stood there and looked out the window. He took her hand and led her up a small flight of stairs to a small room where there was a small sofa and large windows looking out over the town.

"I come up here and watch the sun come up when I can't sleep." He sat her beside him, and she lay across him with her head on his shoulder and cried.

"Sometimes all I hear in my sleep is screaming and my sisters calling for me, and I can't get to them. I am so afraid he will hurt them and I will be too late and all I will hear is more screaming."

She put her hands over her ears, and he held her in his arms until she shook so bad, he could hardly hold her, and then he took her hands away from her ears and said to her, "Listen, Morganna, no screams. They are all in your mind. You are not too late for your sisters."

She looked at him, and then he kissed her again, and this time, she kissed back. She wrapped her arms around him. She told herself it was just for a little while.

He pulled her into him. He was twelve years older than she was, but he wanted her anyway, and he hoped she wanted him. He pulled her into his lap and kissed down her neck and drew her into him. He was holding her so tight, she could hardly breathe.

"I asked your mother if I could marry you before we left all those years ago. Did you know that?"

Morgan looked up at him and said to him, "No, she never told me."

"She told me no. I was on the run with Virgie from General Sherman's men, and you wouldn't be safe, so I left. Also, I am older than you."

She smiled at him and put her hand on the side of his face and stroked across his cheek and lips. "I never cared about your age, and the way things turned out, I probably would have been safer with you. I've always felt safe with you."

"I love you, and I have loved you since you were fifteen, but Virgie says you may not feel the same way about me."

"Have you not looked at the sign on my head? It says, 'Love this woman and you die.' I don't want you to be a casualty of my stepfather's greed as well, so stay far away from me. You will live longer."

He kissed her again, more deeply this time. "You didn't answer the question."

"Don't make me leave loving you. It will be too hard, and I will have to leave soon. The longer I stay, the more risk I put you all in. Just leave it like this."

As he again squeezed her so tight she couldn't breathe, he told her, "You don't leave without me this time. I can't live not knowing whether you are alive or dead. So you might as well admit it. You love me too. I saw your face tonight when you sang to me."

"God help us, I do love you. Now what do we do?"

He just held her. "We will figure it out from here, but you aren't alone anymore."

They just sat there and watched the sun rise as someone else watched them from below.

Virgie had heard something and had gone to see what was going on. When she saw the door open to the roof, she quietly walked up. When she was about halfway up, she saw him holding her across his lap, her head on his shoulder and her hand on his chest. He smiled at her, really smiled, and she hadn't seen him do that in so many years, maybe since he had seen Morgan as a girl. He was wiping away tears from her eyes, and she remembered the last time she had watched him hold a woman like that. It was when they had found him holding Gray Dove on the porch of their ranch and when the place was burning to the ground.

Quantrill's men had raided the ranch, shot and killed Gray Dove, and shot him then torched the ranch. He had married a Comanche woman, and that made him an outcast. They had to knock him out and drag him off the porch and carry her off before it all came down on top of them. Sometimes she thought he would never forgive her for saving him until he saw Morganna, and then he had finally found something to live for again. He had run her plantation for her until they had to run from General Sherman's men, and they took refuge at the ranch of Morgan's mother in Amarillo, Texas.

From the time he first saw Morgan, he loved her. He never touched her, but he never let any other man touch her either. Virgie saw what was happening, as did Morgan's mother, Shannon, but neither knew what to do about it. Morgan was drawn to him, and he was a perfect gentleman. He was even willing to wait a few years for her to be older.

When they were found and started to run again, it was Morgan who led the soldiers away from them till they could get away, and it was all they could do to get Miles to even come with them. They didn't know until later that Morgan told him to go. He would be safer away, and she would see him again.

He hadn't forgiven Virgie or Morgan's mother for not letting him take Morgan with him because it was a little over a year later that she was taken by the Comancheros. He still hadn't forgiven himself for not being there. Virgie was going to have to get someone else to play the piano because he was never going to let her go again. Even if Morgan didn't love him, he would never let her out of his sight. From the look of the woman in his lap, this had already been decided and in his favor. Good for him and for her. They were meant to be together.

"You two need some more sleep. The nights are long around here, and we can't start on the dress for a few more hours. We will work on that dress today, and you can rest until you have to leave. Abigail will do the alterations."

"Wonderful. She is the best. I am glad she is here."

As they walked past her, she stopped Miles and told him, "Justin Winters sent a note we need to talk about later." He was the man who had offered Morgan all that money last night. What did he want from her now?

He continued on past Virgie, got Morgan to her bedroom, shut the door, laid her down on the bed, held her, and kissed her like nobody had ever done. He kissed down her neck and the tops of her breasts, and then he stopped. He realized he was about to start something he was not going to be able to stop, and from the way she was looking at him, she didn't want to stop either.

He quickly got off the bed and was about to leave when she asked him, "Why did you stop? Don't you want me either?"

From the way she had asked, he turned to find she was almost in tears, and he said, "More than anything, but I want it to be more than a quick tumble in the morning. I want it to be something you remember, and you are inexperienced in this."

She just looked at him and turned over in bed and didn't say anything else, and he left the room. He didn't understand the things that had been said to her for so long. She thought he found her as distasteful as Trey did. He didn't understand how badly he had just hurt her feelings.

When he saw her later as she was trying on the dress, he didn't understand but she was different. She had buried the girl from last night, and the hard woman was back in place. The woman you couldn't hurt, who only knew how to survive, was here now. Even Virgie couldn't understand what had happened.

Virgie took him aside and asked him what had happened this morning, and he told her, and she almost hit him.

"You idiot. You start to make love to her, and then you stop? All that man of hers has said to her for days is that she is ruined and that no decent man will have her."

"He says that to her?"

Virgie told him that the first day, he said they should have killed them all. They would never be white women again. They were ruined. Miles wanted to kill that man again, but he had done worse. He had left her thinking he didn't want her. She wouldn't even look at him, much less talk to him. She tried to avoid him all day. She made sure she was not around him. She was in the kitchen with Mama Ruby or with Abigail, the dressmaker, but she wouldn't even look up when he came to the door.

When she was alone with Abigail, she asked her, "Abigail, I need something special in this dress that only you and I can know about. Will you help me with it?"

Abigail looked up at her and then nodded.

"I need a pocket on the right side right here so I can put a small derringer in it, but nobody can be able to see the gun, so it has to be hidden very well. Do you think you can do that for me? We can use some of this extra material from the ruffles to make the pocket."

Abigail looked at the extra material and where she wanted the pocket, and then she looked at her. "I wondered how you were going to walk down those stairs and not get killed, and now I know."

"I am not positive I won't get killed, but it will at least give me a chance."

"I will make sure you have more than a chance. No one will know but us."

Then they smiled at each other and went right on working on that dress.

When the night trade came in, she disappeared, and no one knew where she went to. Miles was in a panic. He was afraid she had gone outside. She was so mad at him, and she was at risk outside these walls. She was just a target outside.

Miles went looking for her and found her in the little tower room all by herself. When he came in, she got up to leave, and he stopped her.

"Please sit back down. I need to talk to you and apologize. I started something this morning and then stopped it, and you think I did it for the wrong reason."

She wouldn't look at him, and she wouldn't talk to him. She just looked straight ahead into the night. He started to put his arms around her, and she moved away. He pulled her to him, but she was stiff, and he could see he had hurt her feelings badly.

"Look at me, Morgan. I want to make love to you, but I want to have the time to do it slowly and not hurt you. I want you to enjoy our time together, and that wouldn't have been this morning. That doesn't mean I don't want you. Look at me, Morganna Linn. You are still the most stubborn woman I have ever met."

She finally smiled, even though she still wouldn't look at him. He had used both of her names, and he only did that when he was mad at her.

"What if I had come back and I wasn't a virgin? What if I had been used by every Comanche brave in the tribe? And you know that was a possibility. What then, Miles? Would you still have wanted me?"

What she was asking was a fair question, but he knew the answer. He had thought about it a hundred times when he was wondering if she was still alive. "I told myself a long time ago I would take you any way I could get you. I just wanted you to survive any way you could. Does that answer your question?"

She sat there and thought for a minute and finally said, "Yes, it answers my question. For now anyway but I am not going to wait forever. I am leaving soon. I have to. I am putting everyone here in danger."

Someone was calling her name, and she got up to leave, then he grabbed her arm and kissed her. "Not long, pretty lady and that man of yours doesn't go with us. Get rid of him, or I will."

She just walked to the stairs and went down them as he followed her. When she got closer to Virgie's room, she heard the man from the other night, Justin, yelling at her.

"I want her, and I am going to have her, or I will have your notes called in at the bank, and you can't afford to pay them, so I will own this place. She is your friend. Make her do it for you, or I will make her do it for me."

They stepped into one of the rooms as he walked out of Virgie's room, and he went down the stairs. When he was gone, Morgan went into Virgie's room and asked her, "What the hell is going on? What has he got on you?"

She looked at Morgan. "It is what he has got on you. He has figured out who you are. He also knows I owe the bank a couple of thousands in notes, and he knows the bank president. He wants you one way or the other. He is threatening to call my notes or contact your stepfather."

Morgan thought for a minute, and then she said, "Your notes, we can take care of in the morning, and as for contacting my stepfather, he will probably do that anyway. We will go to the telegraph in the morning and have the money transferred to pay off your note, and then he can't get to you, and I will leave soon after. We will have the dress fitted by then, and you can send it to Gary Lee in Dallas, and we will be gone."

Virgie looked at her. "I can't let you do that. This is not your problem to fix."

"So you will have a silent partner or, better yet, sell the place and come to Texas and buy a ranch next to me and live there. Mama Ruby would love it. She always did, and you were good at running the plantation. You would be good at ranching. Load everybody up and come home."

"Justin Winters will have a fit. He is used to getting his way, and he wants you."

"Well, too bad. I am not for sale today."

Miles looked at her. They were on a tight schedule. They had to leave soon.

"Come in here. The dress is ready to try on."

Abigail had done a wonderful job. She was Sheri's little sister, and now she did the dresses for the house. She had been hurt badly in an accident when she was a child, so she was protected from the men downstairs. Nobody got too close to her. But she could sew anything. She showed Morgan the little pocket that nobody else could see; it was perfect. They just smiled at each other.

Virgie's dress had ruffles on it where her mother's hadn't. Morgan was fuller breasted, and ruffles weren't needed, so after they were removed; the neckline was quite low cut. She put it on, and they were trying to decide if they needed to put a piece of lace or something across the neck when Miles came in, and his mouth dropped open. His little girl was a beautiful woman.

"It is beautiful. Leave it alone all of it, no hoop skirt, no more petticoats. Come out here. Let the girl's downstairs look and get their opinion. You will see it is perfect the way it is."

He didn't realize Justin was downstairs as well. As she started down the stairs, she looked gorgeous. The dress was indeed perfect on her. She was halfway down the stairs when Justin made his presence known. He walked up the other half of the stairs and took her hand and kissed it. "A woman like you shouldn't even be in a place like this."

She took her hand back. "Is that why you would inform my stepfather where I am so as to make it easier for his hired killers to find me?"

The man in front of her looked like he had been slapped. "He is trying to return you to your home after you were kidnapped."

"Yes, after he hired the kidnappers to kill me. If you have told him where I am, you have signed my death warrant. What did he tell you? That I was yours if you could get me home? I will never get home alive because he can't inherit my land unless I am dead. You told him where I am, didn't you?"

He couldn't look at her face. He turned and walked down the stairs and out of the house.

"We will take care of our business in the morning, and then I will leave. We have run out of time. The dress is wonderful, Abigail."

She said it like it was nothing. She was leaving and on the run again. Miles looked at Virgie. They had done this for months, and it had been a nightmare. They could only wonder what years of this were like.

Miles met her in the bedroom and helped her with the dress and then told her, "I want you to tell Trey he is not going with us. I will take care of you from here on out. Will you do that for me?"

She turned, still dressed in her slip, and nodded as she pulled on a robe. "I will dress and take care of it. Can you find him for me?"

Miles went to find Trey. He was somewhere in the house. He was usually with Sheri, Abigail's sister. He went to her room, and sure enough, he was there, so he asked him to come and talk to Morgan down in the parlor.

He walked out on the stairs, still dressed only in pants, when he looked down and saw her. "What do you want, Morgan? Are you through with my services? Are you and the fancy man going to take off now?"

She could see this wasn't going to go well. He was drunk, and he was always nasty when he was drunk. "Yes. Miles and I are leaving tomorrow. I will pay whatever I still owe you for your services. I was figuring you could keep the horse and saddle as well as another two hundred. Does that sound fair?"

He grabbed the rail, and she looked for Miles. She wanted him near because she was afraid of what was coming. He had held it in for too long. He was going to explode, and she didn't want Miles to kill him. She looked up at Virgie, and she understood, so she started looking for Miles as Trey started on her.

"Do you know my sister was captured by Apaches and I got her back but she wouldn't stay? She wanted to go back to them. She had a kid by an Apache, and she wanted to get back to her, so finally, she stole a horse and went back. When Geronimo was in Mexico, they were starving, but she wouldn't come home. She starved with her kid. She would rather die with that brat than come home."

Miles was in the room by now, and he was standing by her. He had heard most of it and was listening to the rest.

"She loved her child, and you couldn't accept either of them, so she wouldn't come home. That is why I hired you. I knew I was safe with you. You couldn't stand the thought of touching me or any Indian. I was ruined. I'll bet that was how your sister felt too. That was why she ran."

Miles looked down at her. That was how he made Morgan feel yesterday—ruined.

"All those nights we had spent on the range, I would watch you and want you, but then I would think about how many Indian men had been with you, and it would make me so sick to my stomach that I wouldn't even think about bedding you. He can have you—as if he hasn't already."

She had to put her hand on Miles's arm to keep him still. She hadn't had her say, and she had waited a while to say it to him ever since the morning they had attacked the village and he had almost shot her.

"You want to know a secret, you stupid fool? All the men you think I have had? I am a virgin. The Indian man I made that dress for knew that and was waiting for our wedding night and the man beside me has waited since I was fifteen. You are the only one who thinks otherwise."

Trey looked at Virgie, and he looked at Miles. "What about that man the other night who offered you all that money?"

Virgie answered this time. "That is why he offered her all that money. Even he could see she had never been touched."

"I will have the rest of your money in the morning. We are done."

Trey was still staring at her. "Do you still have your knife in your boot?"

She just nodded at Miles as she went to the kitchen. Trey went back to Sheri's room. Morgan was so mad; she went to the kitchen and asked Mama if she still had those brandied peaches she kept for special occasions.

Mama Ruby looked at her and said, "Yes, but your mama never let you eat them. They are almost pure brandy."

"Well, Mama isn't here, is she? And I would like to try some."

Mama Ruby went to the pantry and got a jar out and poured some into a bowl, and Morgan began to eat them. Her eyes almost bugged out of her head; they were indeed almost pure brandy. After a short coughing spell, she ate another, and when she finished the bowl, she got some more out of the jar. None of the women watching realized she was trying to keep a lid on her temper and keep the lady inside from making an appearance. She never drank, and she didn't realize how little it was going to take to get her drunk. Later Morgan headed upstairs with some help from Ivy.

Miles went into Virgie's room as she was packing the gown, and he asked her a question. "Remember the necklace I had you hold for me that was Gray Dove's?"

Virgie smiled and went to her jewelry box and came back with a velvet cloth. She put it on the bed and unfolded it, and inside was a silver and turquoise squash blossom necklace made by a very good Mexican silversmith.

"Don't you think this would look good with that dress?"

Virgie placed it on the dress, and the silver and turquoise blended beautifully with the dress. They were beautiful together.

They heard Morgan coming back upstairs, and Virgie hid the necklace under the bed so she wouldn't see it.

"Well, I think about everything is taken care of. We will take care of the bank in the morning, and if you will send the dress to Gary, it will be waiting on us when we get there. I am going to say good night now. It is going to be a long day tomorrow."

Miles told Virgie to pack the necklace with the dress, and it would be there when they got to Dallas.

"You two watch out. You are not in Dallas yet. Go to your room. It is quieter."

He smiled at her and kissed her head. She knew he wasn't waiting any longer.

She had changed into a nightgown and started to climb into bed when he knocked, and she went to the door.

"You should get some sleep. We need to leave—"

She didn't say any more. He had his mouth on hers and his tongue inside her mouth. When she came up for air, he picked her up and walked down to his room, went inside, and pushed the door shut with his foot, then he put her on the floor and locked the door.

"You taste like brandy. What were you doing in the kitchen?"

She grinned at him and answered, "I had a few bowls of brandied peaches."

"A few bowls? You are drunk. Why did you need that much brandy tonight?"

"So I didn't hurt him."

He just looked at her. She wasn't telling him something, and he was afraid it was bad, but he was interested in something else right now, and maybe it was better that she was a little drunk. Maybe he wouldn't hurt her that way. "Unless you say something right now, tonight is the last time you are going to get to use that virgin speech." She didn't say a word. She just went over to him and started to unbutton his shirt one button at a time as she watched his face. She pushed it off his body and just looked at him. "Did you know I used to watch you swim when you were at the ranch? I always thought you had such a beautiful body, and I wanted to touch it. May I?"

She watched him as he nodded, and she spread her hands wide and ran them up his chest, down his sides, and then over his face. She closed her eyes and felt his hair, and while her eyes were closed, he took her gown off and dropped it to the floor. He got rid of his pants and boots, walked her to the bed, and sat down, but he kept her standing. She was wearing scars, some old, some new. Some, he remembered from when she was a child, and some, like the bandages, were new.

Now it was his turn to touch. He ran his hands up her long legs and her flat stomach to her large breasts, and then he pulled her to him and laid her on the bed. "I don't know what to do. I just know I want you."

He would have to remember not to let her drink. She was a terrible drunk.

"Don't be scared. I will try not to hurt you."

"I have never been scared with you, Miles." She looked into those eyes she had dreamed of since she was fifteen when everything else was wrong. She would close her eyes and think of him till the bad was gone or till she had herself under control.

He kissed her and pulled her up to him as he nipped her neck and went lower to her breasts and found her nipples. As he suckled her breast and ran his hand down her leg to the center of her, she arched up to meet his hand. He used his fingers to start a rhythm to match the one he was using on her breast—pushing and pulling, slipping and sliding—until she was ready for him. Then he was between her legs, and he was kissing her again. When he entered her, he found the tiny membrane and broke it.

The brandy was a pretty good painkiller as far as he could tell, but she was sobering up fast with that bit of pain, and now she was paying attention to what was going on. He had her mouth in his, and she didn't make a sound. He waited a moment until she started the rhythm again. She wanted something, and he hadn't given it to her yet. Then she surprised him and pushed him over. She was on top, and she had the strangest look. She didn't quite know what she wanted, but she was going to find out.

She had spent a lifetime of men touching her and wanting her, and now she was going to find out what it was like to want someone, so she set the pace, and the wicked little smile on her face was priceless. She moved up and down and watched his face as he put his hands on her hips and led her in the rhythm they needed, then she came back to him so he could reach her again. Her hair covered them as he reached for her breasts again, and then he turned her over, and he was on top again.

She was flying, and she didn't know where, but it was wonderful. He got up on his elbows and looked at her. She was coming over the top, and she wanted him, all of him, so she pulled him back to her mouth and found his tongue, and when they came, they came together in an explosion of lights. She held onto him so tight till the inner convulsions stopped, then she just looked at him as she put her hands in his hair.

He was generally so careful not to leave his seed inside a woman, but not this time. He left everything he had inside Morgan. He had always expected this woman to carry his children. He didn't leave her. He stayed where he was and just looked at her as she came back from wherever she was, and she smiled at him.

"Thank you."

"For what? It was just as good for me."

But she wouldn't tell him, so he insisted. "I have never left my seed in anyone except Gray Dove and now you. I want us to have children."

She started to wiggle out from under him, but he wouldn't let her go, and he wouldn't leave her. Now he held her tighter. There was something else going on.

"Tell me what is going on, Morganna."

"You shouldn't have done that. I was going to leave without you so you wouldn't be hurt. I wanted to know what it was like to be loved by someone I loved, but I probably won't survive this, and I don't want to take a child to the grave with me."

He looked at her, and he couldn't believe what she was saying. She had planned to leave without him, and he had her fire the man who was protecting her. What had she planned to do? Go to Dallas by herself?

"The dress and everything else, the money for Virgie—what is that all about? You are leaving everything behind because you are not coming back. Why? What are you planning?"

"If I get there and he doesn't kill me, I am going to kill him for all he had done to me and my family. His men will kill me, so you see, you can't get me pregnant. I still have things to do."

He laid his head on her chest and thought for a minute, and she ran her fingers through his hair some more. Then he started making love to her again, "What are you doing, Miles? Don't you understand?"

"I understand. I am not going to let you die, and if I have to make love to you fifty times a day and get you pregnant just to make you want to stay alive, then that is what I am going to do. As for leaving me behind, forget it. We will go to your stepfather and get your sisters and raise them with our own children, and that is that."

After that, there wasn't much discussion. She was too busy. He either had his mouth on her breast or in her mouth. Either way, if she wasn't pregnant, it wasn't for lack of trying.

CHAPTER 2

The next morning, she watched as he took a bath, and then he was dressing.

"You haven't said much this morning. Are you going to talk to me or just lie there and watch?"

"I thought I would watch for a while longer. It is a lovely sight, and I won't get to watch you wash in a tub for a while. I might as well enjoy it. Do you have a horse?"

He turned and looked at her funny. "This conversation went sideways in a hurry. Yes, I have a horse. What else do you want to know? If I have a gun?"

"Actually, yes. Do you have one?"

Again with the look. "I take it your plan has changed. What is it now?"

She got out of the bed stark naked and got in the tub he had just gotten out of and started to explain. "Well, since you want to come with me, I have decided to go to my stepfather's and take back my sisters and my horses and everything else, and I intend to ruin him in the process. He won't like that, and he will try to prove that I am not the legal heir to any of it, so it is going to be a fight. Are you up to it? Because it is going to be messy, and he will not be nice about what he says about me and anyone with me. You know what they are going to call you if you are with me, don't you?"

"I know. I have been called it before when I was married to Gray Dove, and I survived. Do you think the people who knew you will let him do that to you?"

"Of course they will. He owns them, and he knows it. I am just a hindrance, one he intends to rid himself of and soon."

She got out of the tub, and he helped her dry off, and then she started to dress. He had brought her clothes from her room down to his while she slept last night. She put on her underwear, and he had packed the corset. She didn't need to be riding with that thing on, so he had bought her some decent underwear at the store yesterday. She had come here with nothing but the clothes on her back. She put on her Levi's and then her white boots, and he asked her, "How did you manage not to get blood on the boots? You had it everywhere else."

"The dress was the first thing I grabbed and pulled on. I went outside without anything on my feet. The man I killed cut me as I was coming outside. The men were already dead. Reach in the bag with the dress at the bottom there is a medicine bag. Will you hand it to me?"

As she dressed, he took out the dress, and he then turned the bag upside down. Out fell a white beaded medicine bag, and he could smell the contents inside. He handed it to her, and she put it around her neck.

"What is in the bag?"

"Herbs for fever. White Cloud figured out pretty quickly that I was good with medicine, and I became the medicine woman around our village. I even helped one of the soldiers after the attack with their doctor's bag. We need to get to the telegraph office and get some money and get to the bank. I want to take care of Virgie's debt before I leave. We are going to need supplies and more guns and pack horses as well."

As he pulled her to him, he kissed her. "So my lady has decided to live after all."

"Seems you are not going to let me do anything else, and after last night, there are some things worth living for."

He took his time kissing her, for there wasn't time for anything else. They had to get it done and be on the move. Justin had put a price on her head again, and now her stepfather knew where she was.

They walked down to Virgie's room, and she was dressing.

"All right, how much do you owe the bank so I can have it transferred?"

"I don't think that will be necessary now. He won't come after me because of what you said last night."

"I am going to make sure of that. Virgie, tell me how much you owe the bank."

She looked down at her hands, and then she said, "I owe the bank about three thousand dollars."

"All right, I am going to go to the telegraph and get things started, and you and Miles need to make sure the dress and this list are taken care of at the store." It was a big list of several rifles, pistols, ammo, and supplies. They would need at least one more mule as well as what she had already.

She pulled out a wad of cash and handed it to Miles. "There is a thousand dollars there, and I am getting some more. I will pay off Trey, and then we can leave."

"You don't talk to Trey without me there. Promise me."

"All right, I will meet you at the general store after I take care of the bank. See you in a while."

She reached up, kissed him, and went downstairs and down the street. He knew because he watched, and he had one of the band members follow her.

"What is wrong? What was she going to do?"

"Kill him in cold blood."

"What changed her mind?"

"I told her I might have gotten her pregnant and I was going with her, and she didn't want to see anybody else she loved die or be buried with a baby in her belly."

"Good god, Miles, do you think she would have really done it?"

"I am not sure she still won't if he hurts her sisters. You send that dress and have it there when we get there, and I will see he doesn't hurt her and she gets back what is hers. I am going to marry her, and we are going to Amarillo first, and that is all there is to it if I have to kill him. Send a letter to her grandfather, and tell him we are coming there first so he will be looking for us."

"Here, take this."

"What is it?"

"It is a wide gold wedding band with a diamond in the center. She was playing in my jewelry box while they were fitting her dress the other night. She put that on, and it fit her. I told her to take it, and she said no, it was too much. She is paying my debt today. I think that would be nice for a wedding ring, don't you?"

She took it and put it in a small black box. He hid it in his things so she wouldn't find it, and he started to the general store.

She was at the telegraph office and had sent a wire to Gary and was waiting for him to reply. She didn't have to wait long.

Morgan, what do you need? Someone told him where you are. STOP
I know. Miles and I are leaving soon. I need some more money. STOP
How much do you need? STOP
Thirteen thousand, three for me and ten for Virgie. That a problem? STOP
No, have it there in a bit, then you get gone. STOP
Dress coming from Virgie for me, so keep an eye out for it. STOP
I will. Get going, Morgan. Love, Gary Lee. STOP

After she was through, she went to the bank, and she met with the bank president and waited for the letter of credit to come from the telegraph office. She wanted to be through before Virgie knew what she had done. It didn't take long, and it was there, and she told the bank president she wanted Virgie's notes and two thousand in cash. He was reluctant at first until he saw the name on the wire transfer, and then he got busy.

"I want this done before Virgie gets here. I don't want her to know about the extra money in her account until I am gone. It is a surprise. I will leave her a note."

She didn't trust this man. She suspected he would have just as easily taken the extra money and pocketed it as let Virgie know she had put it in her account. She was going to leave a note in with the papers, and then she would know what she had done. If she ever wanted to leave this life now she had the money to do just that. Besides, if Justin thought he could blackmail him into getting Virgie's notes, he wasn't trustworthy anyway.

He handed her the notes and a deposit slip before Virgie could get there, as well as the three thousand in cash, and about that time, Justin walked in. The president was still counting out money, and she had her hand full of hundred-dollar bills. She took the money, put it in her leather wallet, took the papers, folded them, and put them in an envelope. She then shook this man's hand and walked past Justin and didn't even look at him.

As Justin looked at the bank president, he said, "Is that the woman you wanted?"

He shook his head as he watched her walk out the door.

"She just paid off Virgie's notes and deposited several thousand more into her account and then took three thousand for herself. Do you know who she is?"

He looked at his friend's face. "I do now, and I may have killed her with my stupidity."

"Don't tell me you told Calderon where she is." Justin just nodded.

"You fool. Everybody knows he wants her dead. She is worth more dead than alive. If I had known who she was, I would have told you that."

Justin just looked at his friend. "It is too late now. It is done."

She met them at the general store. Miles had picked out some nice rifles, and she asked the man at the counter if there was any place they could try them out.

"Behind the store, there is a place where some of the men shoot at cans, and your man can shoot out there."

Before she could get outside, she saw a doctor's bag, and she picked it up and looked inside. It was filled with instruments, and the bag was in fairly good condition. "How did you come by this?"

"The doctor who had it died, and I took it to pay his bill."

"Well, add it to mine, and do you have any laudanum? If you do, put several bottles in the bag and charge me for all that as well."

Then they walked outside. She gave a small boy a half dollar to set up some cans while she loaded a Winchester, and Miles just watched.

"You any good with a rifle? I know you are good with a pistol."

"It has been a while since I had a good rifle. We will see."

Morgan aimed and missed the first one. The rifle was pulling to the right, so she tried again, and she hit it and the next and all the rest of them, and then she looked at him. "Guess I am not too bad."

He just smiled. "Want to try this pistol? They had a light one, but he says it has a light trigger. It was carried by a small man."

She had the boy set up the targets again while she put on the gun belt and tied it down to her leg. They had drawn an audience by now, and one of them was Trey.

When the boy was through, she drew, and she was fast. She hit every one of the targets, and then she looked at Miles. "I like it. It is perfect for me, much better than the one I am carrying now, much lighter. Do we have everything else we need?" When she turned, she saw Trey.

"You are as good with a gun as you are with a knife. Did you know I killed the old man?"

She still had her hand on the pistol, and Miles held her hand. He knew what she wanted to do. He turned to Virgie, and then he said to her, "We still owe him two hundred dollars. Will you see he gets it? We are leaving."

Morgan was breathing hard, and it was all Miles could do to get her to the horses. She hugged Virgie goodbye and handed her the envelope with the papers in them that gave her back her house, and all Virgie could say was "Thank you, darlin'. I will never forget this. Please contact me and tell me when you get to safety. I will be waiting. Miles, you watch out too. Take care of each other."

They rode out of town and were well on their way.

Later that night, Virgie was putting the papers away and found the deposit slip. Morgan had left seven thousand dollars in her account with a note.

Virgie,

If we make it home in one piece, come home with us. This will give you enough money to get there, and if it is not enough, contact Gary Lee. He has directions to help you. He also has instructions upon my death to see to it you have a tidy sum in my will. Come back to Texas. It is where you belong.

She put down the letter and just cried. Morgan had provided for her in her will. She really didn't expect to survive this.

Mama Ruby was knocking at the door with her drink for the night before she went downstairs, and she had her come in. Mama couldn't read, so Virgie read the letter to her. Mama just looked at her and said, "That child has had the Lord looking down on her since she was born, and I don't think he has taken his eyes off of her yet. Miles will help her, and she will get home. I think you should start packing. We are going back home to Texas."

Virgie just looked at the old woman, and they started packing the next day.

Miles was making camp in a little bunch of trees, and in this country, there weren't many trees. Morgan was gathering firewood as he got the horses unpacked and the supplies set down. They would have bread and beans tonight. Mama had packed them special for them. They wouldn't be so lucky. Soon, she would have to cook whatever they could catch or kill.

"How much did you leave her? And don't lie. I know you better than that."

She just smiled as she broke the wood into smaller pieces and started a fire. "Seven thousand dollars."

That got his attention. "I thought we decided you wanted to live and you weren't going to die."

"Just in case. I left it for her and asked her to come to Texas and live by us. Maybe Mama Ruby will talk her into it." She didn't tell him about the will.

He smiled at her this time. "Now that would be nice, and I bet she could talk her into it. They are probably already packing. You would like Virgie close, wouldn't you? She is as close to a mother as yours was."

"She would like a baby to raise if you are as good as you think you are, and Mama Ruby would be in heaven, wouldn't she? There is a ranch close, and she would be out of the trade and back into ranching."

She was sitting, making a fire, and talking about ranching. That was better than last night when she was talking about being killed. He walked over with the supplies and sat down and unwrapped the bread and beans. They sat and ate and made small talk like they hadn't been separated for almost four years.

He had found out today that Gary had given her some idea of why her stepfather wanted her land and money so badly. She was worth almost one hundred and fifty thousand dollars in land and money, and that didn't include the horses. Her father had owned two Appaloosa stallions, and the breeding rights he had left to Morgan were worth another fortune. Ramon Calderon couldn't inherit unless he could prove she was dead, and now that she had proved to Gary she was alive, he was determined to make her dead one way or another.

Gary Lee was her cousin, and he was the only one who knew those things about her, and she knew it. Gary had control over her estate as long as she was alive, and they could prove she was alive. Ramon had men looking for her everywhere.

They finished supper and lay down. He held her to him, and they went to sleep. The only thing he was worried about right at this moment was rattlesnakes.

When she woke in the morning, he said, "Be still. We have company."

She didn't see anyone at first, but then she saw two braves on her left and two more on horses watching them.

"Well, they aren't going away. We might as well see what they want or start looking for cover. I will talk to them. You get closer to the horses."

She stood up. The two Comanche's on horseback came toward her, and they came slowly. She stood her ground and waited; the other two stayed right where they were.

When they were close enough to hear her, she asked in Comanche what they wanted. They looked at Miles, who by now was at the guns and ready. One of the men looked at her boots and her medicine bag and asked in English, "Are you the daughter of White Cloud? Are you the medicine woman?" He looked at her strangely.

She answered, "Yes, I am Running Knife."

The man looked at her again. He didn't believe this white woman could be the woman his chief had sent him for, so he got down off his horse and grabbed her arm. Before he knew it, she had him on the ground, and her knife was at his throat.

"My father gave the name for a reason, and now you know the reason."

The other men were watching. Miles had his gun drawn on the two at her side, and the man on the horse was still sitting.

She looked up at the man on the horse and asked him in Comanche, "Well, chief, are you going to tell me what you want, or are we going to stand here all day?"

The man on the horse smiled. "How did you know I was the chief?"

"You let him do your dirty work to see if I was who I said I was, then you just watched. What is it you want from me?" She pushed the man on the ground away from her and sheathed the knife in her boot.

He started to go after her again, and the chief stopped him. "Enough. We have a fever in our camp, and we were told you might be able to help. We went to your old campsite, and they are all dead. What happened?"

"People are looking for me and are willing to kill to get to me. Are you sure you want me in your camp?"

He looked at her again. "One of the sick children is my son. I will take the chance."

She didn't say any more. She just went over to Miles, and they loaded up the horses and started following the Indians.

"Can you help with the fever?"

"We had it last winter, and I found a pretty good way to treat it, and maybe it will work with this one. It is a trick Daddy taught me."

"Don't turn your back on the other one. He doesn't like you."

"What else is new?"

It took them till the late evening to get to their camp, and they were out of Colorado and headed toward New Mexico. They were headed in the right direction anyway.

When she got there, she could hear children coughing from the distance, and it was bad. When she got into the camp, she told the chief she needed a tepee all to herself and some large rocks and water and to bring the children to her. Miles just followed her around and did what she said.

She sat a ring of round stones in the middle of the tepee, and she started a fire. Then she took out a metal pan that miners used to pan gold, sat it in the center, filled it with water and some foul-smelling herbs, and started them to boil. Then she added water to the rocks and started the fire to steam the inside, and it became a steam bath with stinky herbs.

They brought her the children, and some of them could hardly breathe. She had the mothers hold them upright and let them breathe the steam. It wasn't long before they were breathing easier. She had also made a tea to reduce the children's fever and was giving it to them in small amounts when they stopped coughing, and her method seemed to be working.

The chief brought his son in, but he said his wife had died giving birth to him, so Morgan held the baby and got next to the fire and let him breathe in the steam. The child was about a year and a half old and should still be nursing, so there had to be a wet nurse somewhere.

She told everyone to gently beat on the children's back with a doubled-up fist to loosen the stuff in the children's lungs. It seemed to be working; some of the children weren't coughing and had even fallen asleep.

She just held the baby and rocked him. He was a beautiful child. He was not a full-blooded Indian. His mother was white; he had blue eyes and black hair. She didn't realize she was smiling as she rocked him. The chief was watching from the corner.

She added more water to the fire to keep the steam going when Miles noticed her arm was bleeding. "Morgan, your arm is bleeding. This heat and holding the baby have opened it again."

She looked down, and sure enough, it was bleeding pretty badly this time. She handed the baby to Miles, and she started to the opening.

"That brave grabbing me didn't help either. He probably pulled the stitches out. Give me a minute. I will rewrap it, and I will be right back."

She added more water to the fire and some more herbs to the pan and went outside. She hadn't noticed the chief had followed her. She went to the pack horse, opened a saddlebag, pulled out some linen and some salve, and then turned around, and he was right behind her.

"You startled me. I didn't hear you."

He didn't touch her, but Morgan could tell he wanted to. "Who is this man you ride with?"

She knew she was going to have to make some decisions right now because he was deciding if he wanted to claim her, and Miles was in the way. "He is the man I love, and I intend to marry him."

He didn't say anything else to her or to Miles, who was standing behind him. The chief walked away past Miles.

"He wants you?" She nodded.

"You told him I was your man and you were going to marry me. Was that just to keep me alive, or did you mean it?"

"I meant every word."

"Good. That arm needs attention." He thought about the small black box hidden in his belongings. He was going to find a church out here somewhere and use it.

When they found a spot where they could open her shirt and look at the arm, they discovered she had pulled most of the stitches loose, and the arm would have to be stitched again. She had torn it open nicely.

"Just put the bandage back on, and grab the doctor's bag. We will have to redo this later, and we don't have much linen to waste. I will put the needle in some boiling water, and you can do it later."

He looked at her. "Me."

"I don't have anybody else, and I didn't do such a great job the first time."

He leaned down and kissed her and then grabbed the bag, and they went back inside.

She again picked up the baby and poured more water on the fire and started to rock the baby again. The baby was cuddled on her shoulder, and she was rocking it back and forth.

A very pretty Indian woman came in later and took the baby. She was the baby's wet nurse. She started to feed him, and he was eating well. It seemed he hadn't eaten for days because of the cough, and both women were very pleased.

She didn't want to, but her arm needed attention, so she woke Miles. The needle had been boiled, and she had taken some laudanum a while ago for pain, so they might as well do it. They went into the corner of the tepee, and she took off her shirt and laid it over her back so he could get to her arm.

After he took off the bandages, he cleaned the spot and cut out the torn stitches and started to replace them. She told him where they were best placed, and he did what she said. When they finished, she had him put some more salve on it and bandage it, then she put on a clean shirt. She lay down, and he lay next to her.

They hadn't noticed they had been watched this whole time by the chief across the way in the shadows. He had decided before she came that the woman tending to his son, he would take to wife. She was already pregnant with his child. Now he wasn't sure, but the man was a problem. This woman had a reputation, and it wasn't one of a pliable, gentle woman who would put up with anything a man told her to do. She was called Running Knife for a reason. Today, he had seen that reason, but he had also seen her with his child, and she cared for him already. Maybe Little Fox was his way to get her.

The woman taking care of the baby woke her hours later because the fire was burning down, the water was gone from the pan, and the herbs were no longer giving off a smell. She got up stiffly, and Miles started to rise as well, and she told him to go back to sleep. She would take care of things. She got the fire going again, and when she looked up, the chief had more water for her, and she realized he had probably been watching her all night.

She got the steam going again and put some more herbs in the pan, and the tepee was again a steam room. She was going to have to go outside today and see if she could find some more of these herbs to leave behind because she had used almost all the ones she had. She also wanted to look for the trees with the bark she used for boiling to lower the fever with.

The woman with the baby was called Still Water, and she was very pretty. She would be a good mother to the baby. If she got out of here, the chief would start to look at her again. She spoke fair English, and she asked her, "In a little while, if I brush my hair, would you braid it for me?"

She nodded.

"Good. I won't look so white that way, I need to find some more herbs, and I want to look a little more Indian from a distance."

Still Water looked at her boots and her medicine bag and then said, "Looks like some time ago you were an Indian. Why did you leave?"

She smiled kind of sadly. "They killed everybody around me to get to me."

Still Water looked shocked.

"Don't worry. I am leaving soon. I won't put your people in the same position. What is the chief's name?"

"He is Standing Bear."

She nodded to her. She got up and went outside and went to the pack animals, and her things were gone. She looked around, and she saw the chief, and he pointed to a tepee. She went over to it, and he pulled the skin back. She went inside, and there were her things. She turned around, and he just stood there, looking at her. She knew what was on his mind, and she knew she had to stop this right now.

"Still Water is who you need for that baby, not me, and I am not staying, so get that right out of your mind."

He walked over to her and took her in his arms and kissed her. It was nice but not like when Miles kissed her. There were no fireworks.

"He is who I want, and you can't change that. No one can. I am sorry you lost your woman, but you can't replace her with me, and you know that."

"I could try. Your man could die, and you want my son. I can see it in your eyes."

She breathed deeply, and then she looked at him. "Do you know why they call me Running Knife?"

He shook his head, and she started to tell him. She didn't know Miles had come looking for her and was now outside, listening. He had even seen the kiss.

"Two days after White Cloud bought me, I escaped, and I stole his knife and ran. He hunted for me for three days, and when he found me, I had killed and eaten some rabbits and survived. He didn't think I could, a young white woman all alone in this country. I should have been dead. One of his men tried to tackle me and bring me to the ground and got cut along the way, as did another, then they backed off.

"White Cloud finally asked me where I was going, and I said home. He looked at me and asked how. I said I would run. My sisters needed me. I didn't know where I was or how to get home, but I was determined. He came over to me and took the knife away. He knew I wouldn't hurt him, and he picked me up and put me on his horse and said, 'You are going home, Running Knife, with me. If you try to go home alone, you will die. He will kill you.' I was his daughter after that, and no one touched me, I carry his knife, and I will use it on you if I have to. They killed everyone to get to me, and they will kill your people too. Do you want that for your son? He is not safe with me here."

Chief Standing Bear watched her and understood. All she was trying to do was help his people, and then she was going to leave.

She would hurt him if she had to, but he would not make her stay, and he would not hurt her man.

They understood each other now, and she started to leave. He grabbed her arm, and she stood still. "When you are ready to go look for your herbs. Call me. I will go with you and stand guard if it is as dangerous as you say. You can't go alone, and you can't take your man with you if they are watching."

She just nodded and stepped outside, and Miles was waiting for her. He had heard everything. He took her arm, and they went around the other side of the tepee, and he kissed her.

"Are you all right?"

"Better now. You heard?"

He nodded, and after the chief left, she went back inside with Miles, and she changed clothes, put on an Indian skirt and shirt, brushed her hair, and grabbed a piece of rawhide to tie it with when it was braided.

"I can braid your hair."

"I figured you could, but not here. That is a woman's job in the village. When we are not here, you can do it for me some other time." She kissed him and went back to the other tepee. "Make sure everything doesn't get too spread out. We will have to leave soon."

"One of your feelings again?"

She nodded. "I feel eyes on the back of my neck."

"Besides Standing Bear's?"

"Yes. We need to leave and soon. We are running out of time." Miles asked her, "You are fond of that child, aren't you?"

She just nodded and left the tepee.

When she got back to the tepee, Still Water was waiting for her. The baby was asleep, so Morgan sat down in front of her, and she started to braid her hair. It was nice to just have a few minutes alone and do nothing but normal things with another woman.

She could tell that Still Water was upset, and she turned when she was through with her hair and asked, "What is it? Have I done something wrong?"

"He wants you."

"He thought he did, but I will be gone in a few days, and his eyes will be on you again. I am not staying, so don't worry. It will be all right."

Still Water just looked at her. "I loved him even when he was married."

She asked her, "How did you become this baby's wet nurse? Where is your child?"

She couldn't look at her, and she thought this wasn't going to be good. "My husband was shot by white soldiers, and I lost my son soon after he was born. It was too soon, but I still had milk, so I am the wet nurse of the chief's son. Now I carry his child."

Well, now she knew. This was getting better and better. She had to get out of here and soon. "You are not wed yet?"

She shook her head.

"You watch the baby, and I will see if I can find what I need in the way of herbs around here, and then I can leave. Can you do this if I am gone?"

She nodded.

Morgan started to get up, and Still Water handed her the silver headband she had on. "Here, take this. You will look even more like a squaw from a distance if someone is looking."

Morgan smiled and thanked her and walked out into the light, and Miles saw her, as well as the chief, and both men thought she was one of the other women. Now she looked Indian.

"Well, are you ready to go? Let's see if we can find what I need around here."

Both men were still just staring at her.

"I guess I will pass for a squaw from a distance now."

Miles said it first. "You will pass for a squaw from up close as well as from a distance."

She grabbed the bag he was holding and started to walk away from the camp and finally had to stop and say, "Well, are you coming, or do I go alone?" Then the chief finally started to follow her. They walked quite a distance from the village until she found the plant she was looking for. It was just wild sage. When she reached down to pick some, the chief grabbed her and pulled her back, and she fell down on top of him.

"Be still till he moves away from you."

She hadn't been paying attention and almost put her hand on a rattlesnake. He was coiled but not rattling, and he would have struck her, and there was not a lot to do about a rattlesnake bite except watch someone die.

She stayed still, and the snake slithered away from her as she sat on the chief's lap. He had his hands on her, and she could tell she had to get out of here as soon as she could; this man wasn't convinced she wasn't his for the taking. In fact, if she didn't get up right now, she was in trouble.

She scrambled away from him and looked down at him and said, "I think it is time to go back. We have enough for today, and I don't see the trees that I need for the fever."

And she started to walk back, and he started to laugh until he saw his men coming in at a run, and one of them was being carried in the saddle. It was the man who had jumped her the first day, Little Deer, and he had a bullet in his back. They had been attacked by some white men looking for a white woman.

When they got the man down, she finally got the chief's attention. One of the other men told him, "They are looking for a white woman, and they described her." They pointed to Morgan.

She looked at him, and she simply stated, "We need to get Little Deer taken care of, and then I will leave, but you need to put out an extra guard. They may well come back looking for me."

The chief gave the orders and asked the men if they had killed any of the men, and they said no; they just chased them off after they told the men there were no white women in the camp.

She had Little Deer brought to the tepee she and Miles were using, and she had them bring plenty of wood in for the more light. He didn't want her to touch him, so she sent everybody out so she could talk to him.

When everybody was gone and it was just the two of them, he tried to leave. He almost fell, and she caught him. He looked at her with such hate in his eyes, and she sat him down and just looked at him and asked, "This is how it is. You are going to let me take care of you or that bullet is going to poison you, and you are going to die, and it is not going to be quick or easy. I have met your wife. Are you going to leave her alone and pregnant this winter to starve because you were too proud to let a white woman take a bullet out of you?"

She just looked at this man and waited to see if his pride was stronger than his will to live. It wasn't.

"All right, woman, take it out."

"Good decision. Let's get to work."

She called in the others, started a bowl of water boiling with the instruments in it, took out the bottle of laudanum, put two drops in a cup of water, and asked him to drink it. He refused it. Of course he would; he was, after all, a warrior. Men were all alike—white or red, stubborn and stupid.

"You are going to need it. This bullet is near your spine, and if you move, I could kill you. Drink the painkiller now."

He finally took the cup and drank it, and she went to pulling out the instruments and setting them aside in a clean bowl. She put down a clean blanket and had him lie down on it, and after a few minutes, he was drowsy, and then she had two men hold him down as she sat on his back.

He began to struggle, and she told him, "Try and be still. I will be as fast and as gentle as I can."

She took the tool she needed and looked up at the men and laid her hand on his back and almost petted him, and then she went after the bullet. She found it the first time and got it out.

"The worst part is done. Now a stitch or two, and we are done. Just breathe, and I will be quick." She quickly stitched him up and cleaned the wound and bandaged it, and she was indeed done. His woman was there, and she had watched it all. She knew what to do the next time.

Little Deer was awake, and he looked at her and said, "You need to leave. They will come for you again soon."

She just nodded then stood, turned to his wife, handed her the bottle of laudanum, took her outside, and told her, "He won't want to take it for the pain, but give him two drops in a glass of water for the next few days. Just don't tell him you are doing it."

His wife smiled at her then went back inside.

The chief came outside and said, "You are leaving now?" She turned to Miles. "Are we ready to go?"

He just nodded.

"The extra herbs are in the other tent, and Still Water knows how to use them. Little Deer is taken care of." She took her medicine bag off her neck and handed it to him and told him, "Take a pinch of the bark and boil it in a tea and have him drink it for the fever four times a day. We are going now. Keep a guard on your camp. They will still be looking for me."

Before she could mount, he told Morgan, "There is a cabin in the mountains about twenty miles south. It is old but warm, and there is a storm coming. If you can get there, they will lose your trail. I had my men pack some meat for you. That should get you through the storm. Take care, Running Knife." And then he kissed her right in front of Miles.

The two men looked at each other. Miles knew that if she wasn't hunted, he would have had to fight for her, but she was in too much danger here, and Chief Standing Bear knew it. She was putting his people in danger as well.

Morgan and Miles mounted, and they started south as the sun was setting. They would go as far as they could till they just couldn't see anymore to get as far away from the camp as possible.

The chief watched as long as he could see them as he held her medicine bag in his hand. It was probably the last time he would ever see her. Miles was a lucky man, luckier than he knew. He would have killed him for her. That woman should have been his and the mother of his son. Somehow, he knew they would meet again.

The moon was high and full, and they traveled long into the night until they found a small cave—well, not a cave, really, but a wall that wind had scooped out a side in. It was a little protection and cover from eyes looking for them. They could sleep and then leave early in the morning and maybe get ahead of these men and into the mountains and to the cabin that the chief had talked about if they could find it.

He wanted her so badly, but there was no way they could make love. They were to exposed, and they were sleeping in their clothes just in case they had to leave in a hurry.

"Are you sorry yet that you got into this mess? I told you I should have left you behind."

He held her tighter and kissed her neck. "I was just thinking I would like to make love to you. It seems like such a long time since Virgie's, but we need to be ready to run. We will find a place soon, and I will make this up to you."

She turned over in his arms, kissed him, put her hands inside his shirt, and ran her hands down his chest.

"If you don't stop that, I won't get any sleep tonight."

"I have learned to take what you want now because tomorrow may not be there."

He looked down at her, and it took them about a minute to shed their clothes—most of them, at least—and then he was inside her. She was still half dressed and had one boot on, but she didn't care. He was suckling her breast, and her hands were in his hair. He was stroking, and she wanted more as she arched up to meet him. Then he turned over, and he could reach everything at once until she leaned up and leaned her head back, and he had his hands on her hips as she moved up and down on him. Then she looked down at him, and the smile she gave him was anything but angelic as she came back down to him as she came, and she wanted him, and she took his mouth in hers. All those lost years exploded, and if this was all they ever got, she was going to see they never regretted one moment of it.

When she could finally breathe again, she got up on her hands and looked down at him and said, "Now you will sleep well, my love." He smiled at her and said, "Not yet." He rolled her over and started again. "I am not quite through yet, my dear. We may not get too much sleep tonight after all."

"Who needs sleep?"

As she grabbed his mouth again, by now, they were off the blanket and on the ground. It didn't seem to be a problem—at least not one that was bothering them.

When he finished this time, they had rolled a ways from the blanket, and he got her off the ground and dusted the dirt off her. She smiled at him as he did the same for her but with a bit more enthusiasm. He turned around and looked at her as she pulled on her pants, and he looked at her beautiful bottom and wondered why he hadn't just taken her with him when he had the chance all those years ago. If he had to do it over again, he would have.

He finished dressing, and they settled down again on the blanket. She cuddled up to him, and he asked her,

"If we find a church or a preacher out here somewhere, will you marry me? If you are pregnant, I want my child to have a name."

She turned and looked at him. "That is the first time you have talked like you won't survive this. I don't like that."

"Will you marry me?"

"Anytime, anywhere. I would have married you when I was fifteen if you had asked me and not my mother."

That was all he wanted to know. Now he could sleep, and now she couldn't. Now she was scared for him. She had always figured she was going to get killed. She couldn't stand the idea of him getting hurt.

CHAPTER 3

They didn't get much sleep, but they were gone before sunlight the next morning. She wasn't talking much, and that worried him. When she didn't talk, something was bothering her. They rode hard, and he noticed she was looking over her shoulder often, but he didn't see anyone following them. When he would look back, she would always smile at him, but he knew her too well. She was planning something, and he didn't like it.

They could see the mountains, and it was almost dark, so they continued on until they couldn't see anymore. When they stopped, the wind was getting very cold.

"If we don't find this cabin soon, we are going to have to find or build a shelter, or we will freeze in this storm that is coming."

"I know. We will start out early, and maybe we can find it in the morning and have some time before it hits tomorrow."

He looked at her sideways and wondered when she was going to tell him what was wrong, but it was obviously not tonight.

They camped in an outcropping of trees—it cut the wind somewhat—and they had a fire. She cooked the last of the beans and added some of the meat, and they settled down together as close as they could to stay warm and slept. They didn't sleep too long. They were freezing, so they got up and ate some jerky and started as soon as they could see at first light.

As they climbed higher, they still didn't see any cabin and were about to give up when Miles saw something. They headed toward it, and it was a cabin—or what was left of one. The door was hanging off the hinges, but they could fix that. What was bad was the back wall was letting in air, and it would soon be letting in snow.

Morgan told Miles, "Take the animals around the side. It looks like there is an old lean-to over there. I will take care of the wall, and then we can gather some wood."

He nodded to her and took the animals around the side. He pushed the walls up and braced them until he could cut a couple of new braces. He went up and around into the forest, found what he needed in a couple of saplings, and cut them with an ax he had bought at the last general store they had come to. After he braced the old lean-to, he got the animals tied up, gave them some grain, and started to unload them.

When he had them unloaded, he went around back to see what Morgan was doing and found her cutting up a horse blanket into strips and forcing it in between the cracks of the logs in the back of the cabin. She had a log that she was using it as a hammer, and she was pounding the material into the cracks. It was working pretty well. She looked at him and asked, "Can you drag some wood to the front of the cabin? And if we can't get it all cut, we can at least pull it inside to cut it for the fireplace because the snow is going to come from this direction." She was right, of course. The wind was almost knocking them down now, and it was getting worse. They didn't have much time till the snow started.

He started to pull down large pieces of wood to the front of the cabin, and when she was through, she went inside and got a piece of leather off her belt and used it to make a hinge for the door. She found a couple of nails on the floor and hammered them in with the log, and the door worked again. She had saved some of the blanket for starting a fire, as well as some dry twigs, and she soon had a small fire going and then a large one. Thankfully, the flue worked.

When he came back in, his arms were full of firewood, and she went back out and grabbed more, as did Miles. After a few more trips, they had enough for a few days. They would be warm and well fed, so they finally just sat down.

They hadn't been sitting more than a few minutes when the storm hit with its full fury. It was blowing so hard with so much snow, you couldn't see in front of your face. Miles looked at her wall, and a few crystals were sifting through but not many. If she hadn't done her patch job, they wouldn't have had enough wood to even stay warm.

"Well, it looks like we are going to be here a while. How about we eat something?"

She looked at the bags behind her. "I think I can round up something for us to eat. Give me a few minutes." Then she kissed his cheek and started to rise.

"I know something is bothering you. Why won't you talk to me?"

"Later."

He nodded. He was going to have to drag it out of her, but he was going to find out what was wrong.

She took some of the meat and made a stew. It would last for a couple of meals. She even found a can of peaches she had bought at the general store and had hidden for a special occasion. She put the blankets on the floor, close to the fire so they would be warm, and they settled down.

He pulled her close, and then he asked her, "When were you planning on leaving me behind, Morgan? When the snow gets soft? Is that when you plan on running so I don't get hurt?"

She started to pull away, but he wouldn't let her, and when she stopped fighting him, he started talking again.

"Virgie didn't tell you all that has happened since we left, did she? Or you wouldn't think about leaving me."

Morgan shook her head.

"After we left and got settled, we heard your mother died. I got hold of your grandfather and asked him if I could marry you, and he said, 'Yes. Please come.' He would do anything needed to get you away from Ramon. He was scared for you to be with him."

Morgan turned over in his arms and looked at him. "But you didn't come for me?"

"I was on my way when Gary telegraphed us. You had been taken by the Comancheros, and he suspected it was Ramon who had ordered it. He told me to stay put till he knew more. They had hunting parties out looking for you. Your grandfather was with the rangers, hunting for you. They never found you. He told me to wait. The Texas rangers had raided the Comancheros' camp looking for you and hadn't found you. They put me to bed every night drunk. I couldn't stand not knowing where you were.

"Then in January, when your birthday came and they still didn't know where you were, Virgie found me up in that room with my pistol. I was going to kill myself. It was Mama Ruby who stopped me. She came up there and slapped my face and told me she could still feel you. You weren't dead. I handed her my gun, and until you told me I needed it, I hadn't picked it up again."

Morgan looked at him. "Mama said I was alive. She always knew. And then what happened?"

"Virgie telegraphed Gary, and he said he was on the next stage and to wait for him. He was coming. Mama didn't leave my side till he got there five days later. Gary told us that you had been bought by the Indian Chief White Cloud and not as a slave. They had seen you carried off in front of him on his horse, so you were still alive and a captive—an honored one. Mama Ruby was right. Gary told us to write, not to telegraph. He thought someone in the telegraph office was telling Ramon everything we were saying.

"You trying to protect me doesn't work. If I don't know where you are, it is worse. You might as well know I can't live without you. If you leave me, I am dead anyway. If you don't want to marry me, that is fine. Just let me watch over you so I know you are alive."

She looked into his eyes and thought a minute, and then she took a deep breath. "I do want to marry you. I am just so afraid for you. It has always just been my life at stake. Now it is your life on the line too, and that scares me more. I want to go home to Amarillo. I want to see a lawyer and put everything I have in your name and Grandfather's name. That way, if something happens to me, he won't get it. Maybe it will take some of the targets off my back. I will buy enough guards to defend the ranch and Grandfather—an army if need be."

"We need to get married, and then what do you want to do?"

"Go and get my sisters and the horses and ruin him, then we can go back home. How does that sound?"

"It is sounding better and better all the time. No more running from me?"

"No more. Now we go home."

"You need to know one more thing. When you were kidnapped, I sent money to Gary from the sale of my ranch to look for you. There is a tidy sum sitting in a bank in Dallas if we need it as well, so I am not just marrying you for your money."

"You are the only man whom I have never thought was marrying me for my money. Maybe my horses."

He looked at her and grinned. "Well, maybe your horses. They are quite handsome."

Then she smacked him as she rolled on top of him, and they forgot what they had been talking about.

They spent two days in an awful storm, and it was wonderful. Nobody could get to them. They could enjoy being together, and they did. He made love to her over and over with no one around to tell them they were doing something wrong. She loved to just touch him. She had spent a lifetime just dreaming about touching him, or it seemed like it. She had men always wanting to grab or touch her, and the only one she had ever wanted to be held by was here with her now.

She was running her hands down his chest and up again and then down to the root of him and was just watching his face as she put her hand around him so very gently. She felt the softness and then the hardness of him as she smiled wickedly at him. He was holding her with just her shirt on when he rolled her underneath him again and entered her. She just closed her eyes and started moving with him.

"Why do you close your eyes when I go inside you?"

She smiled and then opened her eyes. "I always want to remember it like it was the first time you made love to me because I waited a long time for you, and now I have you."

Then she rolled him over again. He liked it when she did that because she used her hands and touched him everywhere—his chest, his legs. She drove him wild till he pulled her back so he could get to her breasts and her sweet mouth, then she came, and he loved watching her go over the top with him. These had been the best days of his life bar none.

She lay on his chest until she could breathe again, and he held her. She had the sweetest smile. How could such a demon in bed have such a sweet smile? He didn't care; she was his demon. He covered them both up, and she was already asleep.

The snow was starting to slow. Their time here was coming to an end. They would have to leave soon. He was so sad at that thought. This had been the best time of his life and of hers, and he didn't want to give it up, but he knew they couldn't stay. They had to move, or they would be found. One more night, and they would leave tomorrow. At least they were going home.

In the morning, she was getting things ready inside. She still wasn't dressed; he had made love to her one more time before breakfast because they both knew it was going to be a long time before they could again. She just had on her shirt and underwear as she packed, and she had started to put on her pants when someone walked into the door.

"I am hurrying. Wait just a minute."

"Don't hurry on my account. I like the view. It is better from here than from a distance."

This wasn't Miles's voice. She didn't know who this man was. She had let her guard down, and now she was in trouble. *Where is Miles? Please let him be all right.*

She turned and looked at the man in the doorway. He was big, and he had a pistol strapped to his hip.

"Who are you, and what do you want?"

From the way he was looking at her, she knew what he wanted, but she didn't want to move too fast. Her knife was still in her boot on the floor.

"Your stepdaddy has a hefty price on your head, dead, but he doesn't say when I have to kill you now or when I am closer to his ranch."

"It is my ranch."

"What?"

"It's my ranch, not his. That's why he has a reward on my head. It's my ranch. I can pay five times what he is offering if you will get me there alive."

He wasn't noticing the change in the woman in front of him. He should have. "That's why he wants you dead?"

She nodded. He was still looking at her legs, and the bulge in his pants told her he was thinking about it.

She started reaching for her knife. He came after her and knocked her down and was on top of her, pulling at her shirt. Big mistake. The other Morgan was back, and she was mad. Nobody but Miles was ever going to touch her.

About that time, Miles hit him from the side and knocked him off her inside the cabin. She was up on her feet and had her knife in her hand. She was looking for her gun. It was on the other side of the cabin when another man showed up at the door, and he was armed as well. He took one look at her and stopped, and that was all it took for her to get to her gun. She took a running dive and knocked it off the table and grabbed it. She shot the man at the door, and he fell. She couldn't get a shot at the other man because he and Miles were still fighting.

When Miles and the other man separated, he ran out the door and got on his horse.

She yelled to Miles, "Throw me the rifle."

He threw it to her, and he watched as a half-dressed woman took careful aim and shot the man in the back. It was like slow motion. He fell off the horse into the snow, and the horse stopped, turned, and then came back to the cabin.

The man on the floor was moaning, and she turned and looked at Miles. He had been hurt badly and had blood all over his face and down the front of his shirt. The man had hit him with something, probably a log. She was surprised Miles was standing. She turned, grabbed the shirt of the man on the floor, pulled him out of the cabin into the snow, and shot him in the head then walked back in and shut the door.

Miles looked at her as she sat him down, and she started to take care of him. She looked at him and said through clenched teeth, "Yes, that is what I was going to do to Ramon Calderon, and I wouldn't have thought about it twice."

That was the first time in his life he had ever been scared of this woman—and the last. Now he would never let her get this out of control again. He put his hand under her chin and had her look at him.

"You promise me right now. Unless Ramon comes after you or your sisters, you will not kill him in cold blood like that. Promise me."

She nodded.

"Say the words, Morganna."

"I will not kill him in cold blood."

Then she went back to taking care of him. He just watched her as the old Morgan came back slowly. He wondered just what it had taken to make that woman he had seen at the door a minute ago, and then he decided he didn't want to ever know.

Her breathing slowed, and she finally looked like herself again. He wondered if she had looked like that the morning they had attacked the Indian village, and he was sure she probably had. That was what Trey had seen. That was why he was afraid of her. That was how she survived. That other woman took care of her.

He had a lump the size of a fist on his head. She was sure he had been hit with a log, but the cut from it was what was worrying her. She had to give him some laudanum in some water while she cleaned him up, and then she had to stitch him up. The man had cut his neck but not badly. Miles had dodged him before he hit him, or he would have slit his throat.

"What are we going to do about the bodies?"

He wasn't sure. They were bounty hunters, but he didn't know what would happen if he took them to the law. Would Ramon be notified of where they were? It might make things worse. Maybe it was better if they just buried them here.

"I am thinking we bury them and leave. I don't think anybody will come looking for them."

She just nodded as she kept cleaning. She had blood on her as well, but it wasn't hers. He just watched her face. It was better now. The demon was back, but he didn't like this one. She wasn't twenty years old yet, and he was afraid to ask how many men she had killed in her life. He finally stopped her and took her in his arms and held her till the old Morgan was back, and the demon went away. If he had to kill Ramon Calderon himself, he was going to make that demon woman go away forever. She was terrifying and deadly.

They didn't leave till the next day. It took them all of yesterday to get the men buried and the horses and the men's packs rearranged. The man she shot off the horse had been shot right in the heart. He was dead before he hit the ground. When that other woman wanted you dead, you were dead. When they finally left, they were better off than before because of the dead men's belongings and food. It got them down the mountain, and Morgan didn't feel like they were being followed.

When they got to Clayton, New Mexico, they found a little Catholic church. They asked if they could be married there, and the priest said yes. He told them to come back at late mass, and he would do it then. They found a little inn and decided to stay a night after they were married because the Texas border was just a few miles away.

"I don't have a wedding dress."

"Shall we go look at the general store and see if they have something?"

She just nodded, walked down the street, went into the store, and looked around. Pickings were slim in the wedding dress section, but there was one that was pale yellow. It would have to do. She bought it, and they went back.

She asked him, "We didn't look at rings. Should we go back?" He just shook his head.

All right, maybe he didn't want a ring.

They went to the inn, and she changed and put on the boots. They were all she really had, and Miles liked them. When he came out of the other room, he had on a new Levi's and a new white shirt and a bolo tie, and he looked wonderful.

"You want to braid my hair?"

"No, not tonight darlin'. Leave it down. It looks beautiful that way."

"Let's go, my dear. Would you take my arm?"

She slid her arm through his, and they walked down the darkening streets till they got to the church. He had on his gun belt, and she had her knife in her boot. They weren't stupid, and they weren't safe.

When they got inside, the priest met them and noticed the gun and asked about it.

"My woman isn't safe, Padre. She has men who would kill her if they could find her. She is Morganna McKinney Calderon."

That took the old man's breath away. Even he knew she had a price on her head. "I understand, my son. We will do this in private where she will be safe. And your name is?"

"Miles Douglas, and we appreciate your discretion, Padre."

He led them to the back of the church, where they were married in private. When they took their vows, she said yes, and he pulled out the ring she had played with at Virgie's. As he put it on her hand, she could almost feel Virgie and Mama Ruby there. It was perfect.

He blessed them, and as they stood, he also said, "I hope you get home safe and you find happiness. I met your mother and father once, and they were nice people. They helped when we had a cholera outbreak. I will pray for you."

"Thank you, Father. We are on our way home now."

When Morgan left, she put two hundred in the box for the poor. She was sure the priest could find some use for it.

They walked down the street of the little town and back to the inn. They didn't feel comfortable on the street—too many shadows. When they were back in the room, he had a meal sent in, and it was waiting for them. It wasn't much, enchiladas and tamales, but after the last few days, it was a feast.

"When did you arrange for this? We have hardly been alone all day."

He looked at her. "The lady who owns the inn has a mother who is an exceptional cook—at least she says she is. We will soon find out."

She sat down in the chair at the table by the window, and the breeze was cool but not too cool yet. The lady's mother was indeed an exceptional cook.

They ate till they were both stuffed, and then he pulled out her chair and said to her, "I wish we had some music. I would like to dance with you again like the first night at Virgie's. Why did you want out of there so badly that night? I could have danced the whole night away with you."

"I didn't like being in front of all those people, especially Trey. I could feel his eyes on me all the time. We were dancing, and I wanted to be alone with you. I had waited for so long for that."

"I have wanted to ask you why you weren't married to Red Wolf.

You were with the tribe a long time, and White Cloud was pushing you to marry him. How did you stall him?"

"Red Wolf was with another tribe for a long time. He had another woman. He was trying to buy her from her father, and he wouldn't sell her to him. White Cloud finally sent for him to come home, and he did. When his father asked him if he wanted me, he said no, and I was thrilled that he still wanted the other woman. We spent a winter together, and I tried to stay as far away from him as I could, but he finally came around to his father's way of thinking that I would make a good wife."

Miles was unbuttoning her dress as she held her hair out of the way.

"About the time they had everything decided, we got a fever in the camp last winter, and I was too busy trying to keep the little ones alive. Even at that, I had lost two babies. I worked night and day to keep everyone well except me, and when I came down with the fever, I almost died. After I got better, I was so weak I could barely function, so they left me alone about a wedding. I was just getting the wedding dress done when they hit the camp. They had finally found me, but they killed everybody else and not me."

"You can't keep blaming yourself for what Ramon does. You are not responsible."

"I know I am not responsible, but I wonder if he didn't kill Daddy as well. His accident was not right, and I have always suspected him."

"Your father fell off a horse and down a canyon side and broke his neck."

She looked at him. "A canyon he shouldn't have been in, looking for cattle that were never kept there, with Ramon, who never worked cattle with him. I did. Ramon wanted my mother, and I think he killed to get her. He doesn't seem to mind getting his hands dirty for what he wants."

He looked at her. She believed Ramon would do that, and after all this man had done to get to her, it wasn't out of the question. Besides, he had watched her work cattle, and he knew how good she was and how bad Ramon was.

"How long after your father died did your mother marry Ramon?"

She thought back. "About six months. It infuriated Grandpa. He told her it was a mistake and not to trust the man. Ramon was furious when the will was read, and the land and money went to Mother and then to me. He wouldn't ever see a penny of it unless both of us were dead. After y'all were gone, he moved us to Dallas, and I was *kidnapped*—or so everyone thought."

She was in her chemise and lying on the bed, and he undressed and lay next to her.

"He finally talked her into leaving and going to Dallas. She was pregnant with Rose. He bought this huge house with her money and settled in. He hated me and made it quite clear I could go back to Grandfather, but Mother said no. She wanted her children with her. He always called me her McKinney daughter. We had been in Dallas a while when Mama died after a rattler bit her on the wrist. We couldn't help her. She took two days to die, and her arm swelled up horribly. He just watched her and then me. It gave me the creeps.

"About six months later, he took the girls and went to town. I wanted to go, but he said I was in trouble about something. A few hours later, the Comancheros attacked and took me. There were at least five people at the ranch. I don't know if they survived or not, but they weren't with me. The leader, Juan Tores, told me later he was supposed to kill me and leave my body behind, but when he saw me, he got other ideas. He told me the man who hired him was Ramon Calderon. That was why I was left alone and he took his daughters with him."

"So he was just going to sell you, and that was it?"

She looked at him. "That was the plan until he shorted White Cloud some guns, and that didn't go over good, and then White Cloud saw me and changed the agreement. I figured I was dead for sure, but instead, he threatened Juan and took me. He put me up on his horse, and away we went. He told me later he thought I would make a better wife for his son than the woman his son had picked. Apparently, he didn't like the other woman."

"Mama Ruby told me once the Lord had eyes on you and was still watching. I think she was right. Maybe he will watch a little longer, and we can get you home."

"Get us home." She reached over, took his head, brought it down to her lips, and kissed him. "What are you supposed to do on a wedding night that we haven't already done?"

"Oh, I will think of something, wife. I like the sound of that.

Morganna Douglas."

He unbuttoned her chemise, pulled it back, kissed her neck, and sent shivers down her neck. Then he pulled one nipple into his mouth and sucked it until she grabbed his head and kissed him. She leaned up, pulled the chemise off, and leaned over him as she kissed his chest and ran her hand down his leg with that little demon smile of hers, and he knew she was going to be his forever now.

He pushed her over and was inside her before she could even think about it, and she looked at him the way he used to dream she would before he knew where she was. He pumped and pumped in a gentle motion until that wasn't what she wanted anymore. She wanted faster and harder, and she wanted all of him, so she pulled his mouth to hers.

"Please don't ever leave me again, Miles."

As he took her over the top and they came in a million stars, she clung to him like her life depended on it.

"I promise."

They both knew it was a promise neither could keep, but they would try, come hell or Ramon Calderon.

They spent the morning in bed, and it was so nice. They were safe and could just sleep. Miles had put a chair under the doorknob so no one could get in even with a key so they could sleep.

Someone knocked, and he pulled on his pants and asked who it was, and they answered, "Breakfast."

He opened the door, and in came eggs and bacon and bread, toasted. They hadn't eaten this good since Colorado.

After he shut the door again and had the chair under the doorknob again, they ate, and she asked him, "Don't we need to get ready to go?"

"I thought we could take one day and act like married people on a honeymoon. It is still a long way to Amarillo."

She smiled. "I think that is a nice plan." She looked at the chair shoved up against the door.

"We aren't most newlyweds, are we?"

She just shook her head and then asked him, "Sorry about any of this?"

He came over to the bed and took her in his lap, just covered in a sheet. "Nope. You?"

She reached up and kissed the side of his face. "No, sir not a bit."

"Well, let's eat before it gets cold."

She reached for her clothes, and he said, "Just wrap the sheet around you. It will be easier to get off later."

She just grinned. "Oh, really?"

"Yes, really. I didn't say we were leaving the room, did I?" He wiggled his eyebrows.

They stayed all day in bed, just talking and making love, and the next morning, they were on the road to Amarillo.

It was just a few miles to the Texas border but still a hundred miles to where they were going, and it didn't seem that far now to Miles, but to Morgan, it seemed like a thousand. Every night, when they bedded down, she seemed to be more nervous and afraid, and he couldn't figure out why.

He was going through the backpack on the third day after they had left New Mexico and came across the extra linen in the medicine pack, and it finally dawned on him what was wrong. He kept his mouth shut until that night when they had settled down in a small cave at the side of a road, and he asked her, "How long has it been since we left Virgie's?"

"I don't know. I haven't kept track."

He pulled her over and looked at her. "You are a terrible liar, Morgan. Every night lately, you don't sleep. Your heart beats like a hammer, and you are terrified, and I couldn't figure out why. Then it hit me. We have been on the road almost two months, and you haven't bled. You are pregnant, aren't you?"

"Maybe. If I am, that is just one more thing to lose."

He held her to him. *So that was what was wrong. One more thing to lose.* "We are almost home, and you are not going to lose anything."

"What if he has men looking for me at home and we are ambushed before we get there?"

Well, she had a thought that Ramon might have men watching for her at her ranch as well as Dallas. Maybe they should consider that.

"When we get a little closer, we will check and see if he has men watching and find out before we go to the ranch. Just sleep now, and we will find out when we get a little closer."

She was shaking in his arms, and he just held her. "Is there anything I can do?"

"No. We are so close, and I am afraid we got this far and I still won't get home, and I have a headache that just won't go away."

He sat up and put her in front of him and started to rub the sides of her head, and soon, she was leaned back against him as he rubbed her head. After a bit, she was asleep on his chest. He just left her there. He put his head back and held her with his arms around her, and he pulled the blanket up around them. They slept the whole night. When she awoke in the morning, she felt better than she had in days. They didn't even eat. They just started toward town.

There was a small ranch, and she said she used to know the people who lived there. Miles told her to pull her hat down, and they would ride up, see if they could get some water, find out if the same people lived there, and maybe get some information.

As they rode up, the older man shuttled his children inside and grabbed his rifle and met the two riders and asked them what they wanted.

Miles asked, "Could we get some water for our horses? We will pay."

The man looked at Morgan and said, "Why is he hiding his face? What do you really want here?"

Morgan took off her hat and told him, "Allan Barns, I just want to know if I am going to get shot if I try to ride into my own ranch or not. I don't know who to trust anymore."

He sat the rifle down and went to help her off the horse and called to his wife. "Becky, come out here quickly. You put the horses around the side in the barn before someone sees them. Shut the door, and come in the house. I will meet you out back. Becky, take her inside. It is Morgan McKinney. Hurry before anybody sees her."

Becky grabbed Morgan and hustled her in the house, and Allan helped Miles around to the barn and got the horses settled, and then they started to the house.

Before they went in, he stopped Allan and asked him, "Morgan is afraid her ranch is being watched by the people trying to kill her. Is it?"

"It is being watched by someone, and they have been there for about two months. Nobody goes in or out without being searched by them."

Great. How are we going to get in? He grabbed Allan's arm and asked him, "Why are you helping us?"

"I don't know who you are."

"I am her husband, Miles Douglas."

He shook his hand. "Glad to know you. Her daddy helped us when we first got here and didn't have a dime. Our eldest daughter got pneumonia, and he spent five days keeping her alive, and when it started to rain, he helped me pitch hay in that barn. When he left, he never asked for anything, and he delivered my next two children. When he died, I always wondered what had happened, I watched him and that little girl ride here in weather that would have made Indians think twice. I paid him whenever I could but never enough. Maybe now I can repay what I owed him by helping his daughter."

Miles just nodded. Morgan was right. She wasn't the only one who thought something wasn't right with her father's death.

They went inside. Morgan was sitting at a table with a little girl on her lap, and Becky was putting plates of food out for them.

"She said they didn't eat this morning because they didn't want to be seen by anybody in town, so she needs to eat, and so does he. Now sit down while it is hot."

"Yes, ma'am. It looks delicious."

Morgan was eating fresh eggs and feeding bites to the little girl sitting in her lap, and she was smiling. Allan was standing behind her and looked at Miles, and when he was through eating, he motioned him outside.

"The people in town don't know you, so why don't we go to town and see some of the people who are friends of the McKinneys and see if there isn't a way to get you two into the ranch without bloodshed?"

He nodded and then went back inside to talk to Morgan. He got her out back where no one from the road could see her. They sat down on the side of the well.

She said to him, "They are guarding the house, aren't they?" He nodded.

She just sighed. "How are we going to get there without getting shot?"

"Allan and I are going to town. He knows the people who are loyal to your grandfather, and we are going to figure something out. Do you trust him?"

"Yes. He would do anything for Daddy. He would never betray me either. Take some money with you. They are living hand to mouth. Go to the general store and stock up. Tell him we might be here a while, and we will need the supplies. Get the children some candy. Be sure you don't ride one of those bounty hunters' horses. Somebody might recognize one of them."

He hadn't thought of that. They needed to get rid of them.

They mounted up and started to town and talked along the way. Allan told him that Morgan's grandfather had hired a lot of men lately to guard the ranch and that a wagonload of women had arrived a week ago. Nobody knew why they were staying at her grandfather's ranch. He knew there were men all over asking about Morgan and keeping an eye out for her, and they said there was a reward for her dead. Twelve hundred dollars was the price he had heard.

He looked at Miles and asked him, "Who wants to kill her?"

Miles looked at him and said, "Who do you think? Ramon Calderon. He can't inherit until she is dead."

Allan looked at him kind of funny. "I thought he had already inherited. He has that big house in Dallas and her daddy's horses. Aren't those his now?"

"No, they are hers, and that is why he wants her dead. Her daddy left it all to her, and he can't get it till he can prove she is dead."

"Well, that is just not right. We have to get her back home. I never did like that man. Let's go to the stables. The owner there is a good friend of Donald Roy's, Morgan's grandfather, and maybe we can make a plan with him."

Miles just nodded, and they headed down the main street past the auction arena to the stables and went inside. Amarillo was the main cattle auction area for miles around.

It was dark and cool inside the stable, and finally, Allan called out, "Arnold, you here?"

There was silence, then someone at the back of the stables answered them, "I'm here. Who's looking for me?"

They rode a little farther back until they saw the older man. He was putting a saddle up on a rack, and he turned and looked at Allan. Then he stopped for a second and looked at Miles and said, "I know you. You were with Virgie's group when those soldier boys were hunting her, and Morgan led them on a merry chase through the canyon." Then he stopped and shut up and just looked at both men. "Come with me."

He led them to a little office down at the end of the stables. When they were inside, he shut the door, and he turned and was almost screaming. "Where the hell is she?"

He looked at both men like he was ready to kill someone when Allan finally said, "She is at my place. She is safe for now, and this is her husband."

"She isn't safe here." He was still yelling at Miles.

"She isn't safe anywhere. She has almost been killed twice just getting here, and she is not home yet. She is not safe anywhere till he takes the price off her head. He killed a whole Indian village trying to get to her."

"Ramon did this, all this, to Morganna?" Miles just nodded.

"I knew it. That son of a bitch. He had her kidnapped, didn't he? Donald Roy was right all along. Well, how are we going to get her to the ranch without getting her killed?"

They both looked at him. "We were kind of hoping you might have a way."

He finally sat down in his chair and folded his hands. He was tapping his fingers on the table, and then he looked at them. "With all these new men and horses, he has to have a lot of hay brought in every other day, and there are always some new men for hire. He said she was coming home, so he is guarding the ranch like he is getting ready for battle. Now I understand why. Allan, don't you have some hay to sell? Miles, aren't you pretty good with a gun?"

"All right, that gets us in, but what about Morgan? She can't just ride in."

"No, we are going to have to rig a wagon somehow so we can hide her inside and sneak her past the guards outside the ranch. I will come out tomorrow, and we will see what we can rig up on one of your wagons. If we can't use yours, we will get one of mine. Miles, I knew your face. Be careful. Someone else might know you as well." It was getting dark as they left. They were heading out of town, and Miles made Allan stop at the general store. He had asked him if any of the people inside had been here when he was here the last time, and he told him they had sold out and these people were new. He went inside and helped him get what Morgan told him to get, along with the extras Allan wouldn't have picked up, and paid for all of it. Then they left town.

As they left town, a lot of armed men were riding in, and some of them, he had seen before. They had come through and had been at Virgie's house, and he knew what they did for a living. He wondered if they were hunting for Morgan even then. He lowered his hat so they didn't see his face. He just wished he could get word to Morgan's grandfather she was here.

Allan and Becky made them feel right at home, and the next day, Arnold came to the ranch. They pulled out Allan's wagon to see if there was anywhere they could put her so that she wouldn't suffocate. They finally decided under the seat would work if they drilled some holes in the front and back sides toward the hay, but it was still going to be very hot. It was a long ride from Allan's ranch to her grandfather's—about ten miles. That was a long day inside a box. They just couldn't think of any other way to do it. If they started out early in the morning, it would be the coolest, so they decided that was the best thing to do.

They loaded the hay the night before, and when they were done, Becky put jars full of water inside the seat so she could at least have something to drink. They were going to use the bounty hunters' horses as extra horses so they could move faster. They went to bed and tried to sleep.

"Are you scared?'

"I am Terrified. If something happens, I can't get out to help you. I am trapped."

"I will be right there, and Allan will talk to you so you will know what is going on. Just keep thinking tomorrow night; you will be home with your grandfather."

"And you please be careful. I want you there too."

Early the next morning, before the sun was up, she was in the barn with Becky and Allan. She climbed into the box under the seat and watched as Miles mounted his horse and tied hers behind the wagon with her belongings on it. Allan closed the lid, and they were off. She was already feeling closed in. They had poured water all over her to try and keep her cool for as long as they could.

It was about an hour before they were in town, and she could hear the people around her talking, but they just kept going. She took a drink. It was getting hot and dusty in there. She wet a cloth and put it over her mouth and nose so she didn't choke or cough. They passed the stables, and she could see Arnold as he watched them go by. Everything was going as planned, but she was getting so hot. It was now the middle of the day.

Another hour and another, then some men stopped them and asked where they were going, and Allan said, "Mr. McKinney bought some of my hay, and I am delivering it to him, and this man is trying to get a job with him. Let us pass."

When the men wouldn't let them go farther, she heard them say, "You ought to hire on with us. We get paid good, and we don't have to do much—just stay here and guard this place and make sure some girl don't get in, and if she does show up, we are supposed to shoot her."

Miles just turned in his saddle and looked at the men and said, "I don't shoot women." Then he turned back around, and they continued on.

She didn't know how much farther, but she couldn't take much more. She was burning up in there. She took some of the water and drank it and then poured the rest over what she could reach of her body.

They rode a ways farther and stopped again, and this time, the men talking said, "What's going on here? We weren't expecting any hay today, and we don't need any strangers, so get out of here now!" She recognized that voice, and she was too hot and tired to take any lip from him. "Dennis McKinney, is that you?" She would have loved to have seen the look on his face as he pulled a gun on these two men.

"Who is in there?"

"It is me, Morganna, and I am dying from the heat in here. The man on the horse is my husband, so you better not hurt him, or I will hurt you. Get me to the barn so they don't know I am here."

He looked from one man to the next when a voice from inside the wagon said, "*Now*, Dennis."

They walked as slowly as they could and still looked like they were just going to the barn as her grandfather came out.

"What the hell is going on?"

Then he recognized Miles, and Dennis told him, "Come with us, Grandpa. Now."

He followed them—he already knew why—but where was she? He looked all over the wagon, and he couldn't see her anywhere, but she had to be there. Gary had said she was with Miles.

They got the wagon into the barn and shut the door, and Allan quickly got off the seat and opened it, but she was so hot, she couldn't get up. She was pouring sweat. Miles was there by then, and he picked her up and handed her to Dennis, and she was as limp as a wet rag.

Miles got down and ran to the well and got a pail of water. By the time he got back, her grandfather had her in his lap and was sitting on a bale of hay, cradling her like a baby. Miles had the pail of water in his hand, and he poured it on her from head to foot and then went to get another one. When he got back this time, she was at least looking at her grandfather, and then he hugged her and wouldn't let her go.

He looked at Miles as he held his granddaughter, the one he had never expected to see alive again, and told him, "Gary wrote and said she left with you and you were going to Dallas, but he hoped she was coming here first. I hoped you would take care of her, and you did. You brought her home. I see a wedding ring. Yours?"

Miles smiled and nodded.

"Good. Let's go inside and get her cooled off."

Miles picked her up. She was still so hot, she could barely function. The heat was pouring off her. He carried her into the house, and they had a cool bath waiting for her. Miles undressed her, and she sat in it as he poured more cold water slowly till she cooled off. Then he dried her off and put her in a nightgown and put her to bed, and she went to sleep.

While she slept, he talked to her grandfather and her cousin Dennis. They wanted to know what had been happening, so he told them. Her grandfather didn't say much. He knew most of it already. He had ridden with the rangers, looking for her, and he had suspected Ramon of all of it. He had even suspected him of other things Miles didn't know about.

Miles told them about the cabin and how she had killed the bounty hunters, but Donald Roy suspected he wasn't telling them all of it. He knew there was a dark side to his granddaughter. He had seen it when her dad had died. His wife had been a woman you didn't mess with. She had protected her children and her family with her life against Indians, and he saw that woman in Morgan. He was afraid she wasn't through. She wanted her sisters back. He couldn't get them, but she could, especially now that she was married, and he was afraid she was going after them.

Miles had told him she wanted a lawyer to make a will that would leave everything to him and Miles so Ramon couldn't get it. That would infuriate him, but he wasn't sure it would protect her. They would talk tomorrow. Tonight, he would triple the guard just so there wasn't another accident.

The men sat down to dinner, and as they ate, she walked into the room. She was wearing her shirt and tight pants, and she was barefoot. He almost didn't recognize her. She was so grown up. He could see now what Miles was worried about. This woman was different from the little girl who had left here so many years ago, and he was worried about why.

"That smells delicious. Can I join you?"

Her grandfather pulled the chair out beside him, and she sat down. He pulled her over to him, and she kissed his cheek.

"You feeling better little girl your color is better."

"Yes sir much better and much cooler. I don't recommend the underside of a wagon seat for long travel. Did Allan get home all right?"

Dennis nodded. "I had two of my men see to it he got home, and I paid him triple for the hay he brought. Miles said you told me to."

"He took a big risk getting me here, and the hay is good, isn't it?"

"Yes, it is very good."

"Then stop bitching."

Her grandfather just starting laughing. It was the first time in a long time he had laughed about anything, especially the price of hay. He just sat at the table and watched his grandchildren argue like they were twelve years old, and he felt better than he had in years.

After supper, they went outside to the back porch, where there was a fire pit in the center, and sat down. Morgan stood behind her grandfather as Miles and Dennis sat on either side of him. They were just talking when she leaned down to kiss the top of her grandfather's head. When she did, a bullet hit the wall behind her with a thud.

Miles jumped up grabbed her around the waist and almost threw her inside the door. Another bullet hit the door frame not more than two inches above her head.

"Damn him. Dennis, the Sharps—get it for me."

She was standing beside the window, looking out into the darkness for something. Dennis was beside her, and she was still watching.

"Load it for me. I want to see where he is. Let's see if he will fire again."

Miles was starting to walk toward her, and her grandfather stopped him. Miles said, "Look at her face. She changes."

Dennis handed her the loaded gun, and she aimed it into the darkness and waited.

"I know. Her grandmother did the same thing. Leave her alone. She seems to know what she is doing."

The gunman did indeed fire again and hit the windowsill above her. He was close, but she didn't even notice. She was watching for the flash of his rifle, and she aimed at that. She squeezed off a shot, and then they heard a scream. She took another shot a little to the right, and they heard another noise and then a horse riding away, then she lowered the gun.

"I got one of them. I don't know if I wounded him or killed him, but the other one got away. Ramon knows I am here."

She turned, and Miles could see the demon lady, and her grandfather saw as well. He had never seen her quite like this. Even her grandmother wasn't like this. She was deadly, and both men knew it.

"That should be all for tonight. They can't see inside these walls. We should be safe. Do you know a lawyer in town you can trust, or do we need to get hold of Cousin Gary? I need to get some papers drawn up and maybe take some of the pressure off me and you. Otherwise, he is going to keep coming."

"There is a lawyer in town I trust. He can take care of what you need, and then we can have it taken before a judge, and at least it will be legal. There is a ranger in town also, so we can have him witness it. He was one of the rangers who were looking for you."

"Can we have them come out here? I don't think I can get to town alive. That man was shooting from a great distance."

Dennis looked at her. "So were you. Grandpa didn't teach you to shoot like that. Where did you learn to do that?"

"You don't want to know. I think I will go to bed now. I will see everyone in the morning."

She looked at Miles, and he nodded at her. "Be there in a minute. I will help the men get the house locked up."

Donald Roy looked at him. "Is it always that bad?"

Miles looked at him. "You haven't seen bad yet. She can kill without a second thought, and she wants Ramon dead with a vengeance. I had to make her promise not to kill him in cold blood because that was her original plan, even if it meant his men killed her for it."

"What is stopping her from doing that now?"

"She is pregnant, and she doesn't want to take a child to the grave with her."

"Then you better watch her carefully because she still intends to kill that man—and so do I—for what he has done to my family and especially to her. He still has two of my granddaughters, and I will have them back."

"They are not really your grandchildren."

"They are Morgan's sisters, so they are my grandchildren as well and always will be."

Great, now he had to watch both of them because her grandfather would help her if he could.

"In the morning, we will get the men she needs to talk to out here and see if she killed the man on the hill. I personally hope she did. It will put the fear of God into some of those bounty hunters. Dennis, you go check on Allan and his family and take some men to stay there and watch over them. You go to her if she is like her grandmother she needs you now. I will see to the house. If I haven't said it before thank you, for bringing her back home to me and her family."

Then he turned and started to the front door, and Dennis turned to him. "He hasn't been the same since they took her. He had died a little every day they couldn't find her. When Gary telegraphed, saying she was with Virgie, he knew you would bring her home, and he has been waiting ever since. As far as he is concerned, Ramon killed his entire family and deserves to die. When he saw your face today, he knew she was on that wagon somewhere. You have my thanks as well."

He shook his hand and headed to the bedroom where Morgan was. This family had lost so much. He was going to see they didn't lose her too. Tomorrow, they would figure out the rest of it and how to get her sisters back.

When he got to the room, she was standing beside the window and looking out. There were no lights in the room, so no one could see her. The curtains were blowing around her body, and she just looked outside and then at him.

"How did they know I was here? Have they been sitting up on that hill, just waiting for me to make an appearance, or did someone tell them?"

"It doesn't make a difference now. After tomorrow, everyone will know you are here, and after you make the changes in the will, he won't have a reason to kill you."

"You really think that is the only reason he has to kill me? I think he accidentally killed my mother trying to get to me."

He pulled her over to the bed and sat her down. "You have to be mistaken. She was bitten by a rattlesnake."

She smiled at him. "There is something you don't know about me. I like snakes. I find bull snakes and put them around the barns and garden to protect everyone against rattlers."

"Why?"

She looked at his face—he had never liked snakes—then she smiled. "Bull snakes kill little rattlers, so I keep them around. I had two big bull snakes in the garden in Dallas and had no rattlesnake problem. Ramon tripped me and broke my toe the night before Mama got bit, and she went to the garden the next morning to pick me some tomatoes—my favorite. She got bit. While she was in bed, dying, I went looking for the snake with one of the hands, Carlos, and we found it. It was a big rattler, and I caught it and killed it. Then we took it out behind Carlos's house because it didn't rattle and warn me it was there. Rattlers aren't generally aggressive. They give you warning to stay away from them. This one didn't. The rattles had been cut off recently, and the stub was still bleeding. Mama didn't have any warning from a mad and hurt rattler, and she was doing a job I generally did in the morning.

"Ramon had found someone to put a snake in the garden to get me, and it got Mama instead. She didn't even get a warning. She was born and raised around rattlers, and she knew to listen for them. I watched her die, and he watched me. He knew. I knew. After her funeral, I laid that snake at her grave and made sure he saw it. One of his hands liked to use a rope and catch rattlers and snap their necks to kill them. That same man had popped a snake into my grandfather's lap on a horse one day, and he fired him on the spot. He disappeared after Mama died. I figured he was the one who put that snake out there, and Ramon got rid of him. It was war from then on. It wasn't long after that I was kidnapped."

Miles looked at her. This was only going to end one way, so he had better be prepared. Money or horses didn't matter anymore. This was a war between them, and she was going to finish it one way or the other.

The next morning, she came to breakfast in a shirt and a skirt with her silver belt on. She looked beautiful. Some men were sitting at the table, talking. One was a Texas Ranger, and he had his hat on when she walked by.

She plucked it off his head and hung it on the wall. "Men don't wear hats at the table. Didn't your mama teach you better?"

The man stood up and looked at her, and then he smiled. *So this was the woman Ramon wanted dead so badly.* He was glad he hadn't succeeded. He was sorry she was already married because he would have liked that honor. She was only a year older than he was.

"Yes, ma'am, she did, but I have spent too much time out on the plains, and I forgot. Pardon me. I take it you are Morganna?"

She nodded. "And you are?"

Her grandfather answered this time. "His name is Ranger Carter James, and he looked for you for months with me when you were taken. He was even there when they wiped out the Comancheros and found out you had been taken by White Cloud."

She looked at him and then extended her hand. "You don't look old enough to be a ranger. How old are you?"

"I am eighteen, ma'am."

"Thank you for trying anyway. What did they tell you when you found the Comancheros?"

He looked at her. She didn't want to be lied to, so he told her. "The leader had been killed in the raid, but some of the men said they had been paid to take and kill you."

"So I can't press charges against him without someone who he actually hired?" She knew the law, and she was right.

"Yes, ma'am, we need someone he actually hired to testify against him before I can arrest him."

She walked away from him to the kitchen. It was back to her. She was going to have to finish this.

Carter asked her grandfather, "What is she going to do?"

He didn't say anything. He didn't want to get her in trouble. He just looked at Miles and shook his head.

Men were coming up the front of the house, and her grandfather met them and brought them inside. The man she had shot at last night, she had killed, and the other one had bled out not far away. His men had brought them to the ranch this morning. Donald Roy had sent for the ranger early before the men had gone up to see if the man was dead, and he had gone with them. He could not believe she had made that shot, much less in the dark. He had already seen the bullet holes in the side of the house, but what was so disturbing was those men had been there for days. They had a campsite and were waiting for her to step out and make herself a target. She had walked into a sniper's line of sight and lived.

She welcomed the men inside. She had a judge and a lawyer she didn't know and now a Texas Ranger, so why didn't she feel safe? She outlined how she wanted everything set up and how it was to be distributed, and they were to do it today and do it here. They all agreed and went to work. Somehow, they didn't feel safe with papers that had anything to do with her, even if they weren't formalized today.

She made sure lunch was prepared—chicken-fried steak, mashed potatoes and gravy, and black-eyed peas. They would eat in a little while. She was looking out a window when her grandfather came up behind her and said, "You know, this is going to take at least a few days until he knows what you have done before you can leave to go and get them."

She turned and nodded.

"What do you need from me?"

She was looking out the window again. "Daddy's derringer the one with the ivory handle, the double-barreled one."

He put his hands on her shoulders. "That is a .45 and a close-up gun, and it has a kick."

"I know. I will need some practice with it. I need to be able to handle it with only one hand. I don't want Miles to know anything about it."

Then she looked back at him, and he nodded at her. "I think when it is safe in a few days we should start riding, maybe to the gulley where your father was killed. No one would see or hear us, and you could practice. I will see to it that it is oiled and cleaned and ready to shoot. I will do it myself."

They just stood a while longer, then they were called to lunch, and they went and talked to the other men. Miles had been watching, as well as Carter, and he said to Miles, "I am getting a bad feeling about whatever they are cooking up."

"You and me both, you know she is going after her sisters. Would you go with us?"

"Let me think about it." He didn't have to think long.

They had finished lunch, and she was helping clean up. She went to the kitchen window in front of the sink to wash dishes when a bullet came through it and hit the wall across the room.

She hit the floor, as did the other women, and then she got up and went to the door and was going to walk outside when Carter grabbed her.

"What in the hell are you doing?"

"Good god enough already, I am sick of this."

Carter dragged her back as several men started shooting, and men in the hills were shooting back.

Her grandfather sat her in a chair and made her look at him, and then he took her face in his hands and said, "I won't let him have you too. You have fought too hard to get back home. Don't let him win now."

"You are absolutely right."

She sat for a minute, wiped the tears from her eyes sighed, and then as he watched, out came the other lady. She got up and grabbed the Sharps and some ammo and went to a window. She got on her knees and aimed, and when she found what she was looking for, she shot, and down went one man then another. The other men around her were hitting men, but she was killing them. Dennis finally stopped firing and just started reloading for her. She was deadly accurate.

Finally, when it was quiet again, they all looked at her, and she said, "Are the papers ready to sign? This is never going to end until they are." Then she walked away, and as she walked past her grandfather, she handed him the gun. The men just watched as she went.

Miles started to follow, and her grandfather stopped him. "This time, I go."

He followed her into her parents' room. She was sitting on the bed, and she looked up at him.

"Do I scare you too?"

He looked down at her and realized she did a little. "Sometimes you are a lot like your grandmother, but she didn't lose so much of herself to the hatred like you do. That is what scares me. I didn't teach you to shoot like that, and neither did your father. Who did?" He laid the Sharps up against the wall and sat down on the bed next to her.

"White Cloud or I taught him with his rifles."

"Tell me. This ought to be good."

She turned her head and smiled at him. "You always did like a good story. When he got his guns, he got everything in the world. There were no two alike. His men didn't have the foggiest how to even load some of them. Neither did I, but I had more knowledge than they did. I taught them what I knew about the ones I had used here and then tried to figure out the rest. There was a .50-caliber Sharps in a case, and I set it aside. I knew what it could do.

"White Cloud watched me, and he could see I was still looking over my shoulder all the time, and he asked me one day if I was still afraid the men would come after me, and I told him I was sure they would come one day. He asked me which rifle I was comfortable with, and I told him the Winchester. He took it and me and a bag of something, and we went to a washed out-creek. There was a dead cactus hanging out the side, and he stuck a branch in it and on the branch, he put one of those gourds that grow all over here, the round ones. Then he said to hit it. I tried twice and missed, and then he said, 'Think about those men that took you. It is their heads you are aiming at.' I hit the next one, and I didn't miss many after that. He had me move farther back each day till he brought the Sharps, but it was so heavy. I had to get used to holding it. For days, I just carried it around until I could hold it up to my shoulder without dropping the end when I shoot. Now I am pretty good.

"That is the understatement of the year. Miles says he made you promise that you will not kill Ramon in cold blood. Now you promise me."

"Even though he killed Mama and I am pretty sure Father."

He took her hand in his and almost crushed it as he looked at her. "Are you sure?" His teeth were gritted so tight together she thought they would break as she nodded. "You put the snake with no rattles on her grave."

Again, she nodded.

"You make him make the first move. You can do it. That mouth of yours always made him mad. Just don't let him get too close to you. Now you promise me."

"I promise I won't kill him in cold blood, but I will kill him."

He just nodded his head. He didn't care if she killed him; he just didn't want her to get killed doing it. He hugged her again and then he said, "They will have the papers ready in a little while. Why don't you rest and I will come get you?"

She lay down on the bed. It was getting hot, and she was already tired. *Lord, is this ever going to end?*

Carter had more men put around the house. They were getting desperate to kill her if they were attacking in broad daylight. Some of the hands and now a sheriff were outside and out in the hills, looking for the men who had been shooting at them. It wasn't long before three men thrown across horses were brought back into the barn. As the ranger and Miles looked at them, it wasn't hard to see who had killed them. The bullet holes in the front weren't too big, but coming out the back, they were huge. They had been shot with the Sharps, and she had hit them right in the chest. The men just looked at each other.

The ranger said to Miles, "I don't want that woman mad at me. Her grandfather is no slouch either. He was with us when we found the Comancheros' hideout, and I have never seen a man of his age go after anybody the way that man did. When we didn't find her, he was devastated. The man who was still alive told us she was with the Comanche's and was riding in front of the chief. I didn't understand, but he did. She was all right for now. They wouldn't kill her, and Ramon couldn't get at her."

Miles looked at the ranger and said, "She has a way of coming out the other side alive, but it is beginning to take a toll on her mind, and I am afraid for her. It is time to end this."

The ranger looked at him. "You asked me if I would ride with you when you leave. Just tell me when we need to go." Good. They would need all the help they could get.

They had the men leave the dead men here in a wagon. They didn't want Morgan to see them. Carter would take them to town with him when he took everyone back tonight. Miles didn't want her to know how many more she had killed.

When they got back in the house, she was at the table, reading the papers, and she had them sit down. She had everything organized. If she died, the land and money went to Miles, with a portion going to her grandfather unless both of them died, then it all went to her grandfather. That meant two thousand acres of land. There was a good portion set aside for Virgie that she hadn't told him about that night. He knew there was something else. She was going to make sure Virgie was all right, and she hoped she came back to Texas, even if she wasn't here.

After everything was signed and witnessed, the judge saw to it everything was legal and would be filed in the courthouse in the morning. Then she wanted a telegraph sent to Ramon that she wanted custody of her sisters as he wasn't legal heir to the fortune or the stallions anymore. The judge said he would take care of that. He had waited years to stick it to Ramon, and after today, it would be his pleasure.

After supper was served, they started to town. It would be a couple of hours before nightfall, so they would be all right, and they had a large escort and a Texas Ranger with them as well as a wagon full of dead men.

There was a large guard set outside, and she felt almost safe. Now if the men got to town all right maybe this was almost over, so why didn't she feel safe?

Miles came to bed. She rolled over to him, and he kissed her. "Well, are you ready to lead a life of ease?"

Shivers ran up and down her arms. He felt them and looked at her. "What is wrong darlin'?"

"Just a bad day, I guess."

He pulled her to him and pulled off her nightgown and was kissing the lips he always loved to touch, and then he was kissing her neck when he saw the light outside.

She turned her head as things were just beginning to get interesting, and she screamed, *"Fire!"*

Bad timing they were both nude, and she hit the floor running. Then it dawned on him the fire was so very bright. He grabbed her before she got too far because she was only half dressed and headed out the door.

Her grandfather was at the back door, and Miles was screaming, "Get down. The fire is lighting up everything. They can see everybody from a mile away. Get the men inside. They are making another run at us."

Sure enough, the bullets started flying all around them, and one of her grandfather's men went down in front of him. He dragged him inside, and Morgan grabbed a towel and wrapped it around his leg.

"Dennis—where is Dennis?" She couldn't see her cousin anywhere.

"I am right here." And he had the Sharps in one hand and a Winchester and bullets in the other. She had wrapped a robe around her.

Morgan told Dennis, "You load, and I will shoot."

"Good plan."

She was already looking for the rifle fire and hunting for the shooters. She wondered how much these guys were getting paid because they sure were persistent. She watched as the barn was burning to the ground. Soon, it was going to head to the house, and there was nothing they could do about it except get shot. They had learned from this morning and were trying to stay out of her range because she had a better gun. The Sharps had a hell of a range. That was why buffalo hunters used it.

They needed to get closer, and when they did, she had them. She thought she had seen one of them by the wall of the property, and she had told Miles to watch for men sneaking up on them from the front. Then one practically crawled through the window, and Dennis brought a rifle stock down on his head before he could use his pistol on Morgan.

About the time the fire was going to take the house, riders circled around them and were shooting the men outside and some inside the wall whom they hadn't seen. They were waiting for them to come out to fight the fire. It was the ranger and the men they had sent to town. They had seen the fire and came back. Carter told her to stay inside.

"When we got to town, all the bounty hunters were gone, and then we saw the fire. It didn't take a genius to figure out where they went.

You stay out of sight. The reward on your head is five thousand if those papers don't get filed. We have guards on the judge in town as well."

She went to work on the wounded man as they put out the fire in what was left of the barn, and the man Dennis bashed in the head was tied to a chair. He just watched her.

"What makes you worth so much money?" he asked as he struggled in the chair. "Why don't you tell me?"

She had the wounded man's pistol in her hand that she was working on and she started to use it, and then she put it back on the floor. She wasn't paying attention, but Miles was watching, as was her grandfather. This time, she had control. You could almost hear both of them sigh. The man in the chair would never know how lucky he was. She had the scary lady under control tonight.

CHAPTER 4

In the morning, when the telegraph went out, the town was empty. The men disappeared. There were several in the jail who had been captured last night at the ranch by the sheriff and the ranger, but they wouldn't say why they were attacking the ranch. The judge sent his telegraph, and when one was sent back, Ramon said he didn't believe that the girl they thought was Morgan was the real Morgan; she was dead, and he wasn't giving anything back till he had proof.

She had pretty much expected that, and she knew she was going to have to go to Dallas all along. Now when she did the people here could swear she was Morganna McKinney. He wouldn't get any more of her money.

Her grandfather kept stalling her and wouldn't let her go. They had been sneaking off in the afternoons and practicing with the derringer, and he had brought a bag of the gourds that White Cloud had made her practice with. They had been having a great time, and she had figured out she had to be about eighteen feet away from him to hit him where she wanted to, and that was real close, especially if he was armed as well. They were sure going to have a good crop of gourds next year though.

As they rode back on this afternoon, she said, "I am going to have to leave soon, Grandpa. You know that. It is a long ride, and I am pregnant. I want this finished."

"I know, but I have a surprise, and it should be here soon. Please stay a few days more."

"All right, a few days."

As they rode up to the ranch, there were men building a new barn and two covered wagons in the front of the house. *Now why would they need covered wagons?*

And then she saw Virgie, and she looked at her grandfather, and he had the biggest grin. "She telegraphed she was on the way. I just couldn't let you leave till she got here."

"Thank you, Grandpa."

And off she went. She barely stopped. She just jumped off the horse and grabbed Virgie. "You came." And then she turned, and there was Mama Ruby, and she hugged her too. "How long did it take you to talk her into it, Ruby?"

"About a minute. We were packing the next morning."

Around the corner came another face she hadn't seen for a number of years—her cousin Gary Lee. She just walked over crying and held him and whispered into his ear, "Are the girls all right?"

He led her aside. "He won't let me see them now, but they were the last time I saw them. We need to talk later. He is furious. That is why I came. You are still in danger."

She hugged him again, and they all walked into the house.

Virgie was looking at the bullet holes, and she was talking to Donald Roy. Then she saw the barn, and she looked at Morgan. "He didn't stop, even here."

She looked again at Donald Roy. She had always thought her grandfather was a handsome man. Morgan just smiled. Her grandfather was a rich man too and had a large ranch as well. He had just been taking care of hers lately so Ramon didn't take it. Donald Roy had always thought Virgie was a pretty woman but trouble. What's a little trouble now and then?

They went inside, and all of them were there, even someone she didn't expect to see. Trey had come as well. It seemed he had fallen in love with Sheri and followed her and her sister Abigail here. After everyone was taken care of, she and Gary went outside to the back porch, and Miles and Grandpa met them there.

"Well, you might as well get on with it."

Gary looked at her. "He got a judge in Dallas to stop all proceedings until you show your face to him in Dallas and prove you are Shannon McKinney's daughter."

"I figured that was what he was going to do. When is this supposed to take place?"

"You have six months to prove who you are, and then he takes it all."

She got up and walked around the porch. "We need to do it sooner than that. I will be too far along to travel by then."

"What do you mean?"

She just looked at him like he was stupid. "As big as this family is, you don't know what I mean? You have a brother and two sisters. I am pregnant."

He just grinned. "That's wonderful, but your timing sucks." She threw a shoe at him. He just ducked and laughed at her.

"All right, plan B. He is having an engagement party in three weeks at his house, and I will bet he is spending a lot of your money to have it. Can you be ready by then? He is marrying a beautiful woman who was raised by wolves as far as I can tell, and the girls hate her. Now shall we see if we can plan a way to get rid of the evil stepmother and get the girls back to you?" And then he threw her shoe back at her.

"Oh, I like the sound of this already. Did you bring my dress with you? The emerald green one?"

"Of course I did. What kind of cousin do you think I am?"

"I won't answer that. We are in mixed company."

Her grandfather started laughing again, and so did her husband. Miles finally said, "Well, we will get ready to leave for this engagement party, then we still have a couple of days before we need to leave. Let's call it a night." He pulled Gary aside and asked him, "There was a necklace inside the dress box. Did you take it out?"

"Yes, Virgie told me about it, so I took it to a jeweler friend and had it put in a nice box so you could present it to her yourself. I will bring it to you later."

Miles just shook his hand and followed Morgan inside. When they both got inside, they were met by Virgie and her grandfather, and they wanted to talk to them.

"We know you are going to leave soon, but I want you to have a wedding party, and Virgie is going to help me with it, and we are going to do it the day after tomorrow if that is all right with you two.”

Morgan smiled and hugged her grandfather and kissed Virgie. “That is so very all right. I would love it, and some of the families are here.”

“There will be more by then, darlin’. You do need to go and see the women you sent me from the village. I have kept them at my ranch. They are doing well. I didn’t want them in the middle of this mess, but they want to see you before you leave.”

“I will go tomorrow. Maybe I can get the ranger to go with me, and I know Miles will.”

About that time, Trey came up behind her and said, “I will go with you to them. This was my fault. I can at least see that you are safe getting there.”

“I don’t think so, not after what you said about White Cloud. I don’t want you there.”

“I lied. I was mad, and I wanted to hurt you, and I knew that would do it. I am sorry. I didn’t hurt the old man or anyone else for that matter.”

“What has changed? I am still the same woman.”

“Sheri told me about you leading those soldiers away from them into the canyons all those years ago. You risked your life to save them, and when you finally turned around and let the lieutenant see you he still wanted to shoot you. His men had to stop him because of who you were. She told me if it hadn’t been for you, they all would probably have been caught, and a fifteen-year-old girl saved them. I was a fool to you and my sister, and now maybe I can make it up to one of you.”

She just looked at him for a minute and thought about it. “All right, you can come with us if you are nice.”

Miles followed her to their room and shut the door. “What really happened after we left?”

“Me and five of the wranglers headed to the canyons, and the soldiers followed. We kept them busy all day until dusk. Then I turned around, and I took off my hat and let down my hair and turned around in my saddle. I looked different than Virgie. He saw me and realized he had been duped, and he pulled out his rifle and pointed it at me. I didn’t run. I just sat there and stared at him. One of his men took the rifle out of his hand, and he still stared at me till I waved at him and rode away, and I never looked back."

"He was going to kill you?"

"He was very unhappy with me. Let's put it that way. I never saw him again, and you were safe, so I didn't worry about it anymore."

He grabbed her. That was why she had insisted he leave—so she could lead them away. And she couldn't do that with him there. A girl had saved their lives, and it had almost cost hers. God, he would have loved to have met her grandmother and her father.

The next day, they headed to her grandfather's ranch. It was several miles away, but at least this morning, it was cool. Her grandfather had come along with them; he wanted to check his stock and the ranch. They didn't really worry about rustlers anymore since they had made the night riders several years ago. When their stock had started being rustled, the ranchers took turns patrolling at night, and it soon became apparent that rustlers would be shot on sight. After two were killed in a raid one night, the rustling stopped. It was rumored there were more than two, but only two bodies were ever found. After that, it was said you didn't rustle McKinney cattle. And they didn't lose any more.

Donald Roy wanted to talk to Morgan about some things privately. Miles didn't like not being part of their conversations; they were cooking up something, and it scared the hell out of him. Miles had braided her hair this morning, and she looked Indian, at least a little bit. She had on jeans and a shirt—not proper Indian attire for a squaw.

When she got there, she could see they were indeed doing well. She could see the children playing in the buildings out back. Her grandfather's ranch was set up differently than hers. It had out building away from the main house. Her granfather had set the women up there so they had their own places.

Two of the men she had sent with the women had stayed because they had fallen in love with two of the white captive women they brought back. They didn't quite know what to do now because they knew they wouldn't be accepted anywhere else with people knowing what had happened to their women. One of the women had an Indian child about five months old.

When she got down, they all came out to meet her, and she was so glad to see they were doing well. They all looked healthy now that they were eating and had a place to stay that was warm and dry. The two Indian women were staying together and were still not as happy. She went in to talk to them by herself.

She was inside for a long while, and when she came out, she talked to Miles, and he wanted to know what she wanted to do.

"They want to go back to a Comanche tribe, and I told them I had been with one for a little while. I told them when this is over and it is safe, I will see that they are taken to Chief Standing Bear and his tribe."

"Will he take them in?"

She looked back at the women. "I think so if I send supplies and some cattle, kind of a bride price, and tell him it is all right now. They aren't looking for me anymore. His people are safe."

"As long as you don't go with them. He won't let you come back, and you know it."

"I will have someone else take them."

"What about the other women? These two want to marry, but you know how they will be treated."

"Not if they stay around here, and I can see to that. I will set them up in a small farm and protect them here. The other woman says she has family in California who wants her to come home to them, and no one will ever know what happened to her. I will make sure she has enough money so that if it doesn't work out, she can come back here."

Trey had listened to this whole conversation, and he wondered if he had welcomed his sister home instead of making her feel ruined if she would have come back with her child.

"Do you really think they will treat those women with respect after what they have been through?"

"I don't know, but I am one of those women, and they damn well better treat me with respect, or they will regret it."

He had heard what she had been doing with a gun lately. He remembered the woman who killed the man that early morning, and he didn't want to go up against that woman.

When she had everything taken care of, she invited all of them to the party, and then she left. As they rode back, the men were admiring the canyons, and she was just enjoying the afternoon when a snake slithered across their path.

Both men went to shoot it, and she said, "Stop it. It is just a bull snake." She got off the horse, put on her gloves, got a bag she always carried, reached down, and picked him up; and he curled around her arm. They were both acting like little girls as she put it in the bag she carried on her saddle. She tied it to the horse, and she got back up. They headed back to the house.

"What are you going to do with that thing?"

"I need one in the garden. The fire scared the other one off, and this one will do nicely."

As she rode ahead, they both looked at each other, and Miles just shrugged.

When they got back, there were more people there than when they had left—a lot more. There were cousins she hadn't seen in years. Her grandfather must have sent out the word the day she showed up. They were here from New Mexico and all parts of Texas. The dinner table was full. She was introducing Miles to everyone, and he knew he was never going to be able to remember everyone's name. It really didn't seem to matter. She slipped away and let the snake loose. Dennis followed her and made sure she didn't get bitten. It seemed nobody around here thought her snake fetish was weird but him.

Every time Miles turned around, Morgan and her grandfather were in a corner with some cousin or uncle, talking about something, and he wasn't included. He was to find out later when they left that they were going to have an escort from here to Dallas with some relative or another guarding the stage all the way there so she wouldn't be ambushed. Turns out there were that many McKinney's or close relatives to do just that. She wouldn't disappear again. Ramon Calderon should never have pissed off this family, and now Trey had decided to testify that he had been hired to find and kill her. That was what they needed for a judge to issue a warrant.

Gary pulled him aside while Morgan was busy, and they went to another bedroom. This house was huge; he still hadn't seen it all. When they went inside, he shut the door, and Gary brought out the dress box and a jewelry box. He opened the jewelry box. He had the squash blossom cleaned and put on black velvet and hung in the box. It was beautifully displayed.

"I thought maybe tomorrow night, you would want to give it to her a wedding gift."

He hadn't even thought about that. She would love it, and he had never gotten her anything he had bought for her.

"It is beautiful Thank you, and also for bringing the dress. Will you be going back with us?"

"Yes, I will. I am going to be the one who tells everyone she is Morgan. He doesn't know it, but I have been taking her money and hiding it from him so he couldn't spend it till she got back, but I can't get the girls or the horses without her. I have a judge friend who is waiting to write the papers turning the girls over to her when we get there. I want to see his face when she shows up, but more than anything, I want to watch her ruin him for what he did to her."

Calderon had separated her from her family, knowing it was the only way to get what he wanted, and now he was scrambling to try and discredit her, but he wasn't going to be able to do that. He had poked a hornet's nest, and now he was going to get stung.

"Put the necklace away till tomorrow night, and I will give it to her then."

He reached down and took the dress box and started to leave. "By the way, your money is safe and has grown into a tidy sum. When you are in Dallas, we will talk about it. When this is done, you are a rich man."

"In more ways than one Gary marrying into this family has been a blessing. Let's just hope everything works out like it's supposed to."

Gary just nodded and smiled.

They spent the next day cooking. It seemed when these people had a party, no one went hungry. There was more food than he had ever seen. There were women everywhere, and the men were setting up tables and chairs, and he didn't know where half of them came from.

Later that night, when they went to bed, they collapsed. They were so tired. She just snuggled up to his side and said, "You are in for a great party tomorrow."

He kissed her head and sighed and went to sleep.

After breakfast, she was helping make the bread mix when Virgie spilt honey all over her hand.

"Oh, I am so sorry."

"Not a problem. Let me wash it off."

She took off her ring and started to wash it when her grandfather started yelling for her. She was at the sink when Virgie said, "Go see what he wants. I will clean up your ring. I will have it ready for you when he is through with you. *Go.*"

She went outside, and her grandfather said, "We have someone to see. Come on, girl, right now."

She was very confused, but she got on the horse, and off they went.

Virgie turned around and said, "All right, girls, we don't have much time. Get to it. Everybody knows what they have to do. Move we are short on time."

All except two women in the kitchen who were still cooking went in separate directions, and Virgie met Miles in the front hallway. They met Dennis and went to town in a hurry. They didn't have much time to do what had to be done. Donald Roy couldn't stall her forever, and the other cousins were already there with a wagon.

She asked her grandfather where they were going, and he said, "I think you need to talk to your father, don't you?" They were going to the cemetery, and it was a pretty long ride.

"Don't you think they need my help back there? It is going to be a big party tonight."

"No, Virgie said she could take care of it, and I think you need to talk to him, so stop stalling. Ramon wouldn't let you come out here before you left last time, and I am not going to let you leave without doing it this time."

"You like, Virgie, don't you? And don't lie." He smiled, but he wouldn't look at her.

"Not even going to answer me, are you?" She looked sideways at him.

"Nope, it is none of your business. I am old enough to take of my own business."

She just grinned. He did, but he wouldn't admit it.

"If this goes the way I want, I am going to have Mama's body brought back and buried here beside Dad. Is that all right?"

They didn't look at each other. They just kept riding. Finally, he said, "I think that would be just fine. She belongs here with the rest of the family."

They were finally at the cemetery, and they got off their horses and started walking to the family graves. Her father's was not far. It was beside her grandmother's.

"You tell him what you are planning. I will be up at my parents'. I will be back."

She just looked, got down on her knees, cleared the weeds away from his stone, and then found herself talking.

"Well, Daddy, guess you already know what I have been up to, and it hasn't been pretty. Don't know how many men I have killed anymore. Indian or white, I stopped counting, but there is going to be one more. He killed Mama and you, and he has my sisters, and I promised my husband and Grandpa I wouldn't kill him in cold blood, but if it is the only way I will. I think this will take me out of the running for heaven, so I probably won't see you or Mama, but I do love y'all. Please believe that. This is something I have to finish. I am tired of running. I love you both. Please believe that, Daddy. Always."

She was crying as a hand rested on her shoulder, and she put her hand on her grandfather's and just knelt there.

"You haven't done anything but protect yourself. Keep your promise to us, and come back alive."

She turned around and held him and just cried as he held her. He didn't know how lost she really was, and she was going after a man who would kill her in a heartbeat. He wanted to stop her and keep her here, but he didn't know how determined she was to go, so they just sat on her father's grave and grieved.

She finally looked up at him and said, "If I don't do this now, he wins, and I am afraid of what he will do to the girls. They are just pawns in this game of his, and this child of mine will be in his line of fire as well. I have to finish this now. You do understand, don't you?"

He nodded. "Come down here to your grandmother's grave. I want to tell you something about her nobody know but me and maybe your father."

They walked down to her grave.

"She died fighting Comancheros. They attacked while the men and I were out with the cattle. Your daddy and his two sisters were with her and two hands, and I thought I had left enough help. I hadn't. It was when we were in Peacock, Texas, before we bought this place up here. She had killed both of her attackers. She was alone, and when I got here, one of them had tried to rape her, or at least I think he tried. She never told me. Neither did your dad. He shot her, but she cut his throat and then pushed him off her. She died in my arms as your father kept the girls' eyes hidden. He saw it all. He never spoke of what happened that day. I moved all of them after that and brought her body here. She used to look like you do when you get mad. She wouldn't lose herself in the hate. You are worse. That is what scares Miles so much. You have to control it, or Ramon will control you. I am just afraid for you. I have been since he took y'all to Dallas."

"I am not alone this time."

"It is time to get back." He was thinking she wasn't alone last time.

Her mother went with her, and look how that turned out.

They walked back to their horses and mounted and started back. He held his hand out, and she took it, and they rode like that for a long time. Sometimes when he looked sideways, he could see that scary woman. He had never asked his son what had happened that day. He had never wanted to know.

When they got back to the house, it was lit up so you could see it a mile away. She looked over at her grandfather and asked, "How many people did you invite?"

"A few, and then a whole lot more."

"Which meant everybody in the whole county?" Virgie was probably going crazy by now. She was going to kill her grandfather.

She quickly got off her horse, and one of the men grabbed it and started to the barn to put it up, and she went in through the back door, where she was met by Virgie and some of the girls. They grabbed both arms and led her through the back halls and wouldn't let her see the main rooms, and she was led to her bedroom. When they opened the door, on the bed was a white-lace wedding gown she had never seen before, but this gown was old, very old.

She turned and looked at Virgie. "What is going on here?"

"Your grandfather said McKinney women don't get married without a family present, so you are getting married tonight. This is your grandmother's wedding gown, and we think it will fit you. We are your bridesmaids or women or whatever if that is all right."

"Oh, that is very much all right. Y'all did this today while I was gone?"

They nodded.

She turned around and went to the dress and held it up. "Well, let's see if it fits. If it doesn't, we are in trouble. I may have to wear the drapes."

They all laughed as she put the dress on, and it was a little big, but Abigail was there, and after a few stitches and minor alterations, it was good as new—at least new fifty years ago. She didn't know where this dress had been hidden. She had never seen it before, and she had been in every nook and cranny of her grandfather's house over her lifetime.

They brushed and braided back just the top of her hair, and they set a crown of tiny flowers on her head, and it was just enough. She looked like a bride.

She looked at Virgie. "My wedding ring. Where is my ring?"

"The groom has it. He will give it back to you at the ceremony."

About that time, the band started to play the wedding march, and the women started out first, and her grandfather was waiting for her at the door.

"So this is why I needed to see my father today?"

"He couldn't walk you down the aisle, so I thought you at least needed to talk to him and tell him you were home."

She took his arm. "I wish they were here."

"They are, and they always will be. You are wearing her dress, and you are his daughter. She would be so proud of you. Be proud of yourself. You stayed alive."

She looked down the aisle at Miles. She hardly noticed the flowers. Where they came from, she had no idea. He was so handsome in his store-bought suit and new boots. All the people around were friends she hadn't seen in years and family as well. The preacher, she knew; he was from the church in town. If he only knew how many men she had killed, he probably wouldn't be here.

She walked up to Miles, and the preacher asked, "Who gives this woman?"

And her grandfather answered, "The McKinney family, all of them present." And the entire room erupted into clapping.

She looked at Miles, and he looked at her. "Now let Ramon try and deny you."

The ceremony went on from there, and when it was over and they got to the rings, he put a wedding band as well as her diamond ring, but this time, Virgie pressed a ring into her hand, a gold band for his hand. She put his ring on his hand as well, to the cat calls from her cousins, but they could see how much she loved him.

Then he pulled her to the center of the room. The band started to play, and they danced. She sang to him again softly, and this time, she knew he was truly hers. They danced and danced, and so did her grandfather and Virgie, and she smiled at him as they passed. She even got up and sang for the crowd for the first time since she had sung for Miles at Virgie's house that night.

Finally, she got the women she had brought to her grandfather's place on the back patio so she could talk to them. She told them she was leaving soon and they were all going to be taken care of, but she really wanted them to wait a while longer for her to come back.

"What if you don't come back?"

"Everything has been taken care of in case I don't. Just like we talked about, you will still be taken care of. Did you not have a pleasant time tonight? Has anyone been unkind to you?"

One of the women said, "No, but this is not everywhere."

She was trying to make them understand she could protect them here. Finally, it was Trey who explained it.

"She is trying to tell you she can make a safe place for you here, where no one will be mean to you, but she can't protect you outside this area because she is a rich woman with influence here, and she will protect you here. This is her house. This is her world. She can't protect you outside this world."

They looked around. They finally understood—the wagon, the houses, the food. She had provided all that she had and kept them safe. No man had. She had, a woman.

"Decide whatever you want. Just take your time and think it over. You don't have to go back tonight. You can stay if you want." Then she went back inside and found Miles.

Trey stayed for a minute more. "She has protected you from the very start. It was always her at the fort and all the way here. She was the one who made sure you were kept safe. Listen to her, and she will always do what is best for you and your children."

"What about Two Wings? What happened to her?"

He turned back around. "She tried to help her. She bound her wrists after she cut them open, but she begged her to let her die, so she took them off and held her while she bled to death, then we buried her. She said she was just too tired to have another family and lose them, and that is my fault for leading them to you." Then he got up and walked back inside. He was a different man from the one she had met that morning at the camp.

When he went back inside, there were petitions being signed by every person who knew Morgan before, now that she was Morgan McKinney Douglas, for her to take to Dallas with her and one to be filed tomorrow in the courthouse. The judge would take another one and mail it to the judge in Dallas as well. The noose was getting tighter around Ramon's neck.

Morgan and Miles danced and danced until he took her hand and led her to the bedroom. They passed Virgie, and she was dancing with Donald Roy. She gave a little wave to her, and they went on.

When they got to the room, Miles shut and locked the door, and

Morgan went over to the window and shut and locked it.

"It may get hot in here without a breeze."

"This way, my cousins won't get to play any tricks on us, and they will try if the window is open. Trust me."

Before she could go any further, he told her to shut her eyes and turn around, and she looked at him kind of funny, then she turned around. He carefully undid the buttons of the dress and let it slide down, and she stepped out of it. He hung it on the hook on the wall, and then he put the squash blossom necklace around her neck. As she put her hand on the cool metal, she looked down at it, and then she turned and looked into the mirror.

"Where did this come from? It is beautiful."

He was smiling at her in the mirror. "Virgie has held on to it for me for years in her jewelry box. I had it made for Gray Dove, but she never saw it. She died before it was finished. Do you mind that it was made for her?"

"No. I know you had a life before me. I am sorry she never got to see it, but I am glad it is mine now. It is beautiful. But I have nothing for you."

"You are all I have wanted for years."

Then out came that wicked little smile, and he began to get hard at just the thought of what was to come.

"Well then, I think for my wedding present, I should get to undress you and take special attention to my new husband, and he shouldn't get to do anything until I say so."

Oh god, she was going to kill him, and he was going to let her do it. Well, they could bury him with a smile on his face.

She just stood there with her slip and boots on and asked, "I can do anything I want to do, and you can't touch until I say so." That smile was so unnerving, but he just nodded.

She came at him and took off his new jacket and hung it on the hook. *Well, that wasn't so bad.* Then she started on the buttons. She undid each one and licked each spot of skin she opened up, even a nipple when she came to one, but when he reached for her, she shook her finger. *No, no.*

When she had his shirt off, she took her time hanging it as he was burning to touch her, and she was smiling. Then she came back, took his belt, undid it, and went after the buttons of his pants, one by one, until she had them all undone, and then she started to pull his pants off his hips.

Then she changed. Her eyes turned to steel, and she said, "Don't move." And not for one second did he think she was kidding.

She was watching something, and when he looked in the mirror, he could see the rattlesnake lying on the bed. If they had lain down when they came in here, one of them would have been dead, and it probably would have been her.

She pushed him aside, reached for her knife in her boot, pinned the snake, and took his head off. Then she picked him up and put him in a hat box with his separated head.

Miles looked at her. "Maybe it is a joke by one of your cousins."

"My cousins wouldn't ever play games with a rattler. Besides, look at his tail."

He had no rattlers. Someone had cut them off. His tail was still bleeding.

"He is still trying to get to me here. You go get Grandpa and bring him here. I will check the room."

He buttoned up his pants as she got her robe. What she had started was gone now. A rattler was a great mood killer.

He walked out of the bedroom without a shirt, and Virgie saw him first. She was dancing with Donald Roy and patted him on the shoulder, and he practically ran to the room.

"What is wrong?"

"You have got to see this for yourself."

Morgan was on the floor under the bed, looking for snakes as they entered, and he smiled until Miles showed him the box.

"That could have gotten in here by accident, Morgan."

"Really? Look at the tail, and it was on the bed."

His smile disappeared. "Someone is in the house. Go to my room."

"Where do you plan to sleep?"

"I will find somewhere."

Then he looked down at Virgie, and she smiled at Miles.

"All right, but nobody you don't know stays here tonight, and knock before you come in. I am sleeping with a gun. Have everybody check their room."

Her grandfather's room wasn't as big as hers was, but he didn't care. They got in, and they took the room apart, looking everywhere for snakes, and found none. Then they took the bed apart and finally went to bed. He pulled her up beside him and held her, and then he pulled her under him.

"By the way, I was enjoying that wedding present you were giving me before the rattler interrupted. It was quite entertaining."

Before he could go any further, she reached down and took hold of him in her hand, and he saw that smile again. "I was trying to please you, but the snake took my mind off of what I was doing." Then she stroked him gently with her hand.

"So very soft and gentle when you want to be." Then he entered her and took over what she had started.

"Miles, I love you so much. I hope I haven't ruined your life by intertwining it with mine."

As he made love to her, stroking and stroking, he could only think that she had given him more love in this short time than he had felt in his entire lifetime. Even when he was married to Gray Dove, he had never felt like this. She and her family had made his life so complete and whole. He held her so tightly, she could hardly breathe, but she was soaring, and she finally came. If this was all there was, it had been worth it. So now they fought for her sisters and his child.

The next day, she had seen her grandfather come out of Virgie's room in the morning, and he didn't see her. Well, she and Virgie would have something to talk about this afternoon.

She was getting everything packed when Gary came in, and he had the box with the dress in it and another dress box.

"Where did that one come from?"

"My mama's bedroom closet in Dallas. She had her mother's dress, and when I said I was coming up here to see you, she sent it. She said Grandpa would want you to get married in front of the whole family.

She said to bring it back she is waiting for you and the girls.”

“You think we can do this and not get killed?”

“I don’t know, but if you don’t try, I don’t think the girls will survive.”

“What are you talking about?”

“This new woman of his doesn’t like them, and the last time I saw them, Dona had bruises all over her arms like she had been pinched hard, but she wouldn’t even let me see Rose. I just know she hates them both, and if she has a child, especially a boy, they are in trouble. People around him tend to have serious accidents. He won’t let me see them at all now, and unless you come, I fear for their lives.”

“We leave tomorrow, so be ready. Here, let me have the dress and the box. I will pack the wedding dress back up, and we will take it back to your mother.”

She walked down the hall into Virgie’s room, and she was hanging her clothes in the closet. She laid the dress on the bed and the box. “Will you help me pack the wedding dress back up so I can take it back to my aunt when we go?”

“Sure, baby, give me just a minute.”

She watched Virgie do just ordinary stuff and wondered when she had lost the ability to do those things. Now all she seemed to be able to do was kill things. Virgie turned and folded the dress and put it back into the box, and it fit, and she put the lid on it. It seemed like such a simple thing, so why was loading a Winchester easier for her to do than that?

“What’s wrong, Morgan?”

“I was just wondering if I would ever be normal again or if I will always be this scary woman Miles is afraid of, and don’t tell me he hasn’t told you about her.”

She sat beside her on the bed. “He did, but maybe there was a scary lady that night I threw that first torch into the house. Sometimes it takes a scary lady to survive, and, honey, I am not sure I could have survived what you have. Mama Ruby says the Lord has his eyes on you. I don’t know about that, but somebody is watching out for you, or you still wouldn’t be alive. People do what they have to, and you did just that. Someday you will think this is boring and wonder why you were ever scary."

She looked at her and smiled. "I am ready for that day now."

"Not yet, baby. You still have some things left to do and there is still a target on your back."

"By the way, was that my grandpa I saw coming out of your room this morning, or was I imagining that?"

She looked at her sideways. "I have no idea what you are talking about."

She smiled. "Still a little fire smoldering in that fireplace?"

Virgie looked straight ahead as she dangled her feet off the bed. "Honey, there is a blaze in that fireplace."

And they both broke into laughter as Miles walked in the bedroom. "What is going on in here?"

"Nothing, dear, we are just talking."

As he walked away they were dying laughing again, and they were both rolling on the bed.

Morgan said, "Good for you. Take care of him while I am gone."

"Oh, I intend to, darlin'. You won't know him when you get back."

"Maybe I should leave the wedding dress here." Then she thought about it.

"No. If he gets married, his daughters will be here, and I have got to see that."

The grin on her face almost scared Virgie. What were her aunts like? Now she was kind of scared.

They were getting packed, and there was a lot of stuff she needed to take with her. She hid the derringer inside her green dress box and put it where she could get at it easy. She knew Miles wouldn't be looking for anything in there. She was wearing her necklace. She was going to wear it as long as she could. She was so proud of it. They packed the wagon and were ready to head to town. They were staying the night there so they could catch the early stage.

She hugged and said goodbye to everyone at the ranch, and when it was time to say goodbye to her grandfather, she didn't know if she could do it, but better here than at the stagecoach. He grabbed her in a bear hug and whispered in her ear, "Remember, just make him mad and stay out of his line of fire, and come back to us with your sisters. We will be waiting."

She didn't say anything. She knew if she tried, she would start crying, so she just nodded and got on her horse. She started to ride away, but when she turned around and looked back, Virgie had her arm around his, and he was crying. She looked at Miles. She had men all around her—a ranger, cousins, and her husband. If this worked, she wouldn't leave here again.

They rode and got to town before dark, and they went to the hotel. This town wasn't very big, but it was bigger than most around here. When they were in the room, she was looking out the window. She was watching some men walking into the salon across the street, and she recognized one of them.

"Miles come here quick."

When he got to the window, she pointed to a man. "See the man in the black hat with the mustache and the goatee in the chaps?"

He looked and said, "Yes. What about him? Who is he?"

She turned and looked like thunder. "He was the man at Ramon's ranch who liked to play with rattlesnakes. He is the one I suspected put the one in the garden that killed mother, the one without rattles."

"You stay here, and I mean it. You don't move."

He went down the hall and got Carter and told him about the man. They both went to the salon, and when they came out, they had the man with them. He was escorted to the jail. He was yelling, and they were saying something to him when he turned his head and looked at her, then the color drained out of his face.

Miles came back to the room and told her, "The sheriff wants you to come down and identify him."

She was ready to go. She had been waiting for him.

They walked to the jail, and she wanted to go inside. She was going to the back when Miles said, "Morgan, the gun stays here, as well as the knife. We need him to testify."

She turned, placed her pistol on the desk, pulled her knife out of her boot, and set it beside the gun. She looked at him and cocked her head at him. "All right now?"

He nodded, and he walked her in with a chair, and as she sat down, he walked a little ways to the side. The sheriff and Carter were listening at the door. They wanted to hear what was going on as well.

"I don't remember your name just your face. They told me they found the rattles in your pocket already. It didn't work on me the first time, so you thought you would try it again."

He had a smug smile on his face. "I figured the way you looked, the first thing your man would do was put you on that bed. That is what I would have done. Guess he had something else on his mind."

"I was entertaining him another way, and we hadn't gotten to the bed yet." And the look she gave him would have melted butter.

"Damn, woman, Ramon should have married you instead of trying to get rid of you."

She just rolled her eyes. "The mealy-mouthed worm wouldn't have survived our wedding night. What is your name?"

"Martin." He was beginning to squirm; this lady could get him killed. There were horses coming at a dead run outside now, and in came her grandfather, but she held up her hand. She wasn't through with this man yet.

"They made you leave your gun and knife at the door. Are they afraid I will hurt you? What do they think I will do to you in here?" He leaned against the back wall of the jail cell as he talked to her, and she just watched him. He thought he was so smart.

"No, they are afraid I will kill you. I need you to testify against Ramon for me."

"They really think you would hurt me in here? Why?"

She just smiled at him with narrowed eyes, and it seemed her face changed. "I tend to kill bounty hunters who come after me, and you have come after me twice now. My husband worries I have no self-control. I left two dead in the New Mexico Mountains and one gutted in Colorado. I don't know how many at the ranch. I could see about leaving a rattler or two in there with you, seeing as how you like them so much."

The men watching at the door weren't saying anything. So she could kill him, and nobody would say a thing about it. The men in the other cells were getting uncomfortable as well. This woman was scary.

"All right, he hired me to put the snake in the garden, but it was to get you, not your mother. When she died he was furious so he told me to run. When I found out how much the reward was on your head, I thought I might try again. Maybe it would work this time. I forgot you are as good with snakes as I am."

"Is that what you need, ranger?" She never took her eyes off him.

The ranger nodded, but before she could leave, somebody in the cell next to him asked her, "Who was shooting the Sharps? We hadn't expected a buffalo hunter when we took on this job."

Ranger Carter walked past Morgan and answered him. "She was shooting the Sharps." Then he took her arm and led her out of the cell block and handed her back to Miles.

Her grandfather was there. He had heard it all. She had been right all along.

One of the men in the cell said, "We didn't get paid enough money for this job."

She turned back around and looked into the cell. "I am curious. What is the price to shoot a woman backlit by her burning barn?"

They didn't answer, but every man in that cell had five hundred dollars on him.

She walked out into the setting daylight and asked Ranger Carter, "What now? Do we have enough to satisfy a judge? Will his word be enough to prove who I am?" She held on to her grandfather's arm.

"It should be, but I am sending a letter instead of a telegraph so he won't be forewarned. That way, he can't cook something else up, and I don't want him to know we are coming either."

They went to the restaurant in town and ate as they talked about what had happened, and her grandfather decided to stay in town for the night. The judge was taking a statement from Martin as they spoke. He didn't want something to happen to him before they could get everything down on paper.

While they talked, she went upstairs and went to bed. She had thought about after he had signed everything, going back and leaving him a gift from her, but she wasn't going to. She had other things to worry about.

When Miles came up, he lay down next to her and said, "I was proud of you today. You didn't lose it like the last couple of times. You were in control."

She rolled over and looked at him. "I don't want to turn into him, and I am afraid that is what I am becoming."

He held her and covered her up, and they went to sleep. Sometimes he was afraid of the same thing.

CHAPTER 5

She had to tell her grandfather goodbye again the next morning, but it wasn't as hard this time. They loaded the stage and were on their way with three extra men for escorts. Dennis, Miles, and Gary sat inside with her. She wasn't allowed to ride outside. She made too easy a target.

The first day wasn't so bad, and then they stayed at Vernon for the night. The next day, they didn't get too far when they broke down with a broken wheel sometime after lunch. They sent men ahead to get another wheel, and she was looking around. There was a stand of trees, and she was walking toward it with Gary. They found a washed-out stream, and she walked partway down the side.

Gary was following her and said, "Where are you going?"

"Down here. There is some running water, and it is sandy and cool. They aren't going to be back for hours."

He started following her. She had no business wandering off. "Give me a hand getting down." And she reached up, and he helped her get down the side of the steep bank. As he watched her, she turned around and asked him, "Well, are you coming or not?"

These two had been raised together and were like brother and sister and fought like them too. "Why? There is nothing down there I want to see. You go prowl around if you are so curious."

She yelled back up to him, "You have been a lawyer too long, Gary Lee. You are a wuss."

Well, that was all it took. He was over the side in a flash. She couldn't call him that. She was just a girl, no matter the fact she was a scary girl. The fact that he was in a suit and his dress boots didn't matter. She had made him mad.

Miles and Carter weren't far away, watching from a rock, and they could hear it all. Carter asked Miles, "Does she always go after him like that?"

"Yep, and he gives as good as he gets. Watch, this is going to be interesting. I don't know what she is doing down there."

Morgan had taken off her white boots and was walking in the water. She was looking at something, and she called Gary over to look. "There is a big catfish caught in these little pools, and we are going to catch it."

"Oh no, we are not. I am in my good suit."

"For god's sake, Gary Lee, take off your boots and roll up your pants. It is only about twelve inches deep. You are not going to drown."

He looked in the pools, and sure enough, there was a fish, and a big one. "What do you plan on doing with it? One won't feed us."

"Two will. There is another one over here, and it is big too." Sure enough, there was another one.

"How are we going to catch it? With our bare hands, Indian woman?" Nobody else in the world could have gotten away with calling her that except him, and he knew it because she didn't take it as an insult from him. It just was.

"No, burlap bags from the wagon. You go on one side and me on the other, and we scoop it up."

"I am not cleaning those things. No way they stink and I am not ruining my suit."

She smiled at him. He hated cleaning fish, always had. "I will clean them, you wuss. So you will help me?"

He just nodded. Then she turned and yelled to the two men watching them, "Miles, go get the bag, please, so we can get ready."

They just looked at each other. They thought they were so sneaky. "You knew we were up here?"

She turned as she was rolling up her pants leg while she sat on a rock. "I heard y'all coming a long ways away. You sound like a bear coming through the woods. Now go get me the burlap sack, and we will get us some fish for dinner."

He went to the coach and got the bag. It had been carrying extra food for the horses, so she would get one at the next stop to replace it. When he came back, he threw it to her, and she took her knife and split it open and handed one side to Gary, who by now had rolled up his pants and pulled off his expensive boots and set them aside. She was smiling—and so was he—as they set the bag over the water and settled it down under the fish. Then they pulled it up and threw the fish on the sand at the side of the bank.

She stood up and told Gary, "Move over to the right slowly and keep your feet in the water." Then she pulled her pistol and fired. He was dancing around as she went behind him. She walked over, picked up a stick, reached down with it, and picked up a copper- colored snake.

"That thing was behind me, and you didn't tell me? What were you thinking?"

"I was thinking if I told you, you would panic and probably step on it. Look, it is dead."

As she held it out for inspection, he almost hit her. The two men up above her were holding their mouths, trying not to let them hear them laughing. It was so funny.

"Morganna Linn, it is not funny, and you know I hate those things. That is as bad as that stupid horned toad you threw at me when we were little."

"But you wouldn't have known it was me if you didn't have scars now, would you? And it wasn't that big. Your horse just got spooked, and you fell on that rock. You bled all over my new saddle, and it was never the same again. It was a really nice saddle, and I never did get the blood off of it."

"You dragged me home across your saddle like a bleeding calf after my horse ran off. Your daddy had to stitch up my butt. My mother was furious for days at you and me."

"She really was, and they wouldn't let me watch him stitch you up. I am sorry. I won't do it again. If I see another copperhead, I will let him bite you first then tell you."

Then she turned and ran as he threw sand in her hair. "All right, no fair Gary Lee. There is sand in my hair and no bath for miles around? I will get you for that." She turned and grinned at him, and he started to smile. "Are we good now? I apologize. Here, I will get rid of it, and we will catch the other fish."

Gary was still pissed, but she did have sand all over her, and she was going to itch all night. Well, that was a start.

She grabbed the snake by the tail and threw it up on the other bank out of the way so they wouldn't step on it, and they were good to go again. Then they went back to catching the other fish.

"Hand me the other end, and let's get the other one."

This was more fun than she had had with Gary Lee in years, and she was going to enjoy it.

"Push that one in that little bitty puddle, and he will stay wet and alive for a bit till we catch this one. Oh, for heaven's sake, he won't bite much."

And they were good again, but the two men up above them were still laughing. It was hysterical.

When she had killed the fish and gutted them, they started back up, and the other two men were there to help them. She had cleaned up in the stream, and the fish were clean and ready to fry. When they got back to the coach, they had the wheel on and were almost finished, but by now, it was dark, and they couldn't travel at night.

The men from the coach had brought back some supplies, and she had enough to make a good dinner with the fish. She filleted them, and there was plenty. The men had brought bread and some beans, and they were good for the night. She had done with less and worse circumstances.

She and Miles slept inside, and after she had found her hairbrush, she brushed and brushed sand out of her hair.

"Was it worth it to play with him today? And don't tell me that is not what you were doing because a blind man could see that."

"He has spent so many years trying to protect what is mine and the girls, and for what? He will get nothing from it, just my thanks and Ramon's undying hatred. I wanted him to know how much I still love and appreciate him, and when this is over, I will see that he is taken care of if he needs it."

"Does he need it?"

"I don't know. He is a partner in a law firm that Granddaddy helped him start, but I wish he was closer. I know he takes care of his mother since his father died, so I will find out when this is done."

"Are you going to tell me what you are planning?"

"Not yet. It isn't done yet, and I know you think I am lying to you, but I have to see what is going on in Ramon's house when we get there."

"How are you going to do that?"

"That is the part of the plan I don't have figured out yet."

She finally settled down. She was thinking, and he was worrying. She had plans she hadn't figured out yet, and they were getting closer.

Almost another whole day on the road, and they were at the next stop. This one was just a way station, but they were to stay the night here. They would leave in the morning. They were fed, and she was about to get up when a man walked in, and Morgan and Gary both looked at the man and at each other and then sat back down. She just watched this man, and then in came a boy. She grabbed Gary's hand, and he looked at her as she looked at him.

"Do you know either of them?"

He shook his head. They watched both of them until they went outside, and then Morgan said, "I am going to talk to him."

Miles looked over at Gary and asked, "What is wrong?"

Gary leaned over the table and said, "You see that man and that boy? If I didn't know better, I would think her father just rose from the grave, and that boy looks like several of our cousins. He has got to be a McKinney, but I don't know who he is."

She followed the man outside. He was loading the coach, and she just asked him, "Who are you?"

He turned and looked at her and then went back to doing his work. "I am just a hired hand, lady. I have got work to do. Go back inside."

"Not the answer I wanted. Who are you? What is your name?" And this time, when he turned around, she was looking at him so strangely.

He told her, "My name is Dolf McKinney, lady. Are you satisfied now?"

She walked over to him and took his face in her hands. "No, not nearly. What is your father's name?"

"Burrus McKinney."

"Did he have any brothers or sisters?"

"He had a brother named Donald Roy. What is this all about? Who are you?"

"I am Morganna McKinney, and Donald Roy is my grandfather, and you look enough like my father to be him. Your son looks like several of my cousins. Why do I not know about you?"

He looked at her like she had slapped him. He had been looking for some family for years and couldn't find any. He had given up, and now this woman said she was a McKinney.

"Talk to me. What is going on? Why don't I know you?"

He just sat down on the wagon tongue and looked at her and started to talk. "When Burrus and Donald Roy were ranching around Peacock, Texas, Burrus killed a man in a bar fight. Their father split what money he had and told him to run and never come back and that is what he did. When he died two years ago, he sent us back to look for family. We came back looking for family but found none, so we stayed here, and I went to work. All I have left is my son Pete. My wife died a few years ago."

"Finish what you have to do out here and then come in. I want to talk some more. Do you want to stay in this place, or would you rather leave here to come meet your people?"

"I would rather leave, but I still have some money I have to work off here before I can leave. My boy was sick last winter, and I had to borrow from the owner to get a doctor."

She knew men like the man who ran this place. He would never run out of debt, not in this lifetime.

As she walked inside, a little boy not more than four was loading up kindling and starting inside. She opened the door for him. He looked up at her, and she smiled, but the child didn't even acknowledge her presence. He was wearing rags and was dirty, and Morgan's eyes followed him across the room as she walked in the room.

He started to set down the kindling when a man tripped him, and he went sailing. The man who owned the place was laughing as he went to kick him.

"You stupid kid. You are more trouble than you are worth. Just for that, you get no supper."

She was in front of the boy by then and helping him up, and then she looked at the man and said, "It doesn't look like you feed him very often anyway. He is starving. What is his name?"

"Don't have the foggiest, lady. He hasn't spoken a word since he walked in here months ago, and then he looked like he had been buried and dug up."

"Was he alone? You didn't go see if there was someone who might need help?"

"Not my business, woman. The kid is lucky I didn't kick him back out into the desert."

She started to lead the boy away, and he reached to grab him. Wrong move. Her knife was in his belly before he even saw her grab it.

"The child is going over here with me and eating supper, and if you like that hand, you will remove it."

As he looked around, there were several men with guns drawn at the table backing her up. He didn't know who she was, but he decided he didn't want to.

She sat him down in her lap and started to feed him. He was skin and bones. She tried to make him say something. He wouldn't say a word, but she could see he did have a tongue. That was all right she was afraid there was something wrong with his mouth.

As she sat there, she told Gary, "The man outside—his father was our grandfather's brother." She then told them the story and how he had been looking for family. She didn't know how he hadn't found some of them already. Lord knows they were everywhere. Maybe because they had been hiding for so long, she sure didn't know her grandfather had a brother till today.

She took Miles aside and told him, "I am not leaving that child behind. I hope you are good with that, but that man will not take care of him. If that is not all right, I will find him a good home, but I am not leaving him."

He had watched her as she was feeding him, and he had already figured that one out for himself. The child was not stupid, but there was something wrong. As for finding another home, she had no intention of giving that child up. Good. Just another reason for her to stay alive.

"We will take him with us. He needs someone."

He just kept eating. She didn't know when he had eaten last, but it had been a while. Dolf came through the door with his son Pete and sat down. The owner began to rail at him, and she finally had enough. The other men just watched her to see what she was going to do. Texas frowned on killing men in cold blood, so they wouldn't let her go that far.

She stood back up with a sleepy child in her arms and told him, "I am taking this child with me tomorrow so you are rid of him. What does this man owe you?"

"Why do you want to know?'

"Because I am paying off his debt how much does he owe you?"

He thought about it and then said, "I guess about sixty dollars." He thought she would back down. He didn't put up with women. They had big mouths.

"That includes the wagon and horses out there?"

"Yes, that includes everything he owes me."

She handed the boy to Miles and took out her wallet, and it was full of hundred-dollar bills. The look on his face was priceless. She pulled out three twenties, threw them on the table, turned, and told Dolf, "Gather everything you own and pack. You are leaving with us in the morning."

The owner started to say something. "Maybe I was wrong about the amount he owed me."

"You told me an amount, and everybody heard, and now our business is done."

"Maybe I won't let you take the child without more money."

She just turned and pointed to Carter. "Talk to him. He is a Texas Ranger. And tell him how you let a child walk in here looking like he had been buried and dug up and how you didn't go to see if anybody else needed help. I would love to hear that explanation, as well as the one where you don't feed him on a regular basis. Well, start talking. We are all waiting."

She just stood there for a minute, staring at him, and he was getting madder by the second. How dare a woman talk back to him like that? A woman was good for only one thing.

"Thought not. Most cowards lose their voices in front of an audience."

She started walking away. The men just watched. That man would have tried to kill her if they had been alone, and she knew it. He would have lost, and they knew that too. She goaded him just to see what he would do. She didn't like to have to watch her back.

As she walked down the hall, she asked Dolf if he had any small clothes for the boy. The ones he had on were literally falling off him.

"I will see if I can find some of Pete's old clothes. Maybe there are some small ones left."

When she got to a room, it was small, and the beds were not much more than cots, but there was a small bath. The boy was almost asleep. That was the only reason he had let Miles hold him while she was paying the owner. She wanted to bathe him if she could, so she woke him and looked at his face and asked him if she could bathe him before she put him to bed. He looked at her and nodded, but when he looked at Miles, he was scared of him. She nodded, and he went outside.

She went to bathe him, and what she found on him scared her. This little boy had been shot. The bullet had gone through his side below his ribs, but still. He had a knife mark and rope burns as well. Something bad had happened. She didn't know what, but it was obvious he had been someone's captive.

She washed him and took her time with his hair. He had a scar on his head that had healed but should have been stitched. He had been hit with something hard, and someone had intended to hurt if not kill him. She was wondering if he had been shot and if someone had buried him, thinking he was dead. He wouldn't talk to her yet, so she would have to find out later.

After she got him washed and dried, Dolf came back with some clothes, and she put some underwear and a shirt on him. It was still too big, but it would have to do for tonight. When they get to a town tomorrow, she would buy him what she needed.

When she laid him down in bed, he wouldn't let her go, so she lay next to him and called Miles in, and he lay on the other bed.

"Tomorrow, you will be going with us. You are not staying here anymore. Is that all right?"

As she looked at him, he nodded then looked at Miles.

"Yes, he is coming too. He is my husband, but he won't hurt you either. I promise."

He looked over her shoulder, and she knew sometime in this child's life, a man had been very bad to him, and Miles was going to have to work harder than she was to gain his trust.

She stayed all night next to him with his hand clutched to her shirt.

When he was asleep, she and Miles talked softly.

"You know, something happened to him, and it was a man who did it. He is afraid of every man who gets near him."

Morgan looked over the child's head at Miles, and he told her, "Really, I had already figured that one out. He will hardly let me close to him or you."

"I will find out what happened. It will just take some time."

As Miles looked at her on the other bed, he said, "Well, I guess I can wait, but not until he is grown, or I will have to find another woman to take care of me." And then he sighed so pitifully, she wanted to gag.

"Really? Get over yourself. With these cots, you weren't going to have any luck tonight anyway."

Then she heard laughter from the other room. "Shut up, Gary Lee, or I am coming in there with a varmint." He shut up.

She looked over at her smiling husband and went, "Schusses." Then she lay back down and went to sleep on this tiny cot with this little boy and two laughing men. She would have to kill them later as she went to sleep smiling. She did have one hell of a family.

The next morning, she dressed him as best as she could, and they got on the coach. She sat down, and he sat next to her, away from all the men in the coach. She tried to get him to talk, but he just looked at her and didn't say a word.

When they got to the next little town, they stopped, and she went to the store and stood him on the counter as she measured him for pants and shirts and underwear.

The owner came over and said, "Don't you know what size your son wears? I don't really like the children standing on my counter."

She stopped and pulled out a hundred-dollar bill and put it on the counter. "Happy? Now go away." And the look she gave him didn't leave much arguing room.

"Do you like these pants?"

The little boy nodded, so she put them aside, and she reached for some boots and measured them against his feet then grabbed some new socks. She put on the socks. She had seen last night he hadn't worn anything in a while. He must have walked barefoot from wherever he came from because his feet were a mess, calloused and cracked. She would get some cream for them. She put on the socks and then the boots and had him walk in them.

"Are they too tight?"

She felt the toes. She thought they might be too tight, so she put him back on the counter, and he tried another pair. This time, she liked the way he was walking in them.

"Do those feel better?"

He nodded vigorously this time.

"And they don't hurt? Because we can try on another pair if they hurt."

He shook his head.

"All right, now you need a hat. Let's see. What color do you want?"

She had the owner bring out the hats that would fit him and sit them on the counter, and he looked at them. She was holding him on her hip as he looked, and she said, "Which hat do you like?"

He pointed to her.

"Are you asking what color hat I wear?"

He nodded again. She pointed to a cream-colored felt one. He nodded, so she picked it up and put it on his head.

"What a handsome man you have there, Morgan. Will you two join me for lunch before we leave?"

"Yes, let me pay the man."

She also got a couple of jars of hand cream for his feet, and then they went to have lunch. At least he didn't shy away from Miles when he came in this time. He held her hand as they walked into the stage's lunch area, and he was decked out, hat and all. They all looked at him. He didn't look like the same boy.

She sat him down, and she told him, "A gentleman always takes his hat off at the dinner table. A lesson I had to teach the ranger the other day. He had forgotten. Just set it down on the bench if there is nowhere to hang it."

The little boy took off his hat and laid it down on the bench beside him and looked up at her, and she smiled and nodded, and he smiled back. That was the first time he had smiled at her. One step at a time—that was all she could do.

They got back on the stage after eating. This child ate like he hadn't eaten in years. She would find out what happened to him. She looked down at him, and he looked at her.

"I know you don't want to talk to me yet, but I have to call you something, and I am not going to call you boy. How about Two Bits? I used to call him that." And she pointed to Gary Lee across from her. "He is my cousin, and he used to love it."

"Hey, I did—"

The look she was giving him would have killed. If the boy could have seen it, he would have known she was lying, but he didn't see.

Gary just went along and smiled. "Yes, I loved that name. It was my favorite." He said it through gritted teeth, and she just kept smiling.

"How about that name until you are ready to tell me your name?"

He nodded, and she put her arm around him and gave him a gentle squeeze.

The next time they got out to water the horses, Gary got her to the side and said, "You owe me one, Morgan. A big one."

"Whatever you want, it is yours. I promise. I just have to get him to trust me, and maybe he will talk to me, and that is not with me calling him boy or, hey, you, unless you have a better suggestion."

"Do you really think he can talk, or is something wrong with him?"

"Something is wrong, but it is not physical. He has seen something, or something has been done to him, and he is just trying to hide from it the only way he can."

"How do you know?"

She just looked at him. "I have been there. I am almost twenty, and there are things I still can't forget and don't want to remember. I am afraid to find out what he has seen. How much longer till we get to Aunt Martha Jean's?"

"We will meet up this evening before the stage gets to Dallas, and we will have horses to take us to my ranch. We will spend the night there. Mama will be waiting on us."

"I have wanted to ask you. Is everything all right there with you?"

"Why do you ask?"

She shrugged. "I don't know, just a feeling something is wrong and you won't tell me."

"We will talk later when we can discuss it alone."

She was right. Something was wrong.

They rode for several hours more, and then they stopped and got out. They unloaded their things into a wagon that Gary provided and the rest into Dolf's wagon, and then the coach went on. She paid the coachman and his guard extra to forget they were ever on board. Then she climbed up on a horse. Miles handed her Two Bits, and he got on a horse, and they were off to Gary's ranch.

It took them another two hours to get there, and it was almost dark when they had arrived. Even in the dark, she could see there were hardly any cattle, and the house needed repairs. He was low on money. Why hadn't he used some of hers?

When she got inside, her aunt Martha Jean met Morgan at the door, and she thought she was going to break her ribs. Then she had her stand back and let Dolf come up, and she thought she was going to faint. Both Gary and Dolf caught her before she did as she was still looking at Dolf. They sat her in a chair.

"Who are you?" She looked at Morgan.

"His daddy is Granddaddy's brother, Burrus. Did you know about him?"

"Daddy's been looking for you for years and couldn't find any of you since you left Peacock. Where have you been?"

Morgan just looked up at Dolf and then said, "They went back to

Peacock, Texas, looking for family after his father died two years ago."

Martha Jean looked at her. "They were there all the time. Great investigators. Daddy will strangle them."

"He has a son who looks like the cousins."

"Which ones of the cousins?"

"Does it matter? We have several to pick from."

Her aunt reached over and kissed her cheek. "God, how I missed you. I thought Daddy was going to die when they took you."

Dolf hadn't been told the entire story behind the ride here and all the secrets yet. They thought they would tell him a little at a time.

About that time, in came two more of her cousins, and Gary's brother Jackson came up behind her and grabbed her and started to tickle her. She was squealing, and she didn't realize it was terrifying Two Bits.

He came into the room, screaming and hitting her cousin and saying, "Get away. Don't you hurt her? Please get away. You are killing her."

They stopped instantly, and he ran. Morgan just turned, and Miles told her, "Go find him. I think now he will tell you what happened to him." He stayed behind to tell the family what was going on.

She searched and finally found him in a closet at the back of the house. She wouldn't have found him, but she heard him crying. She pushed the boots out of the way and sat down. She scooted to the back with him and put him in her lap with his head on her chest and asked him, "Now is it time for you to tell me what happened to you?"

"No, you will hate me. You will want me to go away. I did something bad."

"What did you do that was so bad?"

"I can't tell you. You will hate me. You are a nice person."

"What if I tell you I did something bad? Would you think I was not so nice?"

He looked up at her. "But you are rich and pretty. People like you don't do bad things."

"Well, let's see about that. A bad man wants me dead. He is my stepfather, and he sent some men to kill me. They have tried several times, and I have defended myself. I have killed several men to stay alive. What have you done that is worse than that?"

He looked at her like she was lying to him, but he began to talk to her. "You really killed people?"

"Yes. They were going to kill me if I hadn't defended myself. So what did you do that was worse than that?"

"My daddy drank, and when he did, he beat me and my mother. She would try to hide me so he wouldn't hurt me, but he would always find me. He wasn't my real daddy. He was my step daddy. My daddy died in the war. My mama came out here with him to start over. He always said I was not his child, and he didn't want me. The last time he got drunk, he said I was the reason we were all going to starve. It was my fault, and Mama and I started to run away, and he shot at us. He hit me. We stayed outside all night until we thought he was asleep, and then we snuck back in. Mama said we were going to run away this time and never come back."

The men were at the door listening by now, so she just put up her hand to keep them there so he would continue. She wanted him to finish this story. Maybe he would finally be done if he told it all?

"When we got back in, we didn't see him, but he was there, and he had a hammer. He started hitting Mama first, and then I went to help, and he hit me on the head."

She heard her aunt sobbing in the hall, and she just held him a little tighter. "Go on, finish it." She already knew the rest was bad. She was just stroking his head. She could feel the lump where he had been hit.

"When I woke up, Mama was lying next to me on the ground, and she looked funny. She didn't close her eyes. Our hands were tied together. He had pulled us out of the house. He had dug two holes, and he pushed Mama in first then me. I pretended to be dead. He shoveled some dirt on us and then walked away into the barn. I got out and tried to help Mama, but she didn't talk or anything. She was dead. So I took the hammer and went to the barn. I was going to hit him. When I got there, he was in the hayloft with a rope around his neck, and he looked at me and walked off the side. He had killed the cow and the horse, so I took care of Mama, and I started walking until I came to the stage line house."

She couldn't even cry. She just held on to him. She remembered that feeling of desolation. "How long did you walk till you got to the stage house?"

He thought for a minute, and then he said, "I think it was three days. I was very thirsty when I got there."

"I'll bet you were. What did you do that you thought was so bad?"

He wouldn't look at her. "I left him there like that. I didn't even cut him down, and I wanted to hurt him for what he had done to Mama. Do you understand?"

"Yes, Two Bits, I understand better than you think I do. By the way, will you tell me your name now since we don't have any secrets anymore?" She looked down at his little face.

"Gregory. My mama called me Greg."

"I think that is an excellent name. Would you still like to come with me and be my son?"

He looked at her. "You still want me after what I told you?"

"Very much. I think we belong together, don't you? But with me come my husband and all those people and a lot more. We are a package deal, but they will protect you as I will, and no one will hurt you ever again. I promise."

He nodded. She put out her hand, and they shook on it.

"Let's get out of this closet and go eat something. How about that?"

He got off her lap and started to leave when he turned and asked her, "What do I call you now?"

Miles was there by then, and he was very interested in this question. She looked up at him, and he said,

"This one is yours. Whatever you two decide, I am fine with."

"Whatever you want to call me is fine with me."

He thought for a minute with his fist under his chin, and then he looked up at her and said, "I think Mama will do fine." Then he looked at Miles and asked, "Is that all right with you?"

Miles bent down and picked him up—he didn't struggle much—and then he calmed down. "Yes, sir, that is just fine." He was glad the men in the hallway were gone by now because they all had tears in their eyes by the time this child was through with his story.

When they got to the kitchen, Aunt Martha Jean was barely holding it together. She pulled the ranger aside and asked him if he could check and see if anybody had reported anything like the child had talked about when he went to town. He said he would find out what he could. They sat down to supper. He still wasn't far away from Morgan's side, but he did let Miles sit close to them. It was a little better.

After supper, she went outside with Gary, and they were talking. She asked him, "What is going on around here? This house needs painting, and there are hardly any cattle. This ranch is all but gone."

He turned and went to the end of the porch and leaned against the corner post when she heard the screen door open, and her Aunt came out. "You might as well tell her. She is not going to let it go."

He turned and looked at her. "Ramon has been trying to get me fired from the firm since you disappeared because I handle your accounts. He wants one of the other partners to have access to them so he can get to the money. He is having trouble getting around me because Grandpa started the firm. I have been hiding your money in different accounts and different banks, and they don't know where. He has been making sure my cattle disappear or get killed or my water is poisoned. We have had to borrow money to just stay where we are this last year, and that isn't saying much. Grandpa sent me money to get to Amarillo to see you."

"Why didn't you get some of my money out and use it when it got so bad?"

"That is what he wanted. Then he could say I was embezzling from your account."

"And you couldn't say anything in your telegrams because someone is telling him everything that goes on in the office."

He just nodded.

"Well, this stops tomorrow. Do you want to stay here after this is over?" She looked at her aunt and her cousin.

"Well, I know you have stayed here to protect my interests. Now it is coming down to the end, one way or another. Do you want to stay here or come back home with me and Miles? Talk about it, and decide if you want to come back. That is wonderful. If not, I will see to it this place is paid off and you are free and clear for protecting my interests all this time, but I would rather you come home with me. Talk to your sisters and brother and decide. As for money, Miles pull out five hundred and put it on the table in the kitchen. Please. Enough is enough. Gary, you two talk. I will see you in the morning."

Miles was standing at the door and had heard everything. He let her in the door. They went to the kitchen. He pulled out his wallet and put the money on the counter while she looked into the cabinets. Her aunt had cooked for a lot of people this evening, and she didn't know how there wasn't anything in the cabinets to cook with.

"Just sit down. I want to talk to them when they come back in. How much cash do we have between the two of us?"

She went to the bedroom and got her wallet as he started counting out his money. She walked back in with her wallet and started to count hers. He put his hand over hers and said, "What are you so worried about?"

"I can't get any more money out here without Ramon knowing I am here, and we may need it."

He just looked at her and smiled. "I can, and he won't have people looking for my money transactions."

She looked at him. "That is your ranch money. I don't want to waste it."

"On what? Family like you? We can spend my money just as easily as you do. It is your money too."

"It would be a lot easier, wouldn't it?"

He just nodded. They sat there and waited and counted out the money they had on hand. When Gary and his mother came back in, Morgan had them sit down.

"Well, what did you decide?"

"I thought we had until the morning."

"Changed my mind. You are coming home with us. This is a lousy place to live in."

"Really?"

"Yes. It is time for the McKinneys to go home."

"We agree. Now what do we do?"

"You said you had Miles's money from the ranch here. Can we get to it without drawing too much attention?" She looked at Gary and at Miles and the money lying on the table.

"I think I can get it all out without too much fuss. And then what?"

"We are going to need some wagons to load all this stuff on and some extra horses, but you can't buy them, and neither can Miles. One of you is going to start drawing too much attention. You can't put the land up for sale until this is all done. You understand that?"

He nodded.

"Is there someone you trust to buy these wagons and horses for us and keep quiet about it, or do we need to go to another town and do it? We are running out of time."

Greg came in about that time, and he was all but asleep. He crawled up on her lap, and she put him on her shoulder. He went to sleep as they continued to plan.

"Are your sisters working at the general store? They will need to start bringing home supplies—and lots of them."

"If they get them here, Ramon will know."

"Have them go to Celina, get them, pay cash for them, and get them over a couple of days. We still need someone to buy a couple of wagons and horses. We really won't need the horses if this thing works out in my favor, will we? But just in case."

"No, we won't need horses. Just the wagons. We will get the horses from the ranch when this is over."

Martha Jean had said it. She wasn't going to die, and they would have plenty of horses. They all just looked at her. Well, they had twelve hundred dollars sitting on the table and more in the bank if they could get it out, so they had a plan.

"Well, let's get to bed, and the men will go to town in the morning and see if they can get Miles's money. We will go from there, and maybe we can think of someone to buy some wagons."

She stood up with Miles's help, and they went to their bedroom and laid Greg down on the little bed at the end of their bed. At least they could be together tonight.

She cuddled up to him and put her arms around him. "This is getting more and more complicated by the day."

"If you are going to go to the ranch the day after tomorrow, you are going to have to tell him. You can't just leave. He won't understand."

"I know. I will figure something out tomorrow."

He kissed her, and she went to sleep. She hoped whoever Mama Ruby thought was watching out for her still had eyes on her for a few more days.

Gregory woke her up in the morning and said, "It is time for breakfast. Martha Jean said come on now."

She pulled back the sheet, saw Miles was already gone, looked out the window, and saw her cousins Mary Jean and Mary Jo were already here and talking to Ranger Carter. She thought they would like him. The girls were twins but not identical, but both of them were beautiful. The ranger would have fun picking.

She dressed quickly and went to the kitchen, and her aunt nodded for her to go outside first while she fed the kids. She did notice there was plenty of food this morning. Someone had already gone to town.

When she got to the ranger, he wasn't smiling, and her cousins generally made any man smile. Something wasn't right.

"What did you find out? Was it as bad as he had said?"

"Worse. They found the house about a month ago, and it was as he said. His father had been hanging in the barn until he rotted enough, then he fell and was on the ground. The boy—"

"His name is Gregory."

"Yes, ma'am. Gregory buried his mother and then piled enough stones on her to keep the animals away from her and then put a small cross on her grave. There was another grave next to hers. He had been in it and crawled out. When we went into the house, there was no food anywhere, and the well was dry. He shot the cow and the horse and then hung himself. We even found the hammer on the floor in the barn. There were two pools of blood where they lay in the kitchen, but there was blood everywhere. She tried to protect him. There was no sign of a child in that house. It was as if he didn't exist. No clothes, no toys, nothing. The other rangers talked to the people in town, and they said they came about eight months ago, he said, from the mines back east. They had no other family, and he brought her to town with him. Sometimes even then, she would have bruises or a black eye. No one ever saw a child. They didn't even know there was one."

Morgan just looked at him. "Is that all?"

The ranger looked at her as she went back to the house, and he turned and looked at Miles. "What else does she want?"

"She wants to know why nobody went to help her and why nobody knew a four-year-old boy was wandering the desert alone."

The ranger looked at him. He didn't have an answer to either question.

Miles met her in the house, and they had breakfast, and then Gary and Miles started to town. She and her aunt started packing after Morgan and the girls sat down and talked about what was going on. She gave both the girls money and a list of supplies, and they said they would take care of the list today and the rest tomorrow. When asked about someone they could trust to buy some wagons, neither one knew anybody they trusted enough to ask to do that. Ramon had made this whole family outcast here. It was just another reason to get them all out of here. Jackson went about taking care of what was left of the stock.

Gary and Miles had already decided when he got his money that they would pay any outstanding bills he had in town quietly, so if he left in the middle of the night, he wouldn't leave any debt. They went to a bank he used outside of Dallas, one his firm didn't use, and they had to wait a while for the transaction because it was so big, but they got it done. Part was transferred to Amarillo, and part was taken in cash. Then they walked around town and went to several stores, buying some items and paying off Gary's bills.

When they were through, Gary saw an old friend at the general store, and he stopped him and asked about his family. He told him it looked like they were going to have to call it quits. He just couldn't make it ranching anymore, but he was going to have to sell his ranch first for the money to get some tickets back to his parents' home. Gary told him to come to his ranch this afternoon and talk to him; he might have a way for him to get home if he would help him out but not to talk to anybody about it. He said he would see him in a couple of hours, and they parted company.

"Gary, do you trust him?"

"Ramon is the one who is running him out of here. He is having the same problems with his water and cattle as I am. Ramon wants to own all the little ranches for himself, but he needs Morgan's money. That is why he is so desperate. He is running out of time to do it."

They headed back to the ranch, but someone was watching. One of Ramon's men had been following them all day. He wasn't too concerned. He didn't know who this other man was. Probably some new client of his firm. His boss was getting ready for this party, and he wasn't too concerned about anything else. When they were through with the party, they were going after the McKinney girl again. She was supposed to be at this man's ranch, so it should be easier this time.

They were more careful going back. They were carrying quite a lot of money with them. When they got back to the ranch, it was a different place. The women had packed quite a bit of it up; with things they wouldn't need day to day.

When they got inside, they told her what they had done with the money, how they had paid off Gary's debts, what they had sent to Amarillo, and about the man coming to see them in a little while about the wagons.

"Travis Davis is coming. I remember him. He had a small ranch on the other side of Dallas. Ramon has run him out of business too. What, does Ramon have to have everybody's land?"

"It is the water rights he wants. If he has them, he controls the whole valley, and that makes it his for his horses."

"Kind of screws it up if he poisons the waterholes around here."

"Only if he poisons a few and then comes back and cleans them up."

"Well, that is just stupid."

"We never thought the man was smart, did we?"

"Besides, the rustlers are taking the cattle faster than we can replace them, and it is just certain ranches, the ones Ramon wants."

"Oh, I am sure they have a new brand and they are now part of the Calderon herd. I am sure he has a running iron for every brand around here."

She just shook her head. How many pockets did he have his hands in around here? Now she knew why Gary was almost broke trying to keep her property hers. She didn't know how he had done it this long.

Travis showed up, and when he saw Morgan, she thought he was going to cry as he came to her and hugged her.

"Ramon told us to just give up. We were beat because you were dead. Look at you. What can I help you with?"

"He is going to have an engagement party in a few days, and I am going to make an appearance. If things go well, Gary and his families are coming home with me after that, but we need some wagons, and Gary can't buy them, or Ramon will suspect what is going on. I will pay you to buy the wagons for us if you are willing and then pay your way back home or help you get back on your feet."

He looked at her and then said, "What if things go bad, Morgan?"

She smiled. He knew as well as she did this could all go to hell and she could die. "You will have your money both ways and you can decide the day after the party."

He sat at the table and brushed his hand against his beard. He had never thought he would see her again, so it was time to make a stand. She was. "Tell me what you want done and where you want the wagons delivered. I think I know a man who has some to sell. They are outside of Dallas, and maybe if we are lucky, Ramon won't be too interested in what I am doing. He might just think I am leaving."

"We have an extra ranger we are going to send with you to drive the other wagon and watch out for you. Do you think you can get this done tomorrow?"

He nodded. She started counting out money for wagons and money for him to leave afterward or to pay on his land; either way, he was taken care of. She gave the ranger more money just in case the wagons were more than they thought they should be. They made arrangements to meet tomorrow at Travis's ranch in the early morning so they could get an early start. She, Miles, and Ranger Carter would be gone by then. She gave Travis a hug just in case and thanked him again, and he wished her luck. She was going to need it. They were heading to Ramon's ranch and sneaking in, and Gary was getting his judge friend and the witnesses who were testifying at the party gathered up. They would all meet at the party in two nights.

Greg came in and sat beside her. Miles looked at her and nodded, and they both stood up. He was holding her hand, and they walked out the door and out back to the corrals. She kept walking until they came to a little bench under one of the pecan trees. Her and her cousins used to sit out here and shell pecans for hours and just talk, so she sat Gregory down on the bench and sat beside him, and Miles sat on the ground.

"Gregory, I have to leave in the morning, and I have to leave you here with Aunt Martha Jean."

He was already starting to cry. "Why? What did I do?"

This was the hardest thing she had ever had to do. "Nothing. Listen to me. I have to go and get my sisters. Remember I told you about my stepfather who tried to hurt me? Well, he still has my little sisters. Miles and I are going to go and get them. He is hurting them."

He looked at Miles and asked him, "You are going with her?"

"Yes, and so is the ranger. In fact, so are a couple more rangers."

"So he won't hurt her this time?"

Miles looked up at her. Was she going to lie to him or not?

She took his face in her hands and said, "They are going so they can protect me, but there is always a chance I can get hurt, but if something happens to me, Miles will take care of you, or my family will. They are your family now."

"No, you are my mama now. He still isn't my daddy yet."

"When will he be your daddy?"

"When he brings you back to me alive. That is the only way."

Miles looked at him and held out his hand. "Deal." And they shook on it.

"So now it is official. Mama, you have to come back alive for both of us."

They just sat out there for a long time till the sun started setting, and they went inside. She still had things to do. Everybody was eating, and she was packing her dress when Miles came into the bedroom and sat down on the bed.

"I know you and your grandfather planned something, and you won't tell me, so please tell me you are sure of what you are doing. Tell me you have a plan and you aren't just going in there and letting him shoot you so you can get your sisters back because I don't know how you are going to get a Winchester past the welcoming committee in that green dress."

"I have a plan, and it doesn't include getting shot or killing him in cold blood. My grandfather said to use my mouth. It always made him mad, so I am going to make him confess in front of everybody, including judges and rangers, as I walk down those stairs."

"Do you think he will do it?"

"You have seen me at my worst. Now you can watch me go after someone like I did Justin on those stairs at the bordello that night. And that night, I wasn't even mad. I am going to accuse him of everything he has ever done to me in front of everybody, and he is going to explode, then I will have him. You and the ranger are my backups. Don't let him kill me, please."

He wasn't sure she was telling him everything, but it was all she was going to say.

"I wish we were alone tonight."

"We will be tomorrow night. I will see to it. Go get Greg. It is going to be an early morning."

When he was gone, she pulled out the derringer and ammunition for it and wrapped it back up and put it in her saddlebag. She wasn't going into that room unarmed, even in that green dress. She and Abigail had seen to that.

The next morning, she was dressed in her Levi's and a dark shirt and her boots. The men were waiting for her as she said goodbye to Gregory. He was standing by her aunt.

"Now you remember to stay close to the house and listen to the adults, and I will send word as soon as I can. Now give me a hug and a kiss and be good."

He put his arms around her neck and hugged her, and then he said, "Please come back."

She couldn't say anything. She just turned and got on the horse and put on her hat, and they rode away. She didn't look back; if she did, he would have seen her crying.

Miles said, "Just keep riding. If he sees you crying, it will terrify him."

She just straightened her hat and put her horse to a run.

It was hours before they got to the outskirts of Ramon's ranch, and she got the men to a stand of trees where they could watch what was happening but not be seen. There was a canyon behind them. There were at least thirty cattle being kept there, and she could see several different brands on them. She pointed them out to the ranger.

"So this is where he has been hiding them. When we were watching the ranch, we couldn't see this part."

She was smiling. Two of the cattle had her cousin's brand on them.

"You can't see this spot from the house either. We will wait a while longer, and then we will walk to the house. I have friends there, and we can go inside the outside houses. We can put our horses around the side of the back house. They won't be seen there."

As soon as night was falling, they walked to a small house quite far from the main house and put the horses around the back of it with some others. She carefully looked inside at a Mexican woman singing softly to herself and chopping tomatoes. She watched her for a minute, making sure no one else was with her, and then she went in the back door.

When the older lady put the knife down, Morgan said, "Making salsa for the guests?"

Rosa turned, and she was going to scream. Morgan put her hand over her mouth before she could give them away. Then they just looked at each other until Morgan nodded, and she took her hand away. Rosa leaned up against the counter as a man walked in, and he was almost as bad as Rosa. He too just stood and stared.

"Carlos."

That was all she had to say. They were both on her like leeches. Rosa was sobbing, and Carlos just kept looking at her. Miles had walked behind him and closed the door. They didn't want anybody else to see this reunion.

Carlos looked behind him at Miles and at the ranger and finally asked, "Who are you, and why did you bring her back here? He will kill her."

It was finally Morgan who spoke while she held Rosa to her chest like a child while she cried. "He gave me no choice. Either I had to prove I was alive, or he was going to take everything, and he won't stop sending men to kill me. Besides, I want my sisters, and he won't give them to me until I prove I am alive."

"He says you are not the real Morgan. You are a fake, and the real one is dead."

"Well, what do you believe? You have known the real Morgan since she was born."

"I knew it was you the minute you opened your mouth, but how are you going to prove it? You know he is going to say you are not the real one."

"I have a lot of signatures from a lot of people saying who I am, including a judge. How are my sisters?"

The look on Rosa's face said it all. Morgan took her face in her hands. "What is he doing to them? Tell me, Rosa."

"Not him, her. She is telling them she is going to be mistress and they are not going to be needed when she has a son. They are scared."

"Who is this bitch? Where did she come from?"

"She is Carmella. She used to make your mother's dresses, or her mother did. She would come here and stay when her mother came."

"She is not much older than I am, and she was always making eyes at Ramon when she was a kid. I am going up to the house. I want to see the girls, and I need to do something else. Rosa, don't you need to check on something at the house?"

Rosa looked at her and said, "Of course. I need to see if the girls' dresses are all in order."

Miles grabbed her arm. "Are you crazy? You shouldn't do this. You could get caught."

She kissed his cheek. "There is something I have to do before tomorrow night. Please get the things from the horses. I will be back. Carlos, is the little house behind here in use tonight?"

He shook his head.

She smiled at Miles. "Put our things in there." Then she went out the door, following Rosa.

When they got to the back door, there were too many people inside, so she motioned to Rosa. She was going around, and Rosa knew she was going to climb up to Dona's room. She had done it a thousand times in the past. It used to be her room.

When she got to the lattice, it was covered with vines, but they were no problem, so she started climbing. When she got to the top, she climbed over the railing, snuck into the room, hid in the drapes, and just listened.

When she got to Dona's room, she just watched from the shadows.

"Such pretty long hair, but such a bother. I think after the wedding, I will cut it all off."

Dona tried to move away, and the woman behind her grabbed her hair and yanked it. "Be still." She laid a straight razor beside her on the table and said to the younger girl, "You should be more careful. I could have cut you while trimming your hair, and wouldn't that have been a shame? Now get to bed, and you better behave tomorrow, or you will be sorry."

Her sister just sat there for a minute and then took the razor in her hand. She had seen that look on her own face too many times. She walked quietly in and took the razor from her hand and put it in her pocket.

Dona didn't even look up for a minute, and when she did, she said, "Mama?"

Morgan was still standing in the shadows, and she couldn't see her very well, so she stepped out farther. "No, honey, it's me, Morgan."

She ran to her and grabbed her. "In that light, you looked just like Mama, but it's you. It is really you. Did you come back for us?"

She looked at her. What was she supposed to tell her? That she was going to kill her father so she could take them away? Lord, she looked so grown up since she had seen her last. She was a young woman now. "Yes, baby, I have come to take you back with me if that is what you want."

Her sister looked at her with disbelief on her face. "Please get us out of here before she hurts us. She hates us, and Daddy doesn't care." Then it finally dawned on her. "Daddy said you were dead."

"He was wrong. Can you go get your sister? And don't tell her why, and don't tell anybody I am here. No one can know yet. Quickly honey we have to go."

As she heard her go across the hall and get her sister up and then come back, she was hiding again in the frame of the window. When Rose came in, she didn't see her until she walked out, and she scared her to death. She started to scream, and Morgan grabbed her and took her over to the bed and calmed her down. When she wasn't struggling anymore, she took her hand off her face. Rose jumped her and about strangled her.

"You aren't dead. He said you were, but I knew you weren't. I just knew."

"Well, you were right, but you have to be quiet, or he will find me."

There was a quiet knocking at the door. Dona went to open it, and it was Rosa.

"How are we going to get past them?"

"I will get the girls down the back to the side of the house, and you go out the door. We will meet you outside. If anybody asks, you needed to make alterations on their dresses. Take them with you. We will meet you out back."

Rosa nodded, and Morgan took the girls to the balcony. She went back and turned out the lights in Rose's and Dona's rooms. When they were on the balcony, she could hear someone talking, and it had to be Ramon.

"While the party is going on, hit the ranch and burn it to the ground. If Morgan is there, it will take care of all my problems at once. If she isn't, it will at least get rid of her cousin, and I can have him replaced at the law office and get to the money. Maybe when this is done, I will send the girls to Morgan's grandfather. They are of no further use to me. All I ever wanted was their mother Shannon anyway."

The girls were clinging to her. They had heard everything he had said. She was going to get them out of here if she had to steal them. When they heard nothing else and the doors down below were closed, she helped the girls get down and around the side, and they were met by Miles. He picked up Rose, then she and Dona made a run for it with Rosa. When they got to the house, all the window curtains were shut, and the girls were safe for tonight.

When they were safely in the house, she told Rosa to get out her sewing kit in case someone came looking for the girls and get the extra room ready. Then she turned to the ranger. "Are your men coming tomorrow?"

"Yes. I am supposed to meet them outside the ranch and lead them here later in the day."

"You have to meet them sooner and get them to Gary's ranch. He has ordered the ranch burned to the ground and everyone killed tomorrow night while the party is going on. He hopes I will be there, but if I am not, he is hoping to kill Gary and get his hands on my accounts at his firm. You have to get word to them."

"I will leave before first light, meet them halfway, come back with some of them, and send the rest to the ranch. I will try to have most of them gone before they even hit the ranch, and Gary is coming with the judge tomorrow night."

Before they could talk more, Carlos turned and said, "She is coming this way. *Hide*."

Morgan and Miles hid in the pantry while the ranger was across from them, and Carlos partially closed the door.

Carmella came stomping in the door and was yelling at Rosa. "Are the girls here?"

Rosa turned with thread in her hand and one of the dresses and said, "Yes, what is the problem?"

"What are they doing out here? They were supposed to be in bed, not out here. You spoil them. Where are they?"

Rosa didn't even blink before she spoke. "I put them to bed. I had to do some alterations on their dresses, and they were tired, so I just let them sleep out here. They do it all the time. Is there a problem? If there is, we can go inside and talk about it with the *patrón*. I am sure he won't mind being disturbed while he is with his friends."

Carmella didn't like being challenged, but she wasn't mistress yet.

"You won't be able to get away with this much longer. I will see to your replacement when I am mistress. There are going to be a lot of changes around here when he marries me, and you two are going to be the first, so you might as well start packing."

Morgan had leaned down and pulled her knife from her boot, and this woman didn't know how close she was to having her throat cut.

"Those brats will be mine, and you won't be able to tell me what I can and can't do with them." Then she turned and walked out of the house.

Miles had his hand on her arm and was holding her still and saying, "Calm down. Not tonight, Morgan."

Rosa and Carter saw her face, and Rosa had seen her like this once before the day they had buried her mother. She had been going to kill that woman.

"She is gone now. You can come out now."

Miles kept her there until she calmed down, and then they came out. He didn't want her sisters to see her like that. When she was better and breathing slower, they came out.

"Rosa, I have a dress for tomorrow night that probably needs pressing. Can we do it in here?"

She looked at her. "You are going to that party with him?"

"Yes. Oh, by the way, this is my husband, Miles Douglas. Do you remember him? He was with Virgie when she was at the ranch. And the other man is Carter James. He is a Texas Ranger. They will both be with me tomorrow night, as well as some other people."

Rosa just looked at her. "Will that be enough?" They were all wondering that.

She went with Rosa to her bedroom, and they began getting out the dress while Carlos got the men some drinks. As she started to pull out the dress, Rosa instantly recognized it. She jerked her head up and looked at Morgan.

"Where did you get it? It looks like the one your mama has on in the portrait."

"Virgie had one made at the same time. We had to make a few alterations on it, and they aren't exactly the same but close. I want to wear it down the staircase and have him deny me in this dress in front of her portrait. It is still there, isn't it?"

"Oh, it is still there, and there is no way he can say you are not her daughter in this dress. We have to get it pressed and ready. When you leave here, may Carlos and I go home with you maybe you need a cook and help? Seems we are going to need a job after tonight."

"Miles has probably already asked Carlos if you want to come, but this may not work out as easy as it sounds. You know that, don't you? If it doesn't, you two can still go home with him and my family."

"You really aren't going down those stairs unarmed, are you?"

She looked at Rosa, and she took the dress and put Rosa's hand into a pocket in the side of the dress. If you didn't know the pocket was there, you wouldn't find it.

Rosa looked at her and said, "They don't know about that, do they?"

She shook her head. "No one but a dressmaker in Colorado, and I know about that, and now you do. My daddy's derringer will be with me as well."

"Good. You take care of yourself."

"You have to promise me something. When this starts to fall apart —and you will know when—get the girls out of there. Will you do that for me? When I kill him, I don't want them to see me do it."

"I will see to it that they don't see anything." She meant her getting hurt as well.

They kept pulling out the dress. Morgan had been watching the house, and it was getting darker. She still had something to do in there. She went to the back door and was about to go out when Miles put his hand on her arm. Then Carlos and the ranger were talking as she went out again.

"I go with you this time."

She just nodded, and they headed toward the house, and when she got to the back door, she slipped inside. They went to the main hall, and she could see the main staircase. He suddenly stopped, and she turned around. He was looking up at the top of the staircase. There was the portrait of her mother; the portrait was huge, about eight feet tall and five feet wide. Her mother was beautiful in an emerald green dress with a square neckline and fitted silk sleeves and an emerald necklace. He looked down at Morgan, and they did look a lot alike, but where her mother's features were very delicate, Morgan's were fierce. It was like looking at a cat and a mountain lion.

The staircase went straight up and then went off on both sides to two separate landings, but Morgan wasn't looking at that. She was counting steps from the desk beside her in the hallway to the staircase, and she did it twice. Someone upstairs was coming with a lamp and asking who was downstairs. She grabbed his hand, and they left.

When she was outside, she turned and looked back in and saw Ramon looking around. He put the lamp up to his face once, and she saw him. She smiled. She backed up against the wall so he didn't see her, and then he made sure the doors were locked and went back up the stairs.

She took Miles's hand, and they went to the little house behind Rosa's house where Carlos had put their belongings and went inside. She turned around and quickly started to undress, and he did the same.

"I told you we would have tonight. I would see to it. Tonight, cowboy, you're mine."

He didn't care what she had been doing in the house. She wasn't going to tell him anyway, so he wasn't going to waste time. He had gotten rid of his boots and pants, and so had she, and now she was working on his shirt.

Finally, he stopped her. "Slow down. I have waited for days, and I want to take my time, I am not going to ask about what you and your grandfather have cooked up, but you have to promise me you will try to be careful."

She was unbuttoning buttons and had her hands on his chest and her mouth on his neck. "I promise I will be careful. Now stop talking. I have been waiting for days too, and we only have till morning."

He had her shirt and her chemise off, and they slid to the floor. Then he ran his hands down her arms. He felt the healed scar from the knife wound, and he was scared again. He picked her up and laid her on the bed. It was small, but they didn't need much room. He could remember the night he first made love to her. He was hoping this wasn't the last night he had with her.

He started to kiss her, but they were up against a wall, and he said, "This is ridiculous."

She looked up at him and said, "Remember the night on the prairie when we rolled in the dirt? Why don't we put the mattress on the floor?" Then she grinned at him.

He pulled her up and the mattress down and they started again. He kissed her so hard; she thought he was going to inhale her. And then he started on her neck and down, and then she rolled him over and started to play, and out came that wicked little devil he loved so much. She moved over him and teased him and brought her breast to his face, and he was in heaven. Then he turned her over, and he took them both over the top and kept them there until she could breathe again. She put out her tongue and licked the sweat from his neck and almost purred like a cat, only his cat could tear your heart out one way or the other, literally.

He lay beside her and pulled a blanket off the side of the bed and covered them, and she got as close to him as she could. They didn't say anything. It had all been said. Now they just had to see how the cards were going to fall. There wasn't anything she hadn't taken care of, nothing else to do but walk into that room tomorrow night and kill a man, and they both knew it. He put his hand on her slightly rounding stomach and hoped she lived long enough for him to see this child.

"You aren't going to sleep either, are you?"

"No, I am not. That would be wasted time, and I don't want to waste any tonight."

"Miles, do you have any idea how glad I am that you were at Virgie's that night when I came back? I had dreamed so many nights of what I would say to you if you were still there, and you were and still wanted me. I stayed alive just hoping you would be there, and you were. It has been worth all this if this is all I get."

"Don't say any more. This is not all you get. We are going to get through tomorrow night, and I don't care what you have to do or who you have to kill. Just do it and stay alive, and then we can go home with our son, the girls, and this child? Now shut up and come back over here."

When she knew he was asleep, she got up and dressed and went back to the house. She climbed back up to Dona's room and snuck into her mother's room. There was a connecting door to Ramon's room, and she wanted to see him.

As she looked around her mother's room, it hadn't changed. Maybe he had really loved her after all. It still felt like her mother was here, watching over her. Her brushes and combs were still on her dresser, and her bed still was covered in the same bedspread. She got a warm and peaceful feeling in here.

She quietly opened Ramon's door and walked over to his bedside and looked down at him sleeping. She had her knife in her hand. It would be so easy to just cut his throat and be done with it, but she just couldn't seem to do it. She had promised Miles and her grandfather she wouldn't do just exactly this. He had made her into the kind of woman who could get this close to a sleeping man and kill him with no remorse. She wondered if he would be proud of himself. She watched him sleeping next to the woman who was making her sisters' lives miserable and thought, *Just one more day and this will be over one way or another*.

She backed out of the room and silently closed the door, and when she did, he awoke in a panic. He turned up the lantern and got out of bed, looking around the room.

Carmella asked him, "What is wrong? Another bad dream my love?"

"She was here. I know she was here. She is going to kill me. She knows I killed her mother and her father, and she wants me dead."

Carmella tried to calm him. "It was just another bad dream. She is gone, and you don't have to worry about her. She will never get this close to you. Stop worrying. Come back to bed, my love."

Morgan was glad she was the cause of his bad dreams. He had been the cause of so many of hers. She had been right about all of it all along. He had murdered her family, and he was going to pay for it in blood— his blood.

After he was back in bed, she went back to Miles, undressed, and went to sleep. Miles never even knew she had left.

When it was light, they had not had much sleep, but they had slept some. She met the ranger at the door, and he was heading out to meet the rest of the men and warn the ranch of the attack. She took her saddlebag inside Rosa's house, and she had a bath prepared. She bathed, and so did Miles, and then she started to get ready for tonight. Rosa had pressed Miles's suit and her dress, and they were ready and hanging in the other room. She had taken the girls with her and had told Carlos she would keep them close to her today.

Ranger Carter was meeting up with his men, and he told them about the attack on the ranch tonight. Some of them went to meet up with Travis Davis and the other rangers, get the family out, and set up an ambush for the raiders tonight. One of the other rangers was going to the judge in town and tells him about the rustled cattle they had found on the Calderon land last night. He was issuing a search warrant for tonight, and he was going to the party as well. This was going to be some party. Ramon was going to be lucky if he didn't get hanged at his own engagement party.

Travis Davis had bought two wagons, and the other rangers had met them on the road to the ranch. They told them about the raid, and the rangers raced to the ranch. When they got there, they loaded as much as they could and got the family out, and then they set up in the hills around the house and waited. They didn't have to wait long. It was just about sunset when the raiders came, and they hit it hard.

They started with shooting the barn and then the house but were surprised when they were fired upon from the hills. Several of the raiders were killed before they could even figure out where they were being fired at from. They had brought torches with them. Some of them had made it into the barn, and one hit the house, but the rest never hit their targets. Soon, they were being chased by several Texas rangers from their hiding places around the hills and inside the house and several men in the hills were shooting down on them from their hiding places above. They had walked into an ambush and were being massacred. So they ran for it, leaving their dead and wounded behind to take the blame for what had happened. The ranch was still standing, and it didn't take long to put out the fires. They brought the wagons with the family back down to the ranch and got them settled and started to round up the wounded men.

Greg went into the house with Martha Jean, and he asked her, "Do you think my mama is all right?"

She just looked at him and after tonight, all she could say was "I sure hope so, honey, but your daddy is looking out for her." She just picked him up, and they went back inside. She sure hoped she wasn't lying to him and this was almost over.

CHAPTER 6

She had been getting ready for hours, and Rosa had come back to help her with her hair. She was going to put it up, but Miles said to leave it down. They weren't trying to recreate her mother. She was still, after all, Morganna. She put on her makeup and her light pink lipstick.

It was dark now, and she was dressed. Rosa was going back to the party so she could be with the girls when it came time for her to get them out. She had brought her an invitation so she could be introduced properly, and she had brought her a pen and some ink to fill it out.

Before she went out, she took the little bag out of her saddlebag and got the derringer while Miles dressed. She loaded it and slipped it in the pocket in the dress. Rosa watched her as she loaded the gun, and she nodded. "Go with God, little one." She came over to her. Morgan leaned down, and Rosa kissed her forehead, then she turned and left the room.

She had her Indian boots on underneath this gown, and no one would ever know because the gown was pooling on the floor. She wanted the stability she had when she walked in them and not in heels. Before he left her, Miles put the squash blossom necklace around her neck. It was the perfect complement to the dress. It lay perfectly between her breasts. The dress was low cut and different enough from her mother's, so they didn't look exactly alike.

He gave her one last kiss and held her and said, "Please be careful, and don't let him kill you."

She just smiled. If she said anything, she was going to cry. "You be careful too. He isn't going to like the way things are going to go this evening, even if the rangers are here."

"Are you sure you don't want me to walk with you down those stairs?"

"No, darlin' this is between me and him, and I don't want anyone else close just in case."

God, he hated the sound of that. She was going to do something, and it scared him to death because he didn't know what.

Miles went before her and mixed with some of the men, and she wanted it to be dark when she went in. She had filled out the invitation, and she was sure whoever read it would be surprised when it was read out loud.

She started around the corrals, and she saw her stallions, one she had raised from a foal. She wondered if he would remember her. He did. He came up to her and wanted her attention when a man came up to her and said, "What is a pretty woman like you doing out here with the horses? You should be inside."

She didn't recognize the man, thankfully, but it was time to make her entrance.

"I was just waiting for my escort, and he is late. I will go in alone."

"Take my arm. I will take you in. You look very familiar."

She didn't want anyone near her when she went in, but that was soon to be taken care of. A very pretty woman came to him, and she was wearing a wedding band.

"Excuse me. My wife needs me."

She just smiled at him, and he hurried away. She kept walking toward the front of the house. It looked like everybody was in so she might as well do this, so she headed in. She was on the left landing, and she started down.

She saw Miles and Carter coming in the downstairs door with the judge. They were met by some men, and they were trying to escort them out, but then it got very quiet in the room as she got closer, and she handed a servant her card to read.

He looked at it, and he looked at her and said, "I can't say this name. She is dead."

"Do I look dead to you? Say the name so everyone in the room can hear it, and then get out of the way."

He looked at her again and nodded. "Mrs. Morganna McKinney Douglas."

Then she started to walk down the stairs, and the whole room shut up and stared up at her. Ramon just looked up at her, and the men who were backing his play and saying she was a fraud began to back away from him. There was no denying this woman was the daughter of the woman in the portrait to anyone in the room. The judge who came with the ranger was saying they had a warrant for his arrest, and then Morgan began to talk as she pulled off her black gloves one at a time and dropped them on the staircase.

"What's the matter, Ramon? Aren't you going to call me a fake? Maybe you are going to tell these people that I am not the real Morganna McKinney?"

She cocked her head to the side, looking back at her mother's portrait as she mocked him. She knew everyone in the room was comparing her to the portrait above her head.

"She was such a beautiful woman, but she was already married. You wanted my mother so badly. Why don't you tell them that you didn't have anything to do with my father's death? That he accidentally fell off his horse while he was with you? You killed him so you could have her. Or maybe tell them how my mother was killed accidentally while you were trying to kill me. Oh, by the way, I have the man who did that job for you behind bars in Amarillo. He even tried that trick again on me with no success. I have his written confession for her murder as well as my attempted murder. Why didn't you try to keep her from walking into that little trap if you loved her so much?"

People were trying to distance themselves from him, and he was furious because he could see they believed her. The likeness between the two women was unmistakable.

As Miles watched, she had the other woman under control, but she had something in mind, and she was doing it. What was so scary was she was every bit as beautiful as her mother had been as she was walking down those stairs. The room was deathly quiet; they could have been the only two people in it. You could hear a pin drop.

Then he started to scream at her. He finally realized he had lost the game, and after all these years, she had finally won.

"Why couldn't you just die? The Comancheros were supposed to kill you, not sell you to the Comanche's, and then every bounty hunter I sent after you, you killed. You are as good a killer as the men I sent after you. I told your mother to stay away from the garden, but she was getting you some tomatoes, and she didn't listen to me. It was always about you, her precious McKinney daughter. We had two daughters together, but it was all about you and that damn will. I tried to talk her into getting a lawyer to break the will, but she said your father wanted it that way and to leave it alone."

So her mother had tried to protect her from him after all.

Nobody was paying much attention to what he was doing with his hands as he reached into his desk and pulled out a .22 pistol and cocked it. They were all watching her walk down those stairs. Then he pointed at her and fired. She saw the pistol but didn't dodge soon enough, and he shot her in the left shoulder.

She stopped, and she was bleeding badly, but she turned and she kept coming. But now the other lady was coming out to protect her. Morgan was pulling out the derringer with her right hand, but she had to get to the fourth step. She had to be about eighteen feet away. That was what she and her grandfather had figured. She could barely walk. The pain was so bad, but the other lady kept coming. It was finally her turn.

Miles saw the derringer. So that was the plan they had worked out —get him mad, and then she could shoot him in self-defense. Miles didn't think they had planned on Ramon shooting her first.

She kept walking, but she wasn't there yet. When she put her left hand on the rail, it was like lightning going up her arm. There was blood pouring down her arm and the front of her breast. The dress was turning color. The front was almost black instead of green.

"You always were a terrible shot, Ramon. Is that why you didn't do the job yourself? Did you watch as they took me that day?" She had to keep him occupied just a bit longer.

"Yes, he did. He said we couldn't help you. We were too far away." She looked over, and Dona was talking in the doorway.

"You let them watch, you bastard. Rosa, the girls, get them out of here now."

She was almost to the fourth step, and he was cocking the gun again, but she was shaking and bleeding so bad. She didn't know if she could make the shot. Miles and the ranger were running toward her, and she held up the gun and shot, but she hit him in the arm. He was aiming again, then there was another shot, and she saw a hole in his chest. Then she was falling. She hit the stairs and rolled down the last few steps. Then Miles was holding her on the floor. The ranger had killed Ramon.

Somebody was yelling for a doctor. She opened her eyes briefly and looked at Miles. "Is he dead?"

Miles nodded.

"Finally, it is done. Well, I ruined another dress."

And then there was no more as she closed her eyes.

They needed to get her to a bed somewhere. Carlos was holding towels on her bleeding shoulder. As Miles went to pick her up, there was blood all over the floor too. She was losing the baby as well. The doctor was there by then and said, "Let's get her upstairs and soon. She is going into shock."

They worked on her most of the night and finally got things under control. The doctor told Miles she would be all right, but the gunshot and the fall was too much for the baby, and she miscarried. He told him she would have other children just give it time.

She woke up to Miles lying beside her and her shoulder hurting like hell, but someone had already stitched it shut, and she had luckily missed that part. The bullet had gone through, front to back. Then she panicked.

"The baby . . . is it all right?"

Miles couldn't look at her but leaned over her on the bed, took her hand, and told her, "There will be other babies. You suffered too much trauma with the fall and the gunshot wound. You are going to be all right, but we are going to have to stay here a while. You are going to have to heal before we can go anywhere."

"Does the family know yet? You have to go tell them."

"Why me? I can send one of the rangers. I don't want to leave you."

"Remember the deal. You have to be the one to bring him to Mama alive, or no deal."

"You're right. I will go get him and tell your family you are all right. There is a lot of bank stuff that has to be taken care of as well. It seems he was living off what he was supposedly going to get from you, and there are creditors coming out of the woodwork."

"That woman Carmella was still here. Tell Gary to come up here. I want to talk to him before you go."

He leaned down, kissed her, let in her sisters, and told them to be easy getting on the bed, and then he left to get Gregory.

When Gary came up, she told him, "I want that woman off this property right now, and she doesn't take anything with her that she didn't come with. She can have the clothes he gave her but nothing else, and that includes one of the good horses. She can have a hand's horse."

"She has some of Mama's jewelry in her case. She took it last night."

"Rose says she has some jewelry she doesn't own. Maybe you ought to take the girls with you and make sure she doesn't take anything that isn't hers."

Gary loved this. Carmella had made the lives of Morgan's sisters a living hell, and now it was their turn, and as for the creditors, they shouldn't have loaned on nothing. They were still cleaning up the house and the blood, but Gary had seen to it the girls had seen nothing. Maybe it was a good thing the ranger had been the one to kill him and not Morgan. Her sisters wouldn't have to ever blame her for their father's death or any of the rest of it.

After everyone was gone, she just took the pillow and put it over her face and cried for the child she had lost. Ramon had even taken that tiny life from her.

Miles rode to Gary's ranch and was met by everybody at the gate, including Greg. When he got off the horse, the little boy began to cry. He started to run, and Miles had to catch him. When he finally got him calmed down, he turned him around in his arms and said, "Mama is dead, isn't she?" Everybody else was listening as well.

"No, Mama is fine. She got hurt, and she couldn't come for you, so she sent me to come get you. Let's get your clothes, and we will go to her. We are going to have to stay at the other ranch for a while until she is better before we can leave."

Greg went with Mary Jo, and they went to get his things packed while he told everyone what had happened at the party. He told them Gary would be back probably later today and to keep packing. When they got done, everybody would be taken to the other ranch until they could all leave together.

When they had him packed, Miles got on the horse, and one of the men handed him Gregory. They headed to the other ranch. It was almost dark when they got there, and he handed him to one of the hands. Then he got down, and they went inside. He took his hand, and they headed upstairs. He finally told him where she was, and he took off running.

She could hear him running up the stairs to her. As he hit the door to her room, the girls were on her bed, drawing, and they turned around and looked at him.

Dona asked, "Is that him?"

Morgan nodded as Gregory came in with Miles behind him.

He walked over to her and looked at the bandage on her shoulder and said, "You didn't die? Does it hurt?"

"A little bit, so be careful getting up on the bed."

He was having trouble getting on the bed, so Miles grabbed his belt and helped him up.

He turned and said, "Thank you."

"Thank you what?"

He looked at her funny. "What do you mean?"

"Didn't we have a deal that if he brought you to me and I was alive, you would call him Daddy?"

"Yes, we have a deal."

"All right, and these two ladies are my sisters. They are Rose and Dona, and they will be going home with us too, all right?"

"Sure. You better have a big house."

"I do."

Then he crawled next to her and lay down easy and fell asleep. Seems he hadn't slept since she left. He had just watched out the window or sat in the wagon as the rangers fought.

"What is happening at the ranch?"

Miles sat down and told her things were not as bad as they thought.

The rangers had run off or killed the raiders, and the house was still standing. Everyone was still packing, and he had told them to come here when they were done and when she was ready to go home. They would leave from here.

Gary had brought some accountant friends in to start taking the books apart. They were friends of his. Their names were James and Francis Jamison. Gary had been friends with this man and his wife for several years, and he trusted them with the books. Most women around her weren't accountants, but it seemed Francis was as good as her husband was with books, and she had earned her place among the men around her.

It seemed Ramon had been siphoning money off her accounts whenever he could, and there was quite a bit gone. Gary Lee hiding it had been a thorn in his side because he couldn't spend what he couldn't find. He had bought this house, and the proceeds would go back to her when it was sold. His creditors were furious, but there was nothing they could do about it. They had loaned money on funds he didn't have. James had found money spent on feed that couldn't be accounted for and furniture that wasn't in the house and that no one had ever seen. They began to wonder if there was another woman or if he was gambling it away. Either way, it was not accounted for.

It had been three days since the party, and there was a knock at the door. Gregory went to open it, and there was a big man there.

"Hello, young man. Who are you?"

"I am Gregory Douglas. Who are you?"

"I am Donald Roy McKinney, and I am your great-grandfather."

He just looked up at him for a few seconds and then said, "Really? I never had one of those before."

His great-grandfather reached down for him and picked him up, and he didn't even struggle. He was too busy looking at this big man who was now holding him.

"Well, you do now. Where is your mama?"

He just pointed upstairs, and they started up the stairs as he kept looking at him. When they reached the top, he said, "That room." And he pointed to the room on the right.

As he entered, the girls were on the balcony, doing something— he couldn't see what—and they saw him.

"Grandpa, you are here."

They both came running and grabbed him around the legs, and he said, "Wait a minute before you knock me down." He got on his knees and put Gregory down beside him and grabbed both of them, and he hugged them both as they were talking at the same time.

Morgan was just smiling. She had seen him bring Gregory in, and he was letting him hold him. He hadn't let anybody but Miles hold him. She wondered how he had managed that.

"Both my girls, you are so big now, and you are coming back home. What will I do with so many grandchildren? Oh, and great-grandchildren." He gave Gregory a hug too.

Morgan just watched. She couldn't believe how Gregory was acting. He was letting Donald Roy in without question, and that surprised her. She motioned for Greg to come to her, and as he stood by the bed, she told him,

"Go down and tell your daddy to bring Dolf up here. Tell him who is in my room. Hurry."

As he went running by her grandfather, he just looked at her, and she said, "He will be right back. I didn't expect you. When did you get on the stage? The day after I left or the next day?"

"The next day. It was horrible not knowing, so I just got on the stage and came. I figured if he hurt you, Miles and I could kill him."

She narrowed her eyes and looked at the girls, and he shut up. After all, he was their father.

"Girls, why don't you go downstairs and see when lunch is going to be ready to eat? We need to feed your grandfather."

When they were gone, he turned and asked her, "Did you get to kill him?'

"No, I shot him, but he had already shot me, and I missed and shot him in the arm. The ranger killed him before he could shoot me again because he was going to in front of God and everyone. One way or another, he was going to see me dead, but he confessed to killing Daddy and Mother before he died in front of everyone. We were right."

He came over to the bed, sat down, pulled her up to him, and said, "Thank God this is done. When did you bury him?"

"Yesterday, but the girls weren't too sorry. We overheard him the night before when I was getting them out of here talking about killing me and sending them to you because he was through with them."

"They heard that?"

She just nodded, and then she looked behind her. She turned his head, and he saw a man at the door. If he hadn't been sitting down, she suspected he would have fallen.

He looked back at her and said, "That's him?"

She nodded.

"He looks just like your daddy."

"I know. That's what I thought the first time I saw him."

The only problem was the man at the door was staring at her grandfather like he was a ghost. He looked at lot like his father. The two brothers were very similar in their youth, but as they got older, they were almost identical.

He walked over to the older man and stuck out his hand. "I am Dolf, Burrus's son, and you must be Donald Roy."

"Yes, sir, I am. I have had people looking for you for some time now. I understand you have a son as well."

He nodded. He couldn't say much more. He was almost in tears, as was her grandfather. She knew this was hard for them both. There was too much resemblance between the men they had both lost.

"Why don't y'all go downstairs and have lunch and talk and get reintroduced? See that the children eat, please."

Her grandfather leaned down and kissed her cheek and leaned his head on her head. "Ruby said the Lord was watching out for you. I guess he was watching out for the whole family around you and was going to bring them all home. I am sorry about the baby, darlin'."

He walked out the door, and Miles came in. He had never seen happier men in his life. So why did his wife not look so happy?

"What is wrong, Morgan? Everything all right?"

She looked at him and smiled. "Just tired, I guess. Go down and have lunch with the others. I will be fine. Did you see how he took to

Grandfather? It was like he knew him all his life."

"Your grandfather has that effect on little people and some grown women I know. Go back to sleep."

When he left, she put her legs over the side of the bed and got up carefully and then stood up. She held onto the side of the bed and took her time because she was so light headed, then she carefully put on her robe, being careful with her arm. She took the back stairs and went down to the bottom and looked back up at her mother's picture. She looked so imposing standing there. All she remembered was Ramon screaming at her to stand up straight when she was posing for the damn thing. She always wondered why she didn't throw something at him. She would have.

She turned and walked out the back door and walked to her mother's grave, and she was exhausted when she got there. The headstone was quite handsome. He had at least done that right. Even so, she intended to smash it. She didn't want his name on her stone.

She was so tired. She had to sit down, so she did and leaned her head against the stone so she could talk to her. It was shady here. The sun was on the other side of the house, and it was cool. The horses were moving around in the corrals, and she could see cattle out in the pasture. He had fought for what he had wanted, just like she had, but he had killed the people she loved for it too.

"Well, Mama, I am back, and I took everything away from him. I know you think he was a good man, but he wasn't, not even to his own children. I didn't kill him, but I would have to protect the girls. Who am I kidding? I would have killed him for what he did to me.

When I leave, I am having you dug up. I am taking you back and having you laid next to Daddy. You belong there. He killed both of you, and I won't leave you here next to him. Please forgive me if this not what you want. I will take care of the girls like they were my own children, so don't worry. Love you, Mama."

She was so tired, and her arm hurt. She just laid her head on the stone and closed her eyes.

They found her like that about thirty minutes later when Miles and her grandfather went to feed her lunch. Miles carried her back upstairs;

she was unconscious. He couldn't understand why she had to talk to her mother so badly right now.

"I am afraid that is my fault. I made her go talk to her father before she went on this trip, and I guess she thought she had to talk to her mother and explain why she had to see him dead."

"You helped her with the derringer, didn't you?"

"Yes. It was her father's gun."

"She let him shoot her, and still, she and that lady kept coming, and he would have killed her. She just wouldn't quit. By the time she got to him I don't know how she was still standing. Is this enough blood for the two of you? Is it done now? Even that woman she becomes is tired of killing, so can we go home now?"

Her grandfather looked at him and realized maybe he had pushed her to keep going until she was almost lost to the both of them. It was time to stop.

She didn't wake for hours, and the doctor was called out again. Her wound was rebadged because she was bleeding again, not as bad as before but somewhat bad. She had a large bruise on her shoulder where she was bleeding inside, and the doctor told Miles she was going to have to keep it elevated and not use it for several days. It was not going to heal properly if she didn't stop moving around.

When she came around this time, just Miles was in the room, and he was sitting in a chair across from her.

"What exactly did you think you were doing out there this time, Morgan? I can't figure out why you keep putting yourself in danger."

She didn't even bother answering him. She didn't have an answer. It was stupid, and it could have waited, but she felt like she had to do it. She just turned over, put her head in the pillow, pulled the sheet over her head, cried, and tuned him out.

She felt him climb into bed with her, and then he pulled her to him and held her as she cried. She went to sleep without saying a word to him. She didn't know how to tell him she had lived in fear and darkness for so long, she didn't know how to live in the light anymore. Sometimes she didn't feel like there was any light anymore for her.

He held her for hours, just thinking. He didn't understand how she had lived this long, and losing the baby was the last straw. It was something Ramon took, and she didn't know how to deal with it. She didn't need him yelling at her. She just needed to learn how to be normal again, and that was going to take time. Gregory and the girls was the best medicine for what she had lost until they could replace her lost child.

He finally went to sleep, and when he awoke, she was looking at him. "Your color is better this morning. Are you hungry?"

She reached out and touched his face and caressed it. "Are you still angry with me?"

He pulled her closer to him and said, "No, I am not angry, just concerned. I was scared I was going to lose you with the baby and needed someone to yell at. It shouldn't have been you." He pushed the hair off her face and pulled her head to him and hugged her tighter. "I have never been as scared as when he shot you and when I saw all that blood. Then I picked you up off the floor, and there was so much more. We just left him there on the floor and let him bleed while we took care of you."

"Did the girls see any of it?"

"No. Rosa got them out of the house and wouldn't let them back in till she had the mess cleaned up and his body taken care of. They never saw him or you."

"I know you don't understand. I was only a couple of months along, but I feel so empty inside and so heartbroken. That is why I needed to talk to my mother."

He just held her closer as she cried. He didn't know what to do, so he just held her. "The doctor says there will be other children. People shooting you and falling down stairs aren't good for babies."

As she looked up at him, it was the first time she had smiled in days. "Guess it really wouldn't be, would it? I will try harder next time to not do that again."

"I really would appreciate it if you would try."

She wasn't crying anymore. She was feeling better, in fact. Not everything could be fixed, but she could try.

"What happened to the dress?"

"Why? Are you planning on wearing it again? It really is a mess."

"No, I thought maybe we might build a fire some night and burn that one and a white leather wedding dress and maybe burn my past with them." She looked up at his face to see his response.

"I think that is a wonderful idea. Let the past go up in smoke—literally."

She was smiling this time. "I think it is time to start fresh, don't you? And they are a part of the past. I am hungry. Can you help me downstairs so I can eat something?"

"No, ma'am, but I will bring you something up. The doctor says you are to stay here for at least three more days, and that is that. You have to keep that arm elevated, or it is not going to stop bleeding inside and heal. You are going to have enough to do when you are feeling better. Your stepfather was in trouble up to his neck, and your name is on the paperwork."

"Great. Just what I want to do dig Ramon out of a mess with my name on it."

After three more days, she was going crazy, so they put her downstairs at a desk with her arm in a sling, and she started to go over the books with the accountants. She liked Francis. She was smart and funny, so they sat down and started to go over the accounts as the men went to check what was where.

There was a great deal of things bought but not accounted for. He had spent her money like it was going out of style, so it was a good thing Gary had hidden most of it. Some of the bankers who had lent her money were now trying to figure out how to account for what they had lent to him to their stockholders. A lot of money was unaccounted for.

Her horses were in good shape. He had at least taken care of them, only she had a man show up one day with a bill of sale wanting to take one of the stallions.

"I want to talk to the owner, Ramon Calderon. He sold the stallion Thunder to me a month ago, and I am here to pick him up now."

Morgan was walking out to meet the man, and he was furious as he stood yelling at her men. Miles had gone to town with Gary. They had some business to do at the bank, and she couldn't ride yet, so she was here with her grandfather and Francis and James.

"What is the problem here? I could hear you screaming from inside."

The man looked at her and didn't figure she would be much of a problem. Most women weren't. "I am Fredrick Russell. I have come for my horse, and these men won't let me have him."

She looked at him and then held out her hand for the piece of paper in his hand and read it then she handed it to James to read. He read it and said, "It isn't worth the paper it is written on. He has no claim to the horse."

She handed the paper back to the man in front of her, and he was purple. He was so mad. "What are you talking about? I bought the horse from the owner Ramon Calderon a month ago, and I have already paid him for him. What kind of scam are you trying to pull?"

"The horse didn't belong to Calderon, Mr. Russell. He belongs to me and always has. He sold him to you under fraudulent circumstances. I am sorry, but the horse is mine and always has been."

He went to grab for her, which was a mistake. At least three of her men started to draw their guns on him, and her grandfather was outside by now.

"Who are you? He said he owned these animals. He inherited them from his dead stepdaughter."

"Well, I am the stepdaughter, but I am not dead, even though he tried hard enough to get me that way."

"What am I supposed to do now? I paid him five thousand dollars for that horse."

"Five? He is worth three times that much. Let me think on it. Maybe we can come to some kind of an understanding. Are you staying in town?"

"Yes, at the Dallas Hotel."

"I will send word tomorrow, and we will talk again." She turned and went back in the house. It was hot out here, and she was tired. Talking to this man was getting nowhere.

"What are you going to do? He is not going away easy. You may wind up with a lawsuit.”

“I know, and I want to go home, not stay here and get sued.” *Maybe a mare will get him off my back and he will go away.*

The man rode away, and he was going to find a lawyer as soon as he could. It wasn’t going to do him any good, but he was mad and getting madder by the minute. He passed men on the way off the ranch road, but he paid them no mind. He and his men just kept on riding.

Miles looked back at him and wondered who he was. When he got to the house, James told him what was going on now. Great, another creditor, and still, they couldn’t find the money Ramon was taking in, and now it was adding up to a lot of money somewhere.

Gary had gotten her assets out of hiding, and it wasn’t as bad as they thought, but he had still used a considerable amount it. It was nothing she couldn’t live without, but she still wondered where he had used the rest of it. There was no woman and no gambling debts they could find, but there was almost twenty thousand missing, and they couldn’t figure out where it went. Bounty hunters weren’t that expensive, or he would have had better ones than the ones he had hired.

Miles met her in the house, and they talked about the man and the horse. He said, “From now on, I am leaving more men behind when I leave the ranch. I don’t know who is going to show up. Your stepfather had some bad people for friends, and they seem to be coming out of the woodwork lately.”

She looked at him and raised her eyebrow. “You can say that again. I don’t know who to expect when somebody comes down the road anymore.”

“What do you plan to do about the horse?”

She sat down at the desk and pulled out a piece of paper. “I thought I might give the man a registered mare for the money he spent for the stallion, but if that doesn’t suit him, he can go away empty handed.”

He shook his head. “You don’t do it alone. I will be here with some of the men. He was furious when we went past him on the road.”

“I wasn’t planning on doing this one by myself. He is not a happy man about this.”

He took her by the arm, and they went in for supper. Gregory was already yelling for her to come. It was suppertime.

She stopped inside the doorway and asked Miles, "You know I want to take Mama Home with me when we leave?"

He nodded.

"I want to take Gregory's mother too, but I don't know where she is buried. Can you ask and find out where the farmhouse is? I don't want him to know, but I don't want her left here. She deserved better than that hole. She tried her best to protect him."

He nodded. He would find out from the rangers where she was, and he would see it that it was taken care of. There would be two coffins on the train when they leave to go back to Amarillo.

The next day, Fredrick Russell came back to the ranch, and Morgan invited him inside. They sat down, and she started talking.

"I have a proposition for you. I will let you have one of my registered mares instead of the stallion you paid for."

Before she could even finish, he was screaming at her that that was not what he wanted and that he was being swindled. She just waited until he shut up, and then she continued.

"You have already talked to a lawyer and found out that I am the legal owner of the stallions, and you don't have a leg to stand on, so it is the mare or nothing. Stop screaming at me, or I will have you escorted out of here."

She was right. He had talked to a lawyer, and he told him she was the owner. He couldn't do a thing about it, but he was still mad. She was sitting there, so calm and cool, and it irritated him to no end, but she had him, and he didn't want to lose all his money and walk away with nothing.

"All right. If that is the best you can do, I will take it."

She looked up at him and said, "It is not the best I can do. It is the only thing I will do. If you don't like it, leave." And she just sat there, waiting for an apology.

He knew he had pushed too far, and she was pushing back. "I am sorry. It is a very generous offer, and I would appreciate it. Thank you." Then he forced a smile on his face before she took back the offer.

She took the paper on the desk and filled it in and gave it to him. It was the registration papers for a breeding mare of her stock. Then they went outside, and the mare was led up to him. He realized the mare was an older one, but she was also pregnant, so he had a chance of having a foal or a filly.

He turned around and shook her hand. She had given him at least a chance at his own stallion out of her line of champions, and all he had done was scream at her. "Thank you. I will take care of her."

She shook his hand, and they started back down the road of her land. Well, one more crisis done with.

"He seemed pleased with the mare."

"She is older. That is probably her last foal, but she usually has male colts. She is Thunder's mother. He has a chance at his own stallion. He better be good to her."

"Does he know?"

"He will when he reads her papers and looks at her lineage."

"Will you and the children be all right? I was going to help bring Martha Jean and the rest of the family here. We will be gone for several hours, probably until late this evening."

"We will be fine. There are enough men here, and I will have them close the gate."

He kissed her, and he and some of the men were off to Gary's ranch so they could get back before it was too late. She had plenty of paperwork to do, and the children were playing around the house and outside where she could see them.

After supper, everybody was bathed and put down for the night, and she was sitting on the balcony of her bedroom when she heard someone coming up the back stairs. He was being very quiet, so she stood up and got her knife out of her boot and stood by the rail as he came up the stairs, and then he was on the balcony. He stopped and looked at her and then the tray holding the liquor bottles and glasses.

"May I?"

"Help yourself. Do I know you, or do you always make yourself at home?"

He poured a glass of tequila, and then he leaned against the rail on the balcony as well.

"I was looking for Ramon. Have you seen him, senorita?" He was looking at her as he drank the tequila.

"Senora. He is dead. He is going to be hard to talk to now. Why were you looking for him?"

"We had business. Are you his wife? Maybe I can do business with you instead."

"I am not his wife, and I don't think we would make good business partners. What kind of business were you and Ramon in?"

He kept looking at her, but he didn't come any closer to her, and she kept the knife hidden. She didn't want him to know there were no men in the house.

"He started doing business with my brother several years ago, selling guns and cattle to him, and when my brother was killed, he started doing business with me. He was supposed to have a large shipment of guns and cattle waiting for us, but they are not here."

"Was your brother Juan?"

He nodded as he sipped the tequila.

"Then you were looking for the cattle behind the house?"

He nodded again. Now she knew where the money was disappearing to. He was buying guns and cattle and selling them then pocketing the money elsewhere. It was probably in another bank where he didn't have to account for it to anyone as hers.

"You're a Comanchero, and he was supplying you? I thought the rangers wiped you all out when they were looking for the kidnapped girl."

He took another drink of the tequila and looked at her again. "How did you know about that? What is your name?"

"Which one? The English one or the Comanche one that White Cloud gave me when he took me from your brother?"

He stopped drinking and started paying more attention to the woman in front of him. "You are her. You got him killed."

"He got himself killed. He shorted a Comanche war chief, and that was a stupid thing to do." She was just standing there, leaning against the rail watching him.

"He should have killed you like he was supposed to, and he would be alive today."

"I doubt it. He wanted me, and that is what got him killed. He made a deal with the devil, and the devil won. Ramon was never going to pay him. He had probably already told the rangers where to find him."

They heard riders coming up the road, and she looked at him. "What are you going to do now?"

He looked at her, and he started toward her, and she just took the knife and gently smacked it against her leg a couple of times. He saw it, and he realized he hadn't seen her pull it out or even grab it before now, so she had it all along.

"You are the one he sent bounty hunters after, aren't you? What happened to them?"

"They are all dead. Why? Do you want to join them?"

"Did you kill Ramon?"

"No. I shot him after he shot me, but a ranger finished the job. I think you should leave now. You don't have much time. Those men coming are my husband and my grandfather, and the rest are Texas Rangers."

"Why are you letting me go?"

"Your brother didn't kill me, so he bought you one chance, so you better run and keep running all the way back to Mexico because they will be coming after you tomorrow. Take your chance and leave while you still can."

"Maybe my brother was right. You were worth dying for."

He drained the glass and put it down on the table and went down the stairs as quietly as he had come up, and she waited until she heard his horse riding away. She saw him going across the back pasture, and he was gone.

Miles walked into the room, and he walked up to her, and then he noticed she had out her knife. There was a glass on the table, and he picked it up and smelled what had been in it. It was tequila. She never drank tequila. He asked her, "Who was here?"

"I didn't get his name, but he was the leader of the Comancheros, and it seems Ramon was supplying them with guns and cattle. That is where all the money has been going."

"Where is he now?"

She nodded to the man riding out in the pasture, and Miles went running down the stairs, but she knew he had too much of a head start, and the sun was setting too fast. She was good to her word. He would get his chance to run. She headed downstairs, and all the questions, she was going to have to answer, but she put her knife away first.

The rangers were ready in the morning to go after the Comancheros, but she knew they wouldn't find anything; he had enough head start to evade them, and now they were square. She didn't tell them most of the conversation. It wasn't any of their business. Miles was worried about leaving her even more now, but she thought the worst was over. She did have an idea she wanted to talk to Gary about though.

"If Ramon was supplying the Comancheros with guns and cattle, he had to hide the money somewhere, so why don't we put an ad in the newspaper and see if one of the banks will tell us where it is being kept?"

Miles just looked at her and said, "We don't need the money, so why do we need to even look for it?"

"It is not for us. He was the girls' father, and that make them the heirs to his estate. They are entitled to that money, especially after what he put them through."

He hadn't thought about the girls being part of this. So they put ads in the paper, and sure enough, one bank got in touch with them. There was an account with Ramon's name on it, and it had almost eighteen thousand dollars in it. Morgan had her lawyers handle the probate part of the transaction, and the money was transferred to Amarillo and put in the girls' names for later when they would need some money of their own.

They were almost ready to leave. She had sold the house and the cattle. The rustled cattle that were Gary's, they had given to Travis Davis for helping get her family out the night of the attack, and the rest went to their owners. Gary had sold his ranch, and they were ready to go when she was. She had made arrangements with the railroad for cattle cars for her horses. They would be transported by train, as would her family. The household goods would be taken by wagon.

It had been several weeks, and she was riding again. She was supervising the checking of the fences and the moving of the remaining cattle. What was left was going to the auction. They were almost through for the day when she remembered an arroyo she had played in when she was younger, and she decided to check it out. It would have been a good place to hide a wagonload of guns if you didn't want anyone to find them.

The men were taking care of the cattle and didn't notice her ride away from them. She rode down the arroyo, and sure enough, she found wagon tracks in the sand and at the end, she found something covered up with branches. When she got off her horse, she pulled one back, and she could see enough to figure out she was looking at a wagon full of guns covered with a tarp. Then she heard footsteps behind her.

"I see you found what you were looking for. Sorry I didn't get your name the other night."

Then she turned around and was looking at the man from the balcony. "You have the hearing of a bat, and I thought I was being so quiet."

"A couple of years of being hunted like a wild animal will do that for you."

She just looked at him. "I still don't know your name." She asked again.

"Raphael. Does it make a difference?"

She shrugged and started walking to her horse. "I guess not. This is the last time we are going to meet. I just like to know who I am talking to."

He grabbed her arm, and she stopped. "What are you going to do now?"

"What are the guns for?"

"The rebels back in Mexico."

She looked at him and then took his hand off her arm. "You paid for them. If they are for the rebels and not for the bandits around here, then they are yours. We will be off this land in two days. Wait till then and come get them. The new owners won't be here for a month."

"I asked about you. They say you are good with a gun. Are you as good as they say?" He was smiling at her.

"Do you want me to prove it to you? Because that would mean I would have to kill you, and that would ruin my whole day."

He just grinned at her as she mounted her horse, turned him around, and started riding away. He had heard all about her. He knew she was very good with a gun or a knife, and she could have killed him the other night. He understood why his brother didn't kill her as his captive. He wouldn't have either. There was something different about her, and he still hadn't figured that out.

When they were ready to leave, there would be some things to be done that the girls and Gregory didn't know about and wouldn't know about until the last minute. There was one car at the very back that would carry two coffins of two mothers who weren't going to be left behind. She had hired men to get Gregory's mother and wrap her in a tarp and put her in a metal coffin, but she had them leave his stepfather behind.

They searched the house for any information on any relatives and found nothing but a burned picture of his mother with a man and some letters. They assumed it was his father because she was pregnant in the picture at the time it was taken, and it had the year on the back. They were both smiling; at least they had wanted him. She would put up the picture to show him, and he would know later he was wanted by his real father.

After her mother was dug up, she went out and personally started smashing the headstone with a sledgehammer till Miles and her grandfather stopped her and finished the job. Her arm still wasn't good enough to be wielding a sledgehammer. She didn't want Ramon's name anywhere close to her mother's name ever, so they smashed it till it was gone.

On the last night before they left, she had the men build a bonfire in the back of the house, and they all went out there. She took the two bloody dresses, and she threw them into the fire. She watched them burn as Miles held her. The children didn't understand what was going on, but they thought the fire was fun anyway. They all sat outside, told stories about their childhood and about each other, watched the fire burn down, and then went inside to go to sleep so they could leave in the morning.

Everybody was loaded, and they were ready to go when she took the girls' hands. They went back inside the house. She told Miles they would be a few minutes. They walked down the same steps she had walked down the night she had come to the party, and she stopped on the landing. The picture of their mother was gone; it was already packed and loaded and was on the train.

She sat them on the steps and said, "Say goodbye to this place. This is the last time you will ever see this house because I am never coming back here."

The girls looked at her, and then Dona asked her, "We want to talk to you about something. Can we do it now? Do we have time?"

"Of course we do. We have all the time you want. What is it?"

"We saw you smashing Mother's headstone the other day when you dug her up, and we want to know why."

She hadn't realized they had seen her do that. "I am taking Mama home with us, and I am taking Gregory's mother as well. I think they deserve a better resting place than they got, and for the headstone, I couldn't bear to have Calderon next to mother's name, and I am sorry to say that."

"We are not. We would like to know if we can have our name changed as well. Is it possible? After all we have found out about him, we would like to have our last name changed."

She was kind of stunned. She hadn't thought about that. They had heard all the things he had done to everyone and the things he had said to them, and now they didn't want his name. "We can change your name, but what last name do you want?"

"You are going to raise us, aren't you?"

"I had planned on it, unless you don't want me to. I can see if Aunt Martha Jean or Grandfather would if you don't want me to."

"No, we want you to. We would like to have your last name Douglas if that is all right with you and Miles."

"It is fine with me. What would you like to call me and Miles?"

It seemed they had already thought about this as they had a ready answer. "We have always called you Morgan, but we were thinking we could call Miles Daddy if it was all right."

"Is it all right, Miles?"

She turned and looked up at him. She could hear a gnat flying at fifty feet. He could never sneak up on her.

"It would be just fine with me. I would be honored, young ladies."

"What about me?" Gregory was asking as he came around the corner of Miles. He wasn't about to be left out.

Rose answered this one. "You are already our brother, aren't you? So what is the big deal? Don't be a wuss."

"All right, Rose, don't be so snotty. I just had to make sure you weren't forgetting me."

"No way. Let's get out of here and go home."

Morgan had her hand over her mouth so they couldn't see her laugh at them as she followed them. Miles just looked at her and thought, *Wonder where they heard that.*

They all went out the door, and then she turned and said, "Goodbye, Mama. Rest in peace."

Miles turned around and looked at her. "Do you think she is gone?"

"She has been since we broke the headstone. I haven't felt her since."

"What do you mean, felt her?"

"She has been with me since I walked into this house. She was the only reason I got down those stairs that night. I dodged that bullet because she told me to move. She knew he was going to shoot me, and it was all she could do to protect me."

They walked out the door, but at the bottom doors, they were watched by Raphael as they left. He just had to see her one more time.

As they went through Dallas, they made quite a procession of people and horses. When they went by the bank where Ramon had hidden his blood money, she saw the banker watch her go by. She was sure he knew more than he was telling the rangers. She figured he was part of the scheme to sell the cattle and guns. She had told the rangers this, and they were now watching this man quite closely. She was sure he didn't like that.

Raphael didn't know it either, but she had warned him to get his operation out of this country, and she only gave one warning. He had better have listened to her.

When they got to the train, they were waiting on them. They unsaddled the horses and put them and then the people on board, and then came the coffins. She had the women put in metal coffins used in the war. They were bolted together for obvious reasons. The girls knew they were coming, but Gregory didn't. He was standing beside Morgan when they were brought to the landing, and he asked who was in the other coffin.

"It is your mother, darlin'. I had her dug up and put in a proper coffin, and she is going with us. She deserved better than that hole, especially after trying to protect you for all those years. She will be buried with my mother in a cemetery close to my home."

He looked at her. "How did you know what she did for me?"

"The rangers told me what the house looked like. They said it was like a child had never lived there, and your mother died trying to protect you. She wasn't going to stay in that sad, lonely place anymore."

He reached up to her, and she picked him up. He put his arms around her neck while she watched them load her mother and his mother into the rail car. When it was done, she carried him to the other car, and they went inside and sat down.

As they started home, his arms were still wrapped around her neck, and he was crying on her shoulder. She just looked straight ahead as Miles took her hand and held it and gave it a gentle squeeze. She had done the right thing; she had wondered, but now she knew. She didn't tell him about the papers they had found in the house. She would talk to him about those later. She at least knew his mother's name now, and that was something. She would have a proper headstone. He would at least be close to her even if he didn't know who his father was.

CHAPTER 7

They traveled for several hours until they got to Wichita Falls, and then they stopped and rested. Since she had reserved this train for her use, they were on a side stop and out of other trains' way until they were ready to leave again. They all loaded up again after the horses were tended to and were off again, and they would be in Amarillo before nightfall.

When they arrived, there were men waiting for them to unload the horses and get everybody home. Morgan had the stallions and several of the other horses saddled, and she and the men would take the children in front of them and head home. As she rode past the jail, she saw men poking their heads out, watching her. She had found out that the men who had attacked her had been sentenced to five years in jail in the Huntsville prison for attempted homicide. They all watched as she came back with her horses and children. They had backed the wrong man and were going to pay for it.

She had Gregory in front of her, and Miles had Rose. Grandfather and Dona were behind them. She looked back and smiled. "Let's get home." And she kicked her horse into a run.

They were home very quickly and were met by Virgie at the door, and Mama Ruby was not far behind. Several of the hands were waiting and reached to take Gregory, but he wouldn't let any of them touch him. Miles handed Rose to one of them, got down, took him from Morgan, and got Dona from Donald Roy so he could get down. Morgan was dismounting and telling the men where to put the stallions. At least the corrals had been rebuilt; the barn was still under construction.

She took Greg's hand, and they went inside. She looked at his face, and he was shocked. He finally said, "You do have a big house."

"I told you I did."

"Does Grandpa live here too?"

She looked at him and smiled. "No, he has his own ranch not far from here."

Virgie came over to her and told her, "There is a wagon outside that needs your personal attention."

She just nodded and went outside. It was the wagon with the coffins in it, and she told the men to put it in the end of the barn that was still intact. They would deal with burying them tomorrow. The men just nodded and went to put the wagon away as she went back inside.

Both the girls had rooms from before when they had lived here with her mother, and they went to them. Greg didn't have any idea where to go, so Morgan took his hand, and they walked down the hall. She showed him where her room was and then and asked him if he would like to have the room down from hers for his room.

He walked inside, just looked around, turned to her, and said, "This whole room is just for me?"

"Yes, sir, this room is just for you."

She didn't realize the thought of being alone in such a big room was kind of frightening to him, but he was too afraid to say that to her. He just nodded and looked around. Then the girls came into the room, and he was pulled outside to see some more of the house and the yard. Morgan didn't see how scared he was to be left alone in that room, but she would find out tonight.

There were wagons arriving in the yard by now. The sun was going down, and she was needed to get things put in the right places until they could be sorted out and put in the right houses. The children played outside until she had supper ready, and they came inside. She put them to bed, and she finally got to join Miles in their bed.

It was well after midnight when she heard noises, and she went to see what was going on. She found Dona holding Gregory on his bed and talking to him with Rose on the end of the bed.

"It is all right, Greg. What was the nightmare about? You can tell us. We won't tell anyone else."

He was crying, and she was holding on to him. "I am scared in here all by myself. It was like when I was hiding from my stepfather and I was all alone."

Rose scooted up beside him and said, "You want to sleep in my room with me or with Dona? That way, you won't be alone, and then you can come back in here before anyone gets up. Nobody will know but us."

Dona looked up and saw Morgan at the door, and Morgan just nodded at her as if to say, "Handle it your way," then she backed up.

"Could we do that?"

The girls looked at each other and then said to each other, "Of course we can. Who do you want to sleep with tonight?"

"Dona."

Morgan just watched as they closed his door and went to her room and climbed into her bed, and he went to sleep. He needed someone to be with him in the dark, and right now, it was his sisters.

"All right, but let's be quiet and not wake the house."

That was how it was going to go. He traded nights between them and was back in his bed the next morning, and only Dona, Rose, and Morgan knew what was really going on.

Morgan went back to bed and went to sleep. Morning was going to be early tomorrow, and she needed some sleep. Miles just pulled her close to him, and they went to sleep together. She would tell him what was going on in the morning.

She was up before the sun was and was dressed before Miles was awake, and he looked at her when she started out the door.

"What is the hurry? Wait for me."

She smiled at his tired face and told him, "Stay in bed. You can sleep a while longer till the children get up. Grandfather and I have some preparations to make before the service today, and it will be too hot for the children to be out there."

Then she started out the door just in time to catch sight of Gregory sneaking into his bedroom, so she backed into her room. Miles looked at her funny, so she told him what was going on.

He just smiled at her and said, "If that is what works, then it is our little secret."

She just smiled at him, "I knew there was a reason I liked you."

"Liked? Just liked? Is that all I get this morning?"

She smiled that wicked little smile. "That is all for now. I am late.

Go back to sleep."

He wasn't so sure he could do that now, but it was still cool in the room, so he would try with visions of that wicked little smile in his memory. He had a smile of his own on his face now.

She headed to the dining room, and her grandfather was sitting at the table with Dolf. They were waiting for her and drinking coffee. Sometimes when she saw Dolf, she could swear it was her father, and it took her breath away. He wasn't identical but close enough.

She grabbed her gloves off the stand by the door and her straw hat, and they asked her, "Don't you want some breakfast? We have time."

She shook her head. "It is going to be too hot, and I want to get this done. Those bodies need to be in the ground and soon. Even in those sealed coffins, they need to be underground now." She was right. Even though they were at the back of the barn, everybody knew they were there.

They went outside and were met by the men who were going to dig the graves. They got on their horses and led the wagon out to the cemetery and showed the men where to dig. When it was done, the coffins were lowered into the ground and covered. The headstones would be set while they were gone, and the service would be in the afternoon when the canyon was shaded and cooler. Now that the coffins were in the ground, they headed back to the house, and even out of the sun, it was already hot.

Dolf wanted to talk to both of them alone anyway, so he started to talk as they went back to the ranch. "I need to look for some work around here so I can earn a living for me and my son Pete. Do you know of anyone who has any jobs open for a laborer anywhere close?"

Morgan looked at her grandfather and then back at her uncle and just said to her uncle, "After this is taken care of, we will talk later tonight. We have some things to tell you."

They rode the rest of the way in silence. It was too hot, and she was brooding about something.

When she got to the house, she got out the papers the rangers had found in the house, sat them on the bed, and spread them out so she could have a better look at them. There was a woman—she was sure it was Gregory's mother because she was pregnant—and a man standing beside her, but the picture had been burned, and you could barely see him. It was dated on the back and had the names Sandra Williams and Don, but no more could be read; the rest was burned. She was smiling in the picture, so she suspected it wasn't the man who had brought her to Texas, but she didn't know who the man was. She thought he might have been Greg's father.

There was a letter to someone. She thought it was probably from Greg's father, but it too had been burned, and most of it was gone. It looked like she had tried to put out the burning paper with her hands, and she probably got burned in the process. All she could read was,

My Dearest Love,

Our child is not far away, and I hope it is a boy. I would love to name him Gregory like you wanted. It seems like I haven't touched you in years, even though it has only been a few months. Please be careful. I await a letter. It seems like this war is lasting forever.

There was no more; the rest was burned and gone. She wondered how she had gotten here with such an evil man who would kill her and try to kill Greg. She didn't have a way to find out with no names, and Greg had no memories. Maybe that was better. They had found these pictures and this letter hidden under a drawer only by accident when they searched the house at her insistence. The envelope was postmarked Missouri. That lady was a long way from home if that was her home.

It was time for lunch, and they all sat down and had the noon meal. They then got the children dressed and in the wagon and rode out to the cemetery, where they were met by the preacher. She didn't expect the reception she was met with out there. The whole town and the women she had brought with her were all there. She had brought her mother home and laid her to rest beside her father, where she was supposed to be. The headstones were set, and after the service was said for her mother, a shorter one was said for Greg's mother, and the girls and Greg put flowers on their mothers' graves. They all came back to her and held her hand as everyone sang a hymn, and then it was finally done. Both women were home. She had come full circle, and now it was done.

She thanked everyone for coming, and then they went back to the ranch. They sat out on the back patio around the fire pit after supper, and the children were put to sleep.

The breeze was cool. It was clouding over—maybe rain was coming—then her grandfather started talking.

"Dolf, I don't know if you know or not, but my father put aside land and money for both Burrus and me before he died, and I have kept it for you all these years until I found your father or his children."

Dolf looked kind of stunned, and then he started to speak. "Is that why you had people looking for us?"

"Yes. I have been looking for you and your father for a long time."

"No, I mean me and my brother Donald Glen."

Well, that shut her grandfather up. He had a namesake, and he didn't even know it. "Where is your brother? Why isn't he here with you as well?"

"He is dead. He was killed at Vicksburg. He was a Union soldier. He died saving his superior officer. They say he left a wife behind, but we couldn't find her, and she never found us, so we don't know if it is true."

Her grandfather looked heartbroken. He had lost another relative before he had even met him. "Well, son, there are still a thousand acres of land and a small house set aside for your father, so I guess it is yours now. My dad gave each of us kids a thousand acres to start and build from."

Dolf looked stunned. He had land and a house. He didn't know what to say. "Here? I have land here?"

Morgan looked at him and smiled. "Down the road some. A thousand acres is a lot of land."

"Cattle. I will need some cattle, won't I?"

"That is generally how you make a cattle ranch," Morgan said as she giggled at his near hysteria.

"You think this is funny, don't you? I have never had land or a house. I don't have the foggiest idea how to go about running a ranch, so shut up."

"We will help you get started with a good seed bull and some good cows, so calm down. I think you will find it is in your blood once you get started."

Donald Roy propped his foot up on a table and just listened to them argue and leaned his chair against the wall. Now this was home. All he needed was a wife again, and things would be perfect. Miles watched him and wondered how long it had been since he had been this relaxed and was glad things were settling down.

Gary wound up buying the ranch next to hers and settling in. It seemed Virgie wasn't going to need a ranch of her own. Her grandfather had staked a claim on her and was pretty adamant she was his. Virgie was still living at Morgan's ranch, but it looked like that was not going to be permanent.

"When are you going to ask her to marry you? You know they are going to want me to testify against Colonel Martin in Colorado soon. They have already contacted me about being there for the trial."

Her grandfather just looked at her and asked her, "What makes you think I am going to ask her to marry me?"

She looked at him and smacked him on the arm. "Well, if you aren't, I am going to tell Arnold Baxter from the stables he can come calling this Saturday. He has asked twice." Then she started to walk away from him.

He grabbed her arm. "Oh no, you don't. She is mine. I am going to marry her."

"Then you better get to asking because you two are neither one getting any younger, and she is too pretty to just be sitting around. You better make up your mind. She has been looking for a spread of her own."

That set a fire under him. Two days later, they were engaged, and a wedding date was set.

"What did you say to your grandfather? He came in and grabbed me and said, 'Woman, nobody else is going to marry you but me. Agreed? I just nodded, and it was done. Not very romantic but fast. You McKinneys get to the point quick."

Morgan raised her eyebrows and smiled. "Like you said, still a fire in that furnace. I just had to add some kindling." Morgan looked at her sideways.

Virgie was doubled over, laughing. "You little devil. What did you tell him?"

Morgan just walked away and shrugged.

The wedding was a week later. It was as big as or bigger than the one for Morgan, and it was a blowout affair. She had never seen her grandfather so happy, and Virgie was on cloud nine. It was at her grandfather's ranch, which was bigger than hers, and it took three days.

When it was done and they were back home, she had a telegram waiting for her. It was from Colorado. The trial was to begin in three weeks, and she was to be in attendance. The Indian women wanted to go with her, but she had a bad feeling about taking them with her for this trial, so she told them to wait and that she would find out if everything would be all right for them to come to the other Comanche tribe. If it was, she would send for them to meet her.

She began to pack and get ready. They would leave in a week. She had to get the children ready. Virgie would stay at the house, and so would Trey and Sheri. They now lived on her ranch, and Trey worked for her as a hand. Dolf was going with her and Miles. It was a long way, and he wanted to go with her as added protection. She wasn't well liked because of what she was doing; most people thought killing Indians wasn't a punishable crime. Going after a soldier for doing it, they thought, was even dumber.

They were still building the barn, but most of the corrals were up and complete, so the horses were secure. Trey, it turned out, was a good hand, and Sheri worked in the house for now until their first child came, and that wouldn't be long now. Morgan had them set up in one of the small houses on the ranch, and Trey was saving up for a place of his own. He had a place in mind, a small parcel. Morgan was prepared to sell if he wanted it by the canyon. It was where her father had died, and she didn't like to even go there anymore, so she would sell it to him if he wanted it.

The children were the most upset. Greg was sure she wasn't coming back, but she assured him she was.

The night before they left, she put her diamond ring in her jewelry box beside her squash blossom necklace and closed it.

Miles looked at her strangely and asked her, "Why are you taking off your diamond ring?"

"I don't know. I just know I need to leave it here. It will be safe here. Maybe I am afraid we will be robbed along the way. Maybe it is just too fancy for a trial of this kind. I will just wear my wedding band." She lay down beside him, and she asked him, "Do you think I am stupid for pursuing this man for killing all those people? Because if you think so I won't go. I will just let it be."

He looked down at her face as he held her. "White Cloud protected you and died for you, and he should at least have someone stand up for him, and if you are the only one who can do that, then you should."

Then she kissed him, and he started to make love to her. They wouldn't have much time or privacy going to Colorado. He entered her and kissed down her neck to her breasts, then she pushed him over, and that little demon came out. He so loved this one and was glad that the other one was gone, hopefully for good; maybe she wouldn't ever need her again. He stroked and stroked until she was flying, and he took them both to the top and over, and she was lying on his chest.

She lay there, running her fingers through the hair on his chest and across his face when she said, "We need to get this done and get back home. I have to have some more furniture built because some things were burned in the barn."

He looked down at her as she looked up at him. "What is so important that needs to be built that can't wait for the barn?"

"I think maybe a cradle. Mine was in the barn, and it burned."

"Are you sure?"

She smiled at him. "Not positive, not yet, but I am a few weeks late, so keep it between us for now."

He squeezed her so tight, she couldn't breathe. "Should we go? Will you be all right?"

"I am just going to testify. Nobody is shooting at me this time. Are you pleased?"

He turned her over in bed and kissed her again and again. "Oh, you don't know how much. Don't get me wrong, I love Gregory and the girls, but a child of our own would complete everything. It would give us back what he took away from you. A baby. I have never had a baby. Our family is getting bigger and bigger."

She smiled. "We have a big house."

He said as he held her, "We have room for even more."

They took the train as far as they could and then took stagecoaches. It was a long ride. It took five days. When they finally got there, they still had a ride to get to the fort, so they were going to wait till the next day. They were going to stay at the hotel, where she had gotten her bath. It wasn't much, but there wasn't anything else.

When they got inside, they were told they were booked up because of the hanging, and then Morgan asked, "What hanging?"

"They are hanging an Indian war chief for killing a white woman today, and we are booked up."

"What war chief?"

"I don't know. An Indian is an Indian."

Morgan turned to Miles, and she didn't even say a word. They both started running to the stables. While Miles paid for the horses, Dolf saddled the horses. Morgan put her Winchester in the saddle, and then they took off. She knew the way. She had been this way before, so they just tried to keep up.

As they got to the gate of the fort, she could see they were fixing to hang Standing Bear, so she just kept going. The men kept the guards off her, and then she started yelling. She had already pulled her Winchester and had it pointed at the gallows. "What in the hell is going on here?"

Who should step out but Lieutenant Riggs, the man who tried to shoot her in the canyon all those years ago?

"We are hanging this Indian for killing a white woman in his camp a few months ago. He has been tried, and he is going to be hanged, so stay out of it."

"What is this woman's name who he is supposed to have killed, lieutenant?"

The man looked closer at the woman talking and answered her, "It's Captain Riggs now, and the woman's name was Morganna McKinney."

"Well, you know, she is not dead because you know that is me and because you tried to kill me, lieutenant."

He started to drop the lever to hang Standing Bear anyway. She shot the rope, and he dropped harmlessly down onto the ground. Then she got off her horse and started toward the lieutenant. Two guards grabbed Standing Bear and led him out from under the gallows as a major grabbed Morgan before she got to the lieutenant.

"Is this true? Are you Morganna McKinney?"

"Yes, sir, and it is Douglas now, and that man was an idiot and still is one. Why didn't Standing Bear tell you I wasn't dead?"

He walked past her and looked at her and said something to her in Comanche, and then the guards took him away.

Miles looked at her strangely and then asked her, "What did he say to you?"

"I will tell you later."

She watched him walk away, and after him came Little Deer. He was to be hanged too. This was getting better and better. She had just walked into a hornet's nest.

They were being led to a hitching rail and tied to it. Standing Bear was livid. She could see from here. He was ready to kill someone, and she didn't think it mattered who right now. God, she needed to clean this mess up but fast.

She followed the men inside. They had sat down, and that condescending Captain Riggs was across the room.

"What in the hell do you think you are doing, trying to hang a Comanche war chief and his brave in the middle of the day in public? Are you trying to start a war? Now you have him tied up to a hitching post? Let's all go out there and wait to be scalped, you idiot. You haven't gotten any smarter since you tried to kill me. You knew who I was when I rode in here, and you tried to kill him anyway. Where were you when they passed out the horse sense? Digging your own grave? Because I will be glad to shovel the dirt on top of it for you."

"She can't talk to me that way. She is just a woman and a rebel sympathizer who I should have shot that day."

Miles was coming off his chair by now, and Dolf wasn't far behind. The major was just sitting and watching, as was the commander of the post. He had already watched this woman once before and knew better than to get in her way. She could take care of herself, and he didn't like the captain anyway.

"You are still a mealy-mouthed worm and a good-for-nothing lieutenant who is going to get these people killed." She looked at the commander and asked, "Can I shoot him just once? I won't kill him. Just hurt him a little."

"Donald Glen said he couldn't wait to meet you."

That got her attention. "What did you say? You knew my uncle? *Who in the hell are you?*" She was almost screaming at him as she turned and looked at the major more closely this time.

"My name is Major Thomas, and Donald Glen McKinney was my lieutenant, the best one I ever had. He found out about you from a telegraph from the lieutenant about that little dustup you two had. He told me he had finally found his family, and he couldn't wait to meet you—a McKinney woman tough enough to stare down a Yankee lieutenant pointing a rifle at her while she helped friends get away. Now I see his point. You are something."

He turned to Miles, who was holding his head in his hand and shaking it, and asked him, "Is she always like this?"

"You have no idea. She is not even mad yet."

"I have your uncle's effects. Would you like to see them?"

"Very much, but you still have a very big problem outside. You need to let those men go and soon before you have the whole tribe in here after them, and you are running out of time."

"How does she know so much about this?"

"She lived with the Comanche's. She is testifying against Colonel Martin this week. That is why we are here."

Captain Riggs was behind her and starting acting like a real jackass.

"So she is the squaw who is backstabbing the colonel."

She didn't even think. She turned, punched him in the stomach, put him on the ground, and then walked out the door. "You are still an idiot, captain." She said it with such contempt. They all wanted to laugh.

"I want her arrested for assault."

The major and the commander were walking out the door, smiling.

"I didn't see a thing. Did you?"

The other man shook his head. "Nope, I didn't see anything."

Morgan asked the men behind her, "Did they have horses?"

"No. They were dragged in here behind soldiers' horses."

"Oh, this just keeps getting better. What did he say at the trial?"

"He hasn't spoken a word since he was brought to the fort by the soldiers ten days ago. The only time he has said anything was to you."

The hairs on Miles's neck were standing up, and he was terrified for her. Standing Bear was not going to take this lying down? They needed to be gone from here and fast.

"I am surprised you people are still alive, but you won't be much longer if you don't fix this. Miles bring our horses over here. At least they can ride out of here. That will help a little."

The major asked if she would talk for them, and she said she would, but she had a feeling this was not going to be good after what he had said to her earlier. When they got close, she pulled her knife out of her boot. She went to Standing Bear first, cut his bonds, looked up at him, and repeated what the major was saying to her. It wasn't making a bit of difference. He wasn't taking his eyes off her, and he wasn't listening to what she was saying to him.

She went to Little Deer next and cut him loose and told him to take the horses, take Standing Bear, get the tribe, go north, and get away from this place. She looked at him. He was at least listening to her. Standing Bear wasn't. Then Standing Bear repeated what he said earlier as he got on the horse. She again told him to get his people away from here. They turned and left at a full run.

She turned, and Miles asked her what he said to her. She wouldn't tell him until he finally stopped her and turned her around to look at him.

"What did he say to you, Morganna?"

"He said, 'I almost died for you. You belong to me now.'"

Then she turned and walked away. He would be back for her, and they both knew it.

The major was waiting inside, and after Miles told him what was said, he had guards put on Morgan full time. He was watching the Indian's face as she talked to him, and he could see he wanted her. After Miles explained what had gone on before, he was afraid for her, but if she was to testify, she had to stay. The trial was in two days. They could keep her safe that long, and he could tell her about her uncle. She would be guarded from now till they left. Dolf and Miles wouldn't let her out of their sight.

They went to his quarters, and he pulled out a metal box and started to display her uncle's uniform and other objects. He didn't know how she would feel about him being a Yankee soldier.

"My father hadn't taken a side in the war, and Virgie was a friend. When she came, we had hidden her just because she was a friend, not because she was a rebel. My father thought too much blood had been spilt on both sides to justify the war in the first place."

The major agreed. There were letters to a woman, your uncle's wife, and a photo. It seemed he had hidden her from her father to keep her safe.

"Why keep her safe?"

"Her father rode with Quantrill's men, and her marrying a Union soldier wouldn't have pleased him at all. She had a fiancé her father had picked out who she left for your uncle, and that didn't help either."

"What happened to him?"

"I don't know for sure. You see, a cannon shell burst near us, and I was badly hurt. Donald Glen pulled me to safety, but he was wounded in the leg, and he bled out before help could come. I was in the hospital for a long time, and when I went to look for her, she was gone. It seems she had been taken to Texas by her ex-fiancé, trying to find Donald Glen's family, and I never could find her after that. I did find out her father was killed in a raid in Louisiana, so he couldn't hurt her."

Miles looked pleased that several of Quantrill's men had been killed while raiding his ranch. He hoped her father was one of them.

"Here, I think I have a picture of them together."

He pulled out a picture of a pretty blond woman and a man in a blue uniform with his arm around her, and she was pregnant and smiling. As soon as they saw the picture, Morgan smiled and turned over the picture and saw the names on the back—Sandra Williams and Donald Glen McKinney.

"What are you smiling about?"

"The man who took her to Texas beat her to death and almost killed her son Gregory."

"So why are you smiling?"

Miles answered him. "Morgan found Gregory and Dolf, his brother, in a way station going to Dallas, and we are raising Gregory now. His brother didn't even know who the child was. He had wandered in from the desert after his mother had been killed, and the man had hanged himself. She also brought his mother's body back to our ranch and buried it there."

"How did you know?"

"I didn't know. I just knew the child needed a home, and that woman deserved a better resting place. You don't know where he is buried, do you? I would like it if I could bring him home as well."

He looked at her strangely. Most of the dead at Vicksburg were buried in mass graves, but he had made sure he knew where Glen was buried because he had said his family would come looking for him, and now they had.

She kept staring at the picture. She could see Glen's eyes and his mother's lips in Gregory. He was going to be so proud of this picture. He could finally see his father and mother together.

She showed the picture to Dolf, and he looked at her and said, "That child was Glen's all along, and I didn't know, and you come along and take him in like he is your own. How did you know he was under my nose all along?"

"Maybe you were supposed to be there, and you just didn't know that so I could find you both."

"I should be raising him."

"Oh no, he is my child now, and no one takes him from me ever. I am his mama. We have a deal, and that child is not going to ever going to lose another mother again."

Well, that was the end of that discussion. Uncle or not, Gregory was hers now. Glen may have been his brother, but he didn't take care of that child when he had a chance, and now Gregory was hers.

Two days later, the trial started, and it was going to be nasty. Colonel Martin had hired a good lawyer, and he was going to try to break her on the stand and make her look like a ruined woman in front of everybody. He had picked the wrong woman to try that on. They had interviewed several of the men in the troop who were in the raid, and they had confirmed that there had been no Indian raids prior to the raid on the village that morning, but there could have been some they didn't know about.

"You are one of the soldiers who attacked the village that morning."

"Yes, sir, I was. When we went in, everybody was asleep but a few outposts and the dogs."

"When the men awoke, they started firing on you?"

"Yes, sir, they did. We were firing on them, and they were defending themselves and their women and children."

"I won't need you anymore."

As the soldier started to leave, Morgan asked the lawyer next to her to ask the boy some questions.

"Your Honor, may I ask the young man some questions?" The judge just nodded.

"Why did you think you were there that morning? What is your name again? Jared?"

The young man just nodded. "We had been told the Indians were raiding the white settlers, but we hadn't seen any raiding anywhere. The lady beside you helped me after the raid to take a bullet out of my leg, and she took care of me and some of the other men that night. The town doctor told us if she hadn't taken care of me, I would have died or lost my leg, and I never got a chance to say thank you. All I saw was a man trying to kill her and all the other men killing everyone else in that village, including children. I still have nightmares about it. I hope you can forgive us, Running Knife."

She just smiled at him and nodded as several men in the room stood and saluted her, and no one else said a word until they sat back down.

The lawyer said, "Thank you, Jared. You are excused."

He left the stand and walked back to his seat. She didn't say a word.

The lawyer still thought he was doing pretty well when he got her on the stand, and he was going to tear her apart. He was known for breaking people on the stand, and he was good at it. She entered the box in front of the officers convening the court and was sworn in, and then he started on her.

"Mrs. Douglas, you were in the Indian camp the morning the soldiers rescued you from the Indians."

She just looked at him and said. "I was in the camp the morning they butchered everybody, yes."

"That was not the question I asked."

"Then you didn't ask the right question, did you?"

He turned and looked at her. This woman wasn't going to collapse in tears like he had wanted her to, and that young man's testimony hadn't helped.

"Weren't you being held captive by White Cloud, the Indian chief?"

"Yes, I was there for some time. He had rescued me from the Comancheros."

"So you were his woman, a slave."

"No, I was treated as his daughter and protected from the man who wanted me dead and had a reward on my head."

"Really? A reward? You think you are so valuable, someone would pay money for you?"

"Yes, At that time, it was twelve hundred dollars, and that was why the Colonel Martin killed all those people—to get to me."

"Really? Can you prove any of this to anyone?" And he turned and looked at the people around the room.

Miles took a handful of papers from judges to Texas Rangers and almost fifty signatures of other people and twelve bounty hunters in Huntsville Prison in Texas and handed them to the court. When they were through looking them over, the major handed them to the lawyer.

He looked at them and then at Morgan.

She looked at him and smiled. "I think the final price was five thousand."

He just looked at her and then looked at the colonel and sat down.

The major asked the lawyer, "Are you through with the witness, or do you have more questions?"

The man looked over at his client and just shook his head. It was her lawyer's turn to ask questions now.

"You stayed with the Indian tribe for some time. Why didn't you leave?"

"White Cloud wanted me to marry his son, and he didn't think anybody would really kill to get me back to my stepfather. I was planning on running and trying to find the man I am married to because I knew I was putting the whole village in danger, but I just didn't get away in time to save them."

"Is there anything you could have done different to save those people?"

"I don't know. The reward on my head was all they saw, and killing all those people didn't matter because they were Indians."

He turned around and walked back to his chair and sat down, and he was through. She got off the stand and went and sat beside him. It was done now. It was up to the judges.

The officers talked to each other, and the major stood up and looked at Colonel Martin and said, "You attacked a sleeping village of Indians and killed them and tried to kill this woman. I can't prosecute you for the Indians, but I can for trying to kill this woman. Colonel, you will spend the next ten years in the penitentiary for attempted murder."

Colonel Martin looked daggers at her as he was taken away in handcuffs. Well, it was something.

When he went past her, she said, "Ten years is not enough. It should have been ten for each life you took, but it will do for now."

And then they took him away, and she felt like a weight had been lifted off her shoulders. Maybe White Cloud could rest now.

Major Thomas led them out of the courtroom and down the front of the barracks to his office. "Will you have supper with me tonight before you leave in the morning? I will have all your uncle's property ready for you to take back with you. I have already contacted the people in Vicksburg and told them where your uncle is buried and made arrangements for him to be brought to your ranch. It may take some time, but I will keep in touch till it is done. I will make sure you have an escort to the train so you can get back home safe."

"I thank you for your help. Just let us clean up, and we will meet you in about an hour for supper."

Then Miles took her arm, and they walked to their room at the other end of the fort. There was a guard standing in front of the door as they went in.

When she walked in, someone grabbed her and put a hand over her mouth and pulled her back against the wall. A brave grabbed Miles and put a knife to his throat, and it looked like he was going to kill him.

She pulled the hand away from her mouth and turned around to look at Standing Bear's face and quietly said in Comanche, "If you kill him, I swear on White Cloud's soul I will kill everything you love if it takes the rest of my life." And the woman he was looking at now made him believe she would do just that.

He stopped the brave from killing Miles and had him tie him up and put him on the bed as he just watched her, as did Miles. Miles knew what was happening. Standing Bear didn't. She was barely keeping herself under control.

She turned to Miles and said, "I have to go, or he will kill you. I love you. I will find a way back to you. Please believe me. Take care of our children."

Standing Bear was tying her hands in front of her, and then he led her out of the room. She looked back once to see Miles. He was tied and gagged but alive.

Standing Bear led her around the side of the building and down the side to an opening and out, and then they ran to waiting horses. He put her in the saddle of one, and he mounted another, and he had the reins of her horse. She just held on as they rode just as hard as they could for hours until they were on the edge of the mountains. He took her down and told one of the men to watch her and bring her to him.

The man didn't know her or about her and the chief. She wasn't moving fast enough for him, so he hit her on the left shoulder with his fist hard, knocking her down. When she hit the ground, she felt something in her arm tear in that scar. It felt like lightning going up it again, and then he grabbed her by the same arm and pulled her up.

That was it. When she came up, she caught him right between the legs and dropped him to the ground and then hit him on the neck. She tried to get back on the horse, but her arm just wouldn't work, so she ran. If she could get to the trees, she might have a chance. She didn't even look back. She just ran, and she was almost there when he grabbed her around the legs and dropped her to the ground. He had a knife at her throat, but the other lady was out now, and she was in a killing mood. He wasn't ready for her.

She had gotten her bonds undone by now, and she had him between her legs and flipped him over, and now she was on top. They were wrestling for the knife, and she finally got control of it and had it at his throat. Now his life was in her hands.

When Standing Bear got there, he was trying to save his brave, not Morgan. The brave and Standing Bear were looking at a woman who had no problem killing him or anyone else, so he put her in a choke hold that would have taken down most men and was holding her hand with the knife, telling her to drop it. She would do neither. He pulled her off the brave, and she was almost unconscious when she dropped the knife, and he turned her around. He watched as the other lady melted away, and then he understood why she was feared by the bounty hunters. White Cloud had given her a warrior's name for a reason, and he had just seen it, and so had his brave. He reached for her.

"Don't touch me. I can walk by myself, and if he touches me again, I will finish what I started."

So he didn't touch her for now as they walked back, and he put her on a horse, for she seemed to be having some trouble with her arm. He warned the brave to stay away from her, which suited the brave just fine. He had never seen a woman look or act like that.

They rode for several hours more, and then they stopped, and her shoulder was screaming at her. Whatever she had done was enough to remind her that it still wasn't healed. When they stopped, Standing Bear took her off the horse and grabbed a couple of blankets, and they walked away from the rest of the men into the forest. She already knew what was coming.

He stopped in a clearing and laid one of the blankets on the ground and pulled off his shirt. She had to admit he was a good- looking man. He just wasn't the right man. Then he came over to her, and she closed her eyes. Maybe she could do this if she just went somewhere else. It had always worked before. He stopped.

"Open your eyes and look at me, or I will go back and kill him just so you won't be able to think of him alive."

She opened her eyes. He would do it.

He started to unbutton her shirt, which was held together by snaps, and he liked that they just flew open. Underneath was her bustier, which he didn't like. She had dressed nicely for her court date. He started to cut the laces open with his knife. Well, it looked like she wouldn't be wearing that again. He pulled the shirt off and saw the bruise and the scar. He pulled her to him, and that got a moan out of her because it hurt.

"What happened to you?"

He pulled the shirt the rest of the way off and looked at her back and saw the bruise, and a scar was on the back too. Now he knew why her arm wasn't working.

"I got shot by my stepfather, and your man hurt me when he shoved me around."

"Is that why that other woman tried to kill him? Because he hurt you?"

She didn't answer him, and he put his hands on the bruise and pushed with his thumb until the pain made her answer him.

"Yes. She protects me, and she does a good job when she makes an appearance."

He leaned down and kissed her shoulder where he had hurt her a second ago. "Don't make me hurt you just to get an answer from you. There is more, isn't there?"

As he started to lay his hand on her shoulder again, she finally said, "I fell down some stairs and lost my unborn child as well."

He looked at her and said, "Good. I only want you to have my children."

Well, that scared the hell out of her. If she was already pregnant, she had to figure a way out of this quick before he figured that out.

He finished pulling off her shirt. The bustier came off, and he threw it away. He just looked at her. "I wanted to kill him every time he touched you at my camp, even when he was sewing up your arm." He ran his hand down her breast to her stomach and then back to the shoulder and asked her, "Does it hurt to raise your arm?"

She tried, and she could hardly move it. She had done something when she fell, and she grabbed it when she tried to move it.

"I will be careful not to hurt you."

"You could leave me alone."

He looked at her and smiled. "I have waited long enough."

He laid her down on the blanket, picked up her leg, and removed her boots, her pants, and her underwear. He removed his buckskin pants and got on his knees and leaned over her.

"You were always supposed to be mine."

And then he was inside her, and she sucked in her breath. It was like he hadn't had a woman in years. He took his time, and she just wanted it done. He avoided her arm but nothing else. He nuzzled her breasts as he stroked, trying to bring her to the top with him.

"Touch me like you touch him, Morgan, or I will make him pay."

She looked up at him. She could play this game too, so she reached up and kissed him. It wasn't like Miles, but she would not let Miles or her children die, and the sooner he trusted her, the sooner she could figure a way out of this mess. *Close your eyes and think of Miles and just get through this. You have to stay alive and protect your child.*

He used her till he was through, and then he rolled off her and lay beside her and just looked at her. "I know you were thinking of him, but you will come to want me, especially when you carry my child. A woman loves the man who fathers her children." He was right, of course, and that was the problem. She was already in big trouble.

He rolled her on his arm and covered them up with the other blanket. He went to sleep, but she didn't. She lay there and hurt. Would

Miles want her back after this?

She cried as he pulled her closer to him, and it wasn't too long before he rolled her under him and took her again, quickly this time, and in the darkness, he didn't even see the tears.

In the morning, she dressed, and he didn't notice the bruise was bigger and her arm was worse. She put on her shirt, underwear, jeans, and boots before he saw her.

He said, "I want your ring. Hand it to me or I will pull it off your finger."

She gave it to him. She didn't know, but Miles would find it two days later on the end of a knife stuck to a tree, holding her bustier. He wanted to make sure Miles knew she had been his.

"You were always meant to be an Indian woman. When we get to the village, you will dress as one again, like the day we went looking for herbs. No more pants."

She knew her shoulder was bleeding inside, and she didn't know what to do about it, but she knew she needed to rest and not use it. There was no way to tell him that, so they just kept going. When they stopped for a rest at noon, she found a place and just lay down, and he left her alone.

When they went to leave, he came to get her, and she started to get up, but she couldn't. He reached down to grab her and he could feel the heat coming off her. She had a fever. He opened her shirt and looked at her shoulder, and the bruise was twice its size from the night before.

He took the medicine bag she had given him, took out some of the herbs, and had his men put some in a cup and mix it like she had shown him. When it was ready, he got it down her till it was all gone. His men helped him get her in front of him on a horse, and they continued up the mountain till they got to their camp.

They got her down and into the tepee, and he laid her down on some blankets inside. Still Water was inside and saw her; and when she saw Morgan she knew she was being replaced, even though she was very pregnant with Standing Bear's child. Standing Bear had even married her, but it had always been Morgan he wanted. It didn't matter. Morgan was very hurt and sick, and she needed help.

Standing Bear came back in with water and started to fix the tea to give to Morgan.

"Just let me sleep. Go away."

Standing Bear left, went to Little Deer's tepee, got the bottle of laudanum from when he was shot, and added it to the tea. Then he undressed her and looked at the shoulder, which was much worse.

"What do I need to do to make it better, Morgan? It is getting worse."

"It has to be lifted, and I need to not use it till it stops bleeding, or it will continue to get worse."

He found a blanket, rolled it up, and put it under her arm after she drank the tea; then he undressed and lay down beside her and pulled her to him. All the while, Still Water watched. He didn't care what she thought. He held her in his arms, kept her warm, and fed her tea till the fever began to go away; and then he let her sleep.

Still Water could see the bruise and the scar. He told her she had been shot, and secretly, she wished she had died.

When Morgan woke, Standing Bear had left the tepee, and she saw Still Water. She just looked at her and her big belly, and tears came to her eyes. All she could say was "I am so sorry. Please forgive me." Then she closed her eyes and cried.

When Still Water left the tepee, Little Fox came over to her side and just looked at her, and then he lay down next to her. She covered him up, and he went to sleep. Since Still Water had become pregnant with Standing Bear's child, she had been ignoring Little Fox. He was looking for a new mother or at least someone to take care of him, and it seemed that someone was Morgan. Standing Bear had always wanted Morgan for his mother; it seemed Little Fox did too.

Now she was really trapped.

CHAPTER 8

The major had come looking for them when they were thirty minutes late, and when he got to their door, the guard was still posted outside, but nobody was answering. They had to kick down the door, and they found Miles tied up on the bed and Morgan gone. When they got him untied, he was in a rush to tell them what had happened. He started to search the fort and finally found an opening at the back of the fort where they had come in and taken her out.

The major asked Miles, "Why didn't he kill you?"

"Morgan threatened him with something, and it must have been bad because he called off his man and tied me up instead."

"Will he kill her?"

"He doesn't want her dead. He just wants her."

Then Captain Riggs had made an appearance by now and made the mistake of opening his mouth. "Well, she finally got what she deserved. That Indian will show her what's what."

Miles went after him, and it took the major and Dolf to keep him from ripping his head off.

"Captain, if you can't keep your mouth shut, stay the hell away from all of us. You are dismissed." The major turned around and said, "That man needs to be somewhere else besides here, and I am going to see to that."

They had men and horses ready to go in the morning at first light, and they were on the trail. It took the men two days to find the first signs of the Indians that were meant to be found. Morgan's bustier and her ring were found stuck to a tree on a mountainside in full view. Standing Bear had left a knife with her ring on the end of it in plain sight for him to find.

The major just looked at him and asked, "Do you want to go back now, or do we keep looking?"

Miles turned around and looked at him and asked him, "Are you married?"

"Yes. My wife is in Virginia."

"What would you do if this was your wife?"

The major didn't know how to answer the question because he didn't know what he would do if he was in the same position.

"She is my wife no matter what happens to her."

"What if she comes back with a child?"

"I am hoping she will. She is pregnant, and if he finds out, he will kill her or that child, but if she came back with an Indian child, it would still make no difference. She is still my wife, not his. He has a son he has always wanted her to raise. It would not surprise me to find out she steals him and comes back with him, but Standing Bear would probably hunt her down and kill her for that. She told me she will come back to me, and she will. You don't understand, major. She changes. There is another woman who protects her, and when she comes out, she kills without a second thought."

The major just looked at him and then at Dolf, and he just nodded. "You aren't kidding?"

"I have watched that woman protect her too many times, and if he comes after her or her child, she will kill him or get killed trying to save her child, and that scares me to death. She lost a child in Dallas trying to get her sisters back from her stepfather, and she won't let him take another one from her." Miles slipped her wedding ring into his pocket. When he found her, he would put it back on her finger himself.

"Then we need to keep looking."

They looked for another week until the snow started to fall, and then they had no trail left to follow. They had to come down off the mountain. Miles went home but told the major he would be back every month until he found her.

The major prolonged his stay at the fort for another year; he was determined to find her as well. He asked his wife to move to Colorado to be with him and start a ranch, and she agreed. He had the captain transferred to another fort in Arizona. It was the worst fort he could find to transfer him to. He was furious. The captain never got another promotion; the major saw to that as well. He left the army two years later. He started riding with an outlaw band, and people lost word of what happened to him.

Standing Bear spent the night next to Morgan, but the next morning, when he touched her, she almost screamed. The pain was so bad. So he again gave her some laudanum and then went to Still Water and made love to her—if you could call it that. He was angry at not being able to have Morgan, and he took it out on Still Water. He wanted Morgan to watch, but she could at least pretend she was asleep, and he couldn't do anything about it.

When he left, Still Water was crying, and Morgan opened her eyes and said, "I saved him from a hanging, and then he did this. I am no more than a prize he stole from another brave. He will tire of me, and I can escape."

Still Water just looked at her. "No, you can't. You are all he has talked of since you left. He almost went after you. When they took him, he said you would come and be his if you were still alive, and if you weren't, it didn't matter if they killed him. He said you should have been Little Fox's mother from the start. Even though we are having a child together, it has always been you he wanted."

She just looked at her. He had a child coming by Still Water, and still, he wanted her. She was in deeper trouble than she thought. "I am going to get away. He won't be able to keep me here."

"You are wrong. You are all he has talked about. He won't let you go again unless you kill him. Are you ready to do that?"

Still Water was afraid of the look in Morgan's eyes. She was ready to kill him now. Morgan didn't say anything.

Standing Bear came back inside the tepee, so she just lay back down, and he had her eat something and then gave her some more laudanum and looked at her shoulder again. The only thing keeping him alive now was that she couldn't get away hurt like this. She needed to get better before she could go, and Still Water knew this, so she just kept her mouth shut for now. The woman she was looking at would kill the man she loved, and she knew it.

It took four more days before she could even move her arm. The bruising was going away, and he checked every morning. He would use Still Water when he couldn't make love to her because there was no other way to put it; he wasn't even trying to hide how he felt for her anymore. Morgan felt sorry for her every time he went to her. Morgan would just close her eyes and try to at least give her some privacy. She couldn't do anything else.

On the sixth day, he decided she was well enough, so he rolled her over. Being careful of her arm, he entered her and had her. She again closed her eyes, and he stopped and told her, "Look at me, Morgan. I have waited long enough for you." He held her face in his hand until she looked into his eyes, and then he kissed her.

"You will never see him again. You are mine now and forever, just like it was supposed to be."

Then he kissed her, and he waited till she kissed back this time. She figured she had better start playing this game because she was going to start showing, and he had better think it was his child, or she was going to be in big trouble. He took his time, and Still Water left the tepee. That made it a little easier. He didn't care either way.

When he was through, he got up on his knees, just looked at her, stroked her legs, and then told her, "In a few more days, you can dress. I brought your clothes from the fort—your skirt, shirt and boots. You will dress like a squaw from now on, my squaw, but you will be watched from now on. You will not escape from me ever again. You will bear my children and raise Little Fox like I always wanted. He is yours now. You will not be allowed to have any weapons. I have seen what you can do with them, and my men are afraid of you."

He rolled her over, propped her arm back up, covered her up, and left her in the tepee alone, and she started thinking. He wouldn't be watching all the time and she would be able to get away. She just had to watch for the right time, and she would know when.

Still Water came back in and looked at her, and she knew she hadn't given up. She just didn't know what she was going to do yet.

Little Fox came in too and sat beside her, brushed the hair from her face, and pulled the cover up around her shoulder. Still Water grabbed him and pulled him away and was going to hit him as she said, "Don't touch her."

Even hurt, Morgan was up and grabbed her with a blanket wrapped around her and told her, "Never hurt him again. That woman I become doesn't just hurt men. Keep pushing and find out who else she will hurt."

Then Morgan backed away from her with Little Fox, and they went to the other side of the tepee. She sat down, and he sat in her lap till she could settle back down. She lay down and got her arm raised up again. He stayed close to her after that. Standing Bear never knew what happened that day. He just knew his son never left Morgan's side if he didn't have to.

Miles had gone back to the ranch with Dolf, and they had told Donald Roy. He was furious at first, and then he was heartbroken. She was gone again.

Gregory was inconsolable, and he kept saying, "I told them she wouldn't come back." And the girls had to keep him in their rooms at night because he started having horrible nightmares again. Finally, the nightmares got so bad that one night, Miles went into Dona's room, picked him up, brought him into his room, and had him sleep with him, and they seemed to get better. He told him she had said she would come home to them somehow, and she never lied, so he could sleep with Daddy till she did.

The ranch was a dreary place, and on the first of the month, Miles went back to the fort, and there was no sign of her. He would stay a week, and they would go and search for her, and then he would come home. The soldiers were on the lookout all the time but still found no signs of any of the Comanche tribe anywhere. It was like they had disappeared. Standing Bear had taken them into the mountains so they couldn't be found and so they couldn't find Morgan.

She was cooking breakfast one morning when she felt sick, and she had to get outside fast before anyone saw. She got to the edge of a tree and was sick, but Still Water saw her and just looked at her and went to get Standing Bear, but Morgan stopped her and got her inside the tepee.

Still Water said to her, "You are already pregnant, and he doesn't know it. He will throw you aside, or he will kill that baby, and I will be first again. I am going to tell him."

Morgan grabbed both her arms and looked at her face. "If you tell him, he will try and take my child, and I have already lost one child. If he tries to hurt me or my child, he will have to kill me, or I will kill him. You choose. You have heard about how I change. Well, it is true. Now you choose who lives or dies."

Standing Bear came in about that time and asked, "What is going on in here?"

Morgan just said, "Nothing. We were cooking breakfast." And then she looked at Still Water, who just agreed with her.

When he left again, Still Water asked her, "What are you planning on doing? You are running out of time."

"The baby of Little Deer's wife is due soon, and when it is born, I will help, and that night, I will run."

"What if he catches you?"

"One of us will die. Either way, it will be done, and you will be free of me."

She turned around and continued cooking breakfast until Still Water asked her, "You would die to get back to your husband?"

"Yes. Wouldn't you? To get yours back all to yourself and me gone from your life?"

"Yes, I would. What about Little Fox? You love him. I see it in your eyes. Are you going to try and take him as well?"

Morgan didn't know what to do about him. She wanted to take him so badly, but she might die on the way down, and she knew Standing Bear would never stop looking for him. He was his son. She didn't answer her.

Standing Bear killed a large elk that day and brought it into camp, and after the men gutted it and were through doling out the meat, Morgan hung up the skin. She had plans for it. She had it on a rack and was scraping it and stretching it, and one of the braves was bothering her and had been for some time. He thought he could get away with tormenting her. Standing Bear hadn't seen any of this, and Morgan hadn't said anything about it.

This time, when he started on her, she just put up with it until he started to poke her with a lance tip. On about the third time, he was drawing blood, and Little Deer went to find Standing Bear because he didn't figure she was going to put up with this for very long.

She wasn't supposed to have any weapons, and no one noticed when she put the knife she was using in her boot because she had turned around to grab the lance the brave was poking her with, and now she had it in her hands and him on the ground. By the time Standing Bear got there, the other lady was out and in good form, and she was ready to kill him.

She looked at Standing Bear and told him, "You come one step closer, and he is dead." She had him on the ground and the lance at his throat, and she had a smile on her lips. No one had any question in their minds she wouldn't kill him. He could see the blood on her back where he had been stabbing her, and she was going to kill him for it.

"Running Knife let him up right now."

"Or what are you going to do? Are you going to try to kill me? It might be worth it to find out just how good you think you are against me." And the look she gave him was pure evil, and for the first time, he was scared of her. This wasn't Morgan. This was the other woman who even the bounty hunters feared.

"I will take care of this, Running Knife."

She lifted the lance and threw it into the ground, and it went into the ground right beside the brave's head. The edge of the lance brought blood to the side of his face. She just stood up and walked past him. He reached out to touch her, and she jerked her arm away, and he didn't try again. He just let her go.

She went into the tepee, took the knife out of her boot, and hid it under a blanket so no one could see it. She went back outside and walked to the stream into the water. No one stopped her this time.

They were afraid of her now. Good. She didn't want Little Fox to see her like this. It would scare him.

Standing Bear pulled the brave up off the ground and hit him in the face with his fist and told him, "She is my woman, and if you touch her again, I will let her finish what she started." Then he dropped him back on the ground.

He went after her and found her standing in the stream. That water had to be freezing, but she was just standing there.

He reached for her, and she turned and told him, "Don't touch me unless you want to get hurt." That other woman was still there, and she was breathing like she had been running a long distance, and her hands were fists.

He walked into the stream, picked her up, walked back to the tepee, set her on her feet inside, and told Still Water and Little Fox to leave.

She backed away from him, "Don't touch me, or I will hurt you. I can't make her go away this time."

"How did you make her go away before, Morgan?"

She looked at him strangely and said, "I always kill someone, and you didn't let me do it this time."

"You didn't kill someone on the mountain, and you changed."

"You choked me, and I was hurting, and then you raped me. It was different that time."

He looked at her and said, "You could hurt me. Take your rage out on me."

She just looked at him. "Do you have any idea what I could do to you?"

He just nodded. She had to do something or explode.

"Take off your shirt."

She came up to him, and she hit him right in the ribs. He doubled over. She hit him again, and he was on the floor. She took off her shirt and skirt, and he could see blood on her back. Then she got on her knees and straddled him, and she just looked at him. Her eyes were narrowed, and her hands were like claws. All he could compare her to was a big cat, and she dragged her nails down his chest until she drew blood, but he kept still. She didn't dare go after the knife hidden under the blanket. She would kill him. That thought brought a smile to her face. She could smell the blood on him.

She ran her tongue up his stomach and bit until she got to his neck, and then she ran her hands up his arms and found his hands and interlaced them. He came up and pulled her hands behind her. He knew he was hurting her, and that was what she seemed to be wanting. The woman in his arms was dangerous and wicked, and she could kill you just as easy as look at you.

He got out of his britches somehow. He turned her over and entered her, and he wasn't gentle. He was almost brutal. Then he took her face in his hands and had her look at him and said, "Say my name, Morgan. Ask me just once."

"Make love to me, Standing Bear."

And then she kissed him, really kissed him, not Miles him. She was like a wild cat, clawing and scratching, and he was pounding into her. He could feel her changing, getting softer and shaking less and stroking his shoulders like a lover, not like a demon. He watched her face change, and for just a moment, she was his. As he took her over the top, she was his. This time, she was thinking of him, not Miles.

He held her so tightly. He didn't want to let her go, but she was already slipping away from him. He held her face and kissed her again, but he could already tell the difference. She had needed him for a while to get rid of the demon lady, and now she was gone. Now she didn't need him anymore. He held her till she was breathing normally again, and then he rolled off her.

She got dressed, went back outside, went back to the stream, and sat down. She wondered if Miles could ever forgive her for that because she wasn't sure she could forgive herself. She hadn't said another word to him.

As she sat there, she saw movement in the woods across from her. She thought she was imagining things until she saw it again. There was a man trying to get her attention, and then he looked at her just long enough for her to see who it was—Raphael.

He was pointing upstream. She started walking upstream as she watched him follow her until she came to a log that crossed the water, so after she checked to see if she was being followed, she crossed. When she got into the woods, he grabbed her arm and pulled her behind a tree so they couldn't be seen from the village.

"What are you doing here? Are you crazy? They will kill you if they find you here."

"What do you think I am doing here? I am looking for you like half the territory is doing. Your husband is going out of his mind searching for you, and Standing Bear is making sure no one can find his camp."

"How did you find it?"

He looked at her like she was stupid. "Remember what I used to do for a living? I sold guns to Indians, so I still have a few men who know where they camp, and they have been looking for this one. What happened in that camp a while ago?"

"You saw. I got mad, and I protected myself."

"You can say that again. Come with me, and we will get out of here now."

"We won't get halfway down the mountain before he catches me, but I have a plan. One of the women is going to have a baby soon, and I will help with the birthing. That night, I am going to run, and then you can help me."

"What do you want me to do?"

"Maybe keep them off of me on the way down the mountain so maybe I can find a ranch or some kind of help before he catches me again because I won't let him bring me back up here alive."

He thought for a minute, and then he told her. "If you can head west, there are ranches that way at the bottom of the mountain. Just keep going, and maybe I can distract them if they get too close."

"That's all we can do, and I would appreciate it. Stay out of sight and stay warm. It is fixing to storm."

"There is a cave up here I can hide in, and I will stay warm and keep an eye on you as well. Try and give me a sign when you are leaving."

She thought for a minute and then told him, "I have a red scarf. I will tie it around my head or my neck when I am getting ready to leave, so be watching for me to go. I will be getting a horse out of the corral and heading down the side of the village trail. I have got to get back. I have been gone too long. Watch out for yourself."

Then she turned and headed back. She had been gone a long time. When she came back in later, she lay down. Even Still Water could see the small holes in her back from across the tepee, but she just covered up with Little Fox and went to sleep.

The next morning, she was again sick, but he saw this time. He cornered her and said, "You are pregnant with my child. Finally, you are mine."

Still Water was behind them, and she looked at Morgan. She looked at her with a warning look. After yesterday, they were all afraid of her.

He grabbed her hand, took her down by the stream, found a secluded place, and put her on the ground. Since she was wearing skirts, she wasn't allowed any underwear so she was always available to him, and he wanted her now. He was so pleased she was carrying his child. Now she realized she had to get out of here soon before he started to figure out the dates were wrong.

He was so happy. She was almost sorry to disappoint him. He wanted to feel her stomach and her breasts and tell her how she would love him when their child was born, and she tried to smile and please him when he made love to her. She could see the marks she had left on him. She had hurt him badly. The lady was in fine form yesterday.

She had to keep up this pretense a while longer so she could get away. After yesterday, he wanted so much more from her. Today, she took his face in her hands and kissed him like she would have Miles, but she had to close her eyes to do it. She even tried the trick of running her hands down him. He was pleased for today, and maybe that would keep him satisfied for a while. It wouldn't be much longer till she could get away.

When he left her, she walked into the water and tried to wash him off her as she cried. God, she had to get out of here soon before she lost what was left of her mind. When she turned around, Still Water was watching her as she washed her face and climbed out of the water. It was starting to snow.

She took the knife and hid it better outside the tepee, and Still Water told her she thought she had found where he had hidden her clothes, and she would try and get them for her when the time came. She couldn't go down that mountain in just a shirt and a skirt.

She had gone out to gather wood one evening and came back inside, and she was freezing. She finally asked. "Where are the rest of my clothes? I had a coat, and I need it."

He looked at her suspiciously and said, "Still Water can collect the wood, so you won't need it."

"Really is that what you think?" Then she took her foot and pushed him over on the floor and told him, "Maybe from now on, you can collect the wood, and we will stay inside. Still Water is pregnant, I have Little Fox to take care of, and I am freezing, so you can help with the wood."

He got up off the floor and was going to slap her when she said, "Be careful you don't bring out that other lady. She might not be so easy to put away this time."

After he thought about it, he went outside, and he came back with her long coat in his hand.

"Wise choice. You are already marked up pretty bad." He hadn't been gone long, so her clothes weren't far away.

Morgan cooked while Still Water took care of Little Fox, and he seemed to be thriving. Morgan had been enjoying taking care of him, but she missed her own children so.

"What are you going to do about him? He already thinks of you as his mother. Are you just going to leave and let me explain why you left him behind?"

"You know that Standing Bear will never come off this mountain, but the Comanche are almost through up here. When it gets to that point, go to the fort they will find me, and you will have a home with me. He will be mine again if I survive getting down this mountain." She was beginning to wonder if she was going to ever see any of them again.

When she shook out her coat that night, a concho fell out of the pocket—a silver half-moon. She had bought it at a general store at the last stop before Denver and the fort. There were six of them. She was going to use them on a shirt, but all she found was one. She pulled off some of the leather strips on her skirt and made a necklace for Little Fox with the half-moon as the centerpiece on it.

The next day, she took him, and they went down by the stream. She talked to him about her home in Texas and how much she loved him, and then she tied the necklace around his neck and put it under his shirt.

She told him it was their secret. Then she just held him until it was time to go back inside. There wasn't anything else she could do. She couldn't tell him she was leaving. He was too little to understand.

Morgan had taken down the elk hide and rolled it up with some of the things she was taking with her and put it next to the wall of the tepee. When Standing Bear asked about it, she told him, "It will keep out the wind until we need it for a blanket this winter." And it did exactly that, so he left it alone.

Little Deer's wife went into labor three days later, and Morgan went to help just as she had planned. Things were going well until a blizzard hit. They were trying to get everything tied down as she was trying to get a baby born. The wind was howling, and the snow was blowing and drifting as she came back to the tepee.

She told Still Water, "I am still going to try to get down this mountain. Can you see if you can find my clothes?"

"I already did. They are in the elk hide, as well as some food, but do you really think you can get down in this weather?"

She looked at her and said, "If I don't try now, I will never get another chance. In a little while, can you push the elk hide out under the edge of the tepee? I will get it."

She reached down to a sleeping Little Fox and kissed him goodbye. Standing Bear walked in about then and wanted to know what was going on.

"I need the bottle of laudanum you used on me. Where is it if there is any left?"

He reached behind her and pulled out the small green bottle and handed it to her, and she started back to the other tepee.

"Will you be there all night?"

"Probably. This baby isn't ready to come yet."

He turned her around and kissed her, and this time, she kissed back because it was going to be the last time she would ever see him, she hoped, and she could at least leave him with that. Then she looked at Still Water, and one way or another, she was going to be gone from here, dead or alive.

When she went outside, she put the red bandana on her head. She went back to Little Deer's tepee, and the child wasn't far away. She gave her some laudanum to ease the pain, and in about an hour, she had a beautiful little boy.

She went back outside and found the elk hide outside the tepee, and she picked it up and snuck around to the horses and picked out the one she wanted. It was the one she had sent Standing Bear out of the fort with, and he was big and long legged. He should do well in this snow. She walked him to the end of the side of the mountain and down a steep path, and then she mounted.

She rode for quite a ways, and then she got down and rolled out the elk hide and found her pants. She took off her boots and put them on and then put her skirt on top of that. She was freezing. There was a blanket inside, and she put it on the saddle, and when she got back on, she wrapped it around her legs. It helped keep her warm.

She rode as far as she could in the dark, and then she rode into the woods and found some trees for a wind break. She got the elk hide and wrapped it around her and settled down for a short rest until light. When it was first light she was up and on the move again down the mountain. She knew he wouldn't be far behind. She kept to the side and in the trees, anything to hide her tracks.

She kept this up for two days and saw them once. They almost had her, but something distracted them. They turned the other way, and she got away. She got to cover before they discovered her. Maybe Raphael had distracted them. If he had, she hoped they hadn't caught him.

On the third day, the terrain was beginning to look familiar, but she was getting so tired, and the weather was so bad. By nightfall, she was ready to just wrap up in the elk hide and call it quits. She knew she couldn't do that. She would go to sleep and never wake up.

She saw some lights ahead, and she thought it might be a ranch. She hated to involve anybody else in this, but she was running out of steam, and she needed help. This ranch looked pretty big; maybe they had enough people to at least get word to the fort.

When she got to the front of the ranch and saw the name, she had to smile to herself as she rode in. She got off her horse and knocked on the door. Someone came to open it, and she walked in.

There was a man sitting at a dinner table, and he upset his plate he got up so fast. Then he looked at the woman coming through the door.

"Hello, Justin. I need a favor, and I think you owe me one."

"Good god, Morgan. Everybody in three states is looking for you, honey. Sit down."

She did. She could hardly stand. "You have got to get a man to town now and get word to the fort that I am here. Standing Bear is right behind me. You don't have much time. Tell them we need help, and get your men in here where we can make a stand until they get here. Hurry, Justin. We are running out of time."

He turned around and started giving orders. Soon, he had men going to town and men coming inside and closing windows and barricading doors. If they could get word to the fort, they had a chance. They had soldiers looking for her already, and some might have been close.

CHAPTER 9

One of Justin's men did get to town. He rode several hours in the dead of the night to get to the telegraph office and send a message.

Morganna Douglas at Justin Winters's ranch. STOP
Comanches on her heels. Need help. STOP
Will wait for reply. STOP

The young man didn't have to wait long.

Troops on the way. We are not far from you. STOP
We will meet you at ranch. STOP

The young cowboy decided to wait in town. He didn't want to ride back into the middle of an Indian attack.

Miles was at the fort. It was the first of the month. He was just about to go back home when the telegraph came in. The major came running into his room, out of breath, and said, "They found her. She is at Justin Winters's ranch, but Standing Bear is right on her heels. Do you want to come with us?"

"That has to be the stupidest question I have ever heard. Let's go."

They were both running as men were saddling horses and gathering rifles, and then they were on their way out of the fort. Justin's ranch was halfway between Denver and the fort, so they had to ride hard. Standing Bear was riding just as hard, but he got there first. They attacked the ranch, but they were ready for them, so they backed off.

Standing Bear yelled at Morgan to come out and go back with him. She walked out on the porch and stood there and talked to him. "I am going home. I told you when you took me I wouldn't stay, and you didn't believe me, so go back to Still Water and your children."

"You carry my child."

She just stood there and then answered him, "No, I don't. I was pregnant when you took me. This is Miles's child, not yours."

She could hear the scream of rage from where she was standing. Justin pulled her back inside before Standing Bear decided to shoot her. They came again, and she just stood there watching, and then the cavalry was there too.

Justin was shot in the arm, and he was on the floor. She was helping him when someone came through the door, and she went to shoot him. It was Little Deer.

She stopped and just looked at him. "No more." Then she put the gun down. She got up and walked outside and into the line of everyone's fire and said, "Enough." She didn't even say it very loud.

Standing Bear got off his horse, as did Miles, and they were both there. She was talking to Standing Bear.

"You are mine." He put his hand around her neck and started to squeeze as he pulled her to him.

"For one brief moment, and that was all, and now it is done. No more. Go back to your wife and your children and let me go back to mine."

He took his hand off her neck, looked at Miles, and turned around. He gathered up his men, and they started to leave, then she said one more thing.

"Let me take Little Fox with me, Standing Bear. You know he wants to be with me." She had said it in Comanche so only the Indian men knew what she had asked him.

He turned and looked at her and said, "Only if you come back with me and be my wife will you ever be his mother."

She shook her head and backed away. She turned and looked at Miles. He had heard everything, and he had questions. She didn't want to answer them here or now, but he was going to want answers soon.

"What did he mean, you were his for one brief moment?"

"Can we talk about this in private later?" She looked at all the men staring at her. He turned and walked away.

She went inside and started to bind up Justin's shoulder wound when he said, "Morgan, you are bleeding." The little wounds on her back had reopened and were bleeding through her shirt, but he was the only one to notice.

"I know. I assume there is a doctor in town we can take you and these men to, and maybe he can take care of me as well?"

He nodded.

"I will put my coat back on, and no one else will notice."

"What is wrong with Miles? He seems mad at you."

She just shrugged and helped him up and went to the wagon waiting to take her and the men to town. Miles rode next to her on his horse, but he wouldn't talk to her, and he didn't even look at her. When they got to town, Miles helped her down and then stepped away from her like she was dirty, and she got the point.

She went inside the hotel, and she got two separate rooms for her and Miles and then followed Justin to the doctor's office. Miles was helping the major with other things when he went inside and found out she had gotten separate rooms and that she had gone to the doctor with Justin. He followed them down there to see if she was hurt. He hadn't even asked her. When she got to the doctor's office, she wasn't to be found.

Justin was sitting in the waiting room with his arm in a sling, and he said to him, "If you don't want her, just say so. Not all of us are as stupid as you seem to be."

"Where is she?"

He pointed to a room to the right.

He knocked on the door and was told to come in. Morgan was lying on her right side, and the doctor was stitching up two small cuts in her back. There were two smaller healing ones below them.

"We are almost done. I was just telling your wife I think the baby will be fine, and she should stop bleeding if she just rests for a few days. She has just done too much, and it has stressed the baby out, but it seems to be fine. The shoulder looks good. How long did it take before it healed the second time?"

"It was eight days."

"You can hold her hand while I finish this if you want to."

He reached for her hand, and Morgan closed her hands into fists and said, "I am just fine. Are you almost done?"

The doctor saw what happened and said, "Yes, I am almost finished, and then you can dress. Do you have anything else to wear? These clothes are all bloody."

"Yes, I stopped at the store and bought some new clothes to wear."

When he was done, he walked out of the room and let her dress. Miles started to help her up, but she wouldn't let him touch her.

"I can do this myself. I don't need your help."

"Where did you get the money for the clothes?" he asked as she dressed.

"Justin loaned me some till I could get some wired to me."

"Why didn't you ask me?"

"I assumed from your attitude you didn't want anything to do with me. You can barely stand to touch me. You told me once you wouldn't care what happened to me as long as I came back alive. Seems like that was wrong."

He looked at her while she dressed and wondered what had happened. She was so distant.

"You said you were his. I don't understand."

"I stayed alive."

Then she went to the door, and Justin walked her to the hotel. As they walked past the general store, a cowboy tipped his hat to her, and she smiled at him and nodded. Raphael had been with her coming off that mountain, and he was alive. He melted back into the shadows of the building, and she didn't see him again. He just stood there and watched. She was all right now, but he thought he might go back to Texas.

She went to her room, and Miles went to his. She didn't come out again, and he was going insane. She wouldn't talk to him.

Justin was downstairs in the bar, so he went to talk to him. He walked up to his table and sat down and asked Justin, "What happened?"

"She walked through the door and told me she thought I owed her a favor and sat down at my table. We got hold of the fort, and sure enough, Standing Bear wasn't far behind her. I don't know how she was still standing up. She was so tired. He was screaming at her to come back. She was carrying his child, and Little Fox needed her. She walked out on the porch and told him it was your child, and we could hear him screaming in rage from the hills. I pulled her back inside. I was afraid he would shoot her right there. One of his braves got inside, and I guess she knew him. She was going to shoot him, but she stopped and put down the gun and walked outside. That was when he grabbed her by the throat, and then you showed up. I don't know what happened to her back up there. She won't tell me. But you are a damn fool."

"Thank you for helping her, Justin. I will see that you are repaid."

"You really think I did this for the money or for you? I did it for her, and anytime a woman would look at me like she looked at you that night in Virgie's house, I would be a happy man."

He was right. He needed to talk to her and right now.

He went back to the hotel and knocked on her door, and she didn't answer. The door wasn't locked, so he went inside. She was standing next to the window, just looking out at the mountains.

"We need to talk, Morgan. Don't you think it is time?"

She kept looking out the window while he started to ask her questions.

"Why did you say you were his, Morgan? You never loved him.

What happened?"

"My back happened. A brave started poking me with a lance and got increasingly vicious with it till he was drawing blood, and then the lady came out."

"Oh, Lord. What did she do?"

"She went after him with a lance."

"And then what?"

"Standing Bear told me to leave him alone. He would take care of it."

Miles just waited until she turned around.

"She threatened Standing Bear and the man she had on the

ground, and then she walked away. I couldn't make her back down this time. I didn't get to kill anyone, and I didn't have anywhere to go with all that rage. I walked into a mountain stream until he picked me up and took me back to the tepee, and he told Still Water and Little Fox to leave. I had to hurt something to get rid of her, and he told me to hurt him."

"What if you had killed the brave?"

"They would have killed me long and slowly, and he knew it. He was protecting me."

"Finish it. What did you do?"

"You told me once I reminded you of a mountain lion. He took off his shirt, and I hit him, and I clawed and bit until he took me, and he hurt me. But somewhere in there, when I was turning back into Morgan, there was a minute I was his, just his, and he knew it. Just a minute, but it was his minute, and we both knew it, but he wanted it back. Then he found out I was pregnant, and he was so happy, and a few days later, I escaped."

He went over and put his arms around her, and she was his again. She had never really been Standing Bear's. She was right. She had just survived.

"What did you ask him when we were at the ranch?"

"If I could have Little Fox."

"And he told you no unless you went back with him."

"How did you know?"

"That is what I would have said. Besides, he has always known you wanted that child, and he has been using him to get you from the very first day."

He pulled the ring out of his pocket. He had been carrying it since he had found it on the tree. He pulled her hand to him and slipped it back on her finger. "Now it is back where it belongs. The doctor said you needed to rest. Do you want me to sleep in the other room, or can I stay in here with you?"

"Don't you want to know about that night he took the ring?"

"You can tell me or not. It doesn't matter either way. Let's go to bed. You are cold, and it is starting to rain."

He laid her down, put on a second blanket, and they cuddled up together and went to sleep. It was the first good sleep she had had in months.

They slept late in the morning, and then there was a knock at the door. Miles got up and pulled on some pants, and it was Justin inviting them to lunch downstairs. Miles agreed and said, "Give us an hour, and we will meet you there."

Morgan just looked up and said, "Do we have to?"

He sat down on the side of the bed and asked her, "When was the last time you ate, honey? You and that baby have got to be starving."

"You're right. I am. But that means I have to get out of this warm bed." And she looked up at him, and the old Morgan was back with that smile he loved so. Well, he was just going to have to wait till later.

"Come on, woman; let's go feed my son before he starves to death."

"Son. Aren't you the cocky one today?" She just wished the baby would move. She hadn't felt it since she came down the mountain, but she hadn't told anyone that.

They dressed and went downstairs, and Justin was waiting at a corner table. They sat down, and then in came a beautiful woman to meet them.

"This is my sister Shelbee."

She was lovely, with dark hair and green eyes. For some reason, Morgan could see her and Gary Lee together, and she smiled and shook her hand. "I didn't know you had a sister, Justin. She is lovely."

"She runs the general store for me in town. I own several stores around town, including the establishment Virgie used to own."

"He won't let me run that one. He thinks I am too good to be seen in that one." And she gave him a scolding look. Morgan just covered up her mouth to hide the smile. This woman was no shrinking violet no matter what her brother wanted. She was her own woman. She liked her already.

"I hear you are having some new cattle brought into the country. Some new bulls from England called Herefords."

Morgan had heard about them before she left, but Miles knew more than she did. Morgan's grandfather and several other men got together and bought some of the bulls and some cows and had them shipped over here, and they were trying them to see if they could survive this country. So far, they were thriving.

"I would like to see them and your horses. Would it be all right if I came to your ranch in, say, a month and looked at them?"

Morgan answered, "On one condition. You bring your sister with you. I want her to meet my family. We will have a barbeque, Texas style."

Shelbee was thrilled. She never got to go anywhere with her brother, and Miles was curious about this request too. They had a nice lunch, and Morgan ate everything. She didn't realize how hungry she really was.

When lunch was over, she hugged Justin and thanked him for his help and told Shelbee she expected to see her at her ranch in a month. Then they went back upstairs.

"What was that all about with the sister?"

She looked at him and smiled. "Gary likes dark-haired ladies with a little fire. Don't you think she fits the bill?"

He smiled down at her. "Yes, she does. Do you suppose she likes horned toads as well?"

She elbowed him in the side.

When they got to the room, she was changing back into her gown. She was going to lie back down. She was tired, but Miles wanted to check the bandage on her back before she did. She hadn't pushed or asked anything of him. She wanted him to do the asking, so she waited. He would either want her or not.

He checked it, and it wasn't bleeding anymore and looked good. He turned her around and laid his head on her stomach and just held her to him.

"What happened to your shoulder, Morgan?"

"When he was taking me up the mountain, one of his braves pushed me down, and I landed wrong and tore it up again, and out came the lady. The brave chased me down and dropped me again, and I landed on it, and I was going to kill him. Standing Bear choked me till I was unconscious and got rid of her, then he took what he had always wanted, and he raped me. He didn't know how bad I was hurt. I had a fever, and it took eight days before I was better."

"That was when he left your ring?"

"He wanted you to know what he had done to me."

"How did you keep him from killing me?"

"I told him if he did, I would spend the rest of my life taking everything he loved from him, and I swore it on White Cloud's soul."

He just looked at her. She had saved his life the only way she could.

She held his head against her, and she just ran her hand through his hair like so many times before and stood there until he looked up and saw she was crying. He laid her down on the bed, and she closed her eyes. She kept running her hands through his hair.

"I left Little Fox up there, Miles, and that child is as dear to me as Gregory is, but I couldn't bring him down. Standing Bear would have never left me alone. It is tearing me apart. He won't understand why I left him."

"Morgan, you couldn't take him. He wasn't yours, not now anyway."

She turned away from him. He didn't understand. That was part of the problem—no one understood except Standing Bear.

"Morgan, tell me what to do. I know it is not like before, but I don't know how to fix it."

She looked at him.

"Like the first time. Remember, Morgan? Just us in that cabin all alone?"

Then he held her as she cried and cried until there were no more tears. She hadn't done that since the brave had hurt her shoulder so badly.

"I still love you, Morgan, just as much as I did the first time I saw you when you weren't just fifteen years old. I know we can't forget this, but can we get around it and continue with our lives? It doesn't have to end here."

She pulled his head down to her and kissed him, and he pulled her under him and entered her, and they made love. She figured if it was still good, maybe they still had a shot at making this all right.

He stroked and stroked, and then she looked into those eyes she had always loved and said, "You are my life now and always, Miles, if you will just let me back in."

That was all it took. He took her all the way to the top, and as she was riding the waves back down, he held her to him as he came. He watched her face, and he didn't know what Standing Bear had taken of her, but she was his again, and he was never giving any of her back. He held her while she slipped into sleep, and he covered them up and held her while they slept.

Later, she awoke to a tiny flutter in her abdomen, and she said to herself, "There you are, little one." *We go back home tomorrow.*

Up on the mountain, Standing Bear had made it back to his people, and Still Water was waiting. She didn't know if he would come back alive or not. He came into the tepee. He had already ordered the camp to be moved higher into the mountains just in case the soldiers came looking for them.

She looked at him and asked, "Are you finally done with her now? Can we go on with our lives?"

"You knew all along it was not my child?" She just nodded.

"You stayed with me after I treated you so badly?"

"I have always loved you, and she told me I had to make a choice."

"What choice?"

"Her child or you. She said she would kill you if it came to protecting her child. I chose you."

He just nodded, and they started to pack the tepee. They never said her name again.

No one noticed Little Fox hiding her knife in a skin and putting it with his things. He didn't understand where she had gone, but she was gone. He mourned her by himself, but he never forgot her. As far as he was concerned, Running Knife was his only mother. Maybe when he was older, he could find her again.

He never took off the necklace she put on his neck that day by the stream, and it was some time before his father noticed it. Still Water wanted it removed, but his father told her to leave it alone, and she never touched it after that. Still Water was careful to never let Standing Bear see how much she hated his son even more since Morgan was gone. Little Fox learned to just stay out of her way.

In the morning, when he awoke, she was staring at him, and she said to him, "The baby is alive, and I want to go home."

He just looked at her, kind of stunned.

"I hadn't felt it since I came off of the mountain, but I did last night, so let's go home. It is time. Can you get us on a train today?"

He hit the floor running and was dressed in a minute then turned around and went back to the bed and kissed her. "Get dressed, and I will go get tickets."

"Boots. You will need boots, and send a telegram and tell them we are coming."

He sat down on the bed to put on his boots as she started to dress, and he went out the door, came back in, kissed her again, stopped, and said, "I love you. I will be right back."

She went over to the window and looked up at the mountain. "Good luck, Still Water. If you or your child ever needs me, you know where I am. Find me. Bring me my son." Then she turned away, and she never looked back at those mountains again.

They got on a train that afternoon, and it took them three more days to get home, but the girls and Gregory were waiting for them at the station at Amarillo. Her grandfather and Virgie had driven a wagon to town with everybody in it, and they were waiting.

Gregory almost knocked her down. "You, don't ever leave us again."

Dona said, "We have all decided you can't leave the ranch ever without an escort, and you can't ever leave the state again."

"You know what? I agree. I am never leaving home again." She got down and hugged the girls and Gregory and then got in the wagon, and they went home. They even had an escort; the ranger Carter James was riding beside them.

"What is he still doing here?" she asked Virgie.

"Well, this is his territory, but he has been staying close to the ranch lately."

"Why? Or do I want to know?"

Virgie pointed to Dona. "He is only eighteen. Watch how he looks at your sister. I saw another man look at you that way once a long time ago."

"She is only thirteen."

"And you were only fifteen."

"Is she looking back?"

"Yes, she is, but he is keeping his distance. I have seen to that personally."

"She will be fourteen in a couple of months, and if Grandfather or Miles finds out, they will have his head. Keep this between us for now."

Lord, it was good to just see the ranch house again. The barn was finished, and the corrals were finished around it. Morgan was anxious to see the new cattle, but she was too tired today. She went inside, and Gary and Aunt Martha Jean and Mary Jo were inside, cooking supper, and it smelled good. They all sat down and ate, and she got asked all kinds of questions, but Miles was trying to keep them ones the children could hear the answers to.

Finally, she excused herself and went to bed, and her aunt followed her to the bedroom.

"Is there anything you need me to do for you? Miles said you had a bandage on your back that might need changing. Do you want me to look at it for you?"

"Why don't you so he can answer questions and I won't have to?"

She pulled off her dress and pulled up the chemise and let her aunt look at her back, and she said, "These need clean bandages put on, Morgan. Some of these stitches have pulled a little but not badly. Let me go get some clean ones. I will be right back."

The door opened again, and she wasn't paying attention to who it was until Gregory got up on the bed and said, "Someone hurt you again, Mama. You said no one was going to do that ever again." And then he was in her arms and crying. That was what Miles found when he came into the room a few moments later.

"It's all right, honey. Daddy brought me home so I could get better, and I won't go away again."

"You said that last time." Well, she did.

"Well, I promise I won't go away again. I will stay with you, or you will go with me, all right?"

Miles had to pick him up and take him out of the room so Martha Jean could redo the bandages.

"He has been sleeping with Miles. He has had nightmares so bad since they took you. If something else happened to you, I don't think he or Daddy would survive it. You have to stay home from now on."

"Believe me, I am not going anywhere."

"These aren't all the scars you have, are they?"

She just shook her head, and that was the last time her aunt asked anything about it. Her grandfather thought her father was the only one who saw something the day his wife died; from the look on her aunt's face, he was wrong.

She finished bandaging her back, leaned down, kissed her cheek, and left the room as Miles came back in.

"What did your aunt want to know?"

"Nothing, and that is what bothers me. She knows everything."

"How do you know?"

She looked at him funny. "I just do."

"You ready for bed?"

She nodded, and they climbed into the bed and went to sleep.

It hadn't been but about an hour until they hear screaming. It was Gregory, and she went to him this time. She lit the lamp by his bed and held him as he screamed until she calmed him down.

"You are here. You are not dead."

"I am right here. I came home. See? You can touch me. I am real." He was clinging to her as if she was going to disappear again, and she lay down next to him and covered him up and hummed to him, and they both went to sleep. He was again that little boy who wouldn't talk and was clinging to her in that cot.

Miles watched from the doorway, came in, put another blanket on them, and went back to bed. He should have shot Standing Bear for what he did to his family. He hoped that other lady hurt him badly.

She awoke to Greg stroking her face like she was a cat and just looking at her. It was still dark outside.

"Are you sure you are all right? I saw some scars on your back and some stitches. Someone hurt you."

"It will be all right. They will heal, but I am still tired. Can we go back to sleep, or can I go back to your daddy's bed so I can sleep late this morning?"

"You go back to sleep. I will guard you so no one can hurt you again." Then he lay down with his hand on her face and watched as she fell back to sleep, and then he went back to sleep as well.

That was how Miles found them later that morning when he went looking for her in Greg's room. The little boy was guarding his mother from any attackers. They were going to have to start all over with him to prove Miles could take care of her and him so he could sleep at night again.

He followed her around all of that day, and that night, it was the same. He was screaming as she went to him, and she finally asked him, "What do you see in your dreams, Greg? Tell me."

"He comes after you. You should never have left us. It did nobody any good, and it got you hurt."

When she turned around and Miles was at the door, she told him, "In the morning, we go to the cemetery, and Dona and Carter will go with us. Have the horses ready after breakfast. This has got to end."

She slept in his room again, but in the morning after breakfast, they all headed to the cemetery together, and she had the box with the pictures and Donald Glen's effects with her. Martha Jean just watched from the door. She was going to have to have a talk with her soon too, but that was later.

They rode, and when they got there, she could see where the new grave was. Miles had told her the major had seen to it. Her uncle had been sent to the ranch, and they had buried him about a month ago with the rest of the family. Her grandfather had wanted her to tell him about his father, so they waited. She told Dona and Carter to give them a while alone and they would talk in a bit.

She took Gregory's hand. They went to the grave site, and she sat down with him. "You see these two graves, Gregory? I know you can't read the names, but you know that one is your mother's. It says Sandra

Williams McKinney, and the one next to it says Donald Glen McKinney."

He looked at her funny. "What are you talking about? How do you know my mother's last name? And who is that man?"

She opened the box and took out the picture and put it in his hand, and he looked at the face of his mother.

"That is my mama. Who is that man?"

"That man is your father. He is lying right there next to her, and his name is Donald Glen McKinney. I found him when I went to the fort to testify in Colorado, and their names are on the back of that picture."

She sat there a minute as he was figuring it out in his head. "So he was related to you?"

"Yes. He is Dolf's brother and my granddaddy's nephew." That really confused him. "So I am really your family after all?"

"Yes, you are, but I would never have known if I hadn't gone to Colorado to that trial, and you would still be wondering who your real father was."

"Why did he kill her, that other man?"

"She married your father instead of him, and he was supposed to take her to Texas and help her find your daddy's family. He lied to her, and he killed her in a rage. She was looking for us. You found us instead."

He kept looking at the picture in his hands. "I still wish you hadn't gone. Do you think that Indian man will come after you and take you away?"

"No. He is gone, and he won't come for me again. I had to help another Indian man who gave up his life to save mine, but I am done now."

"I will never leave this ranch ever."

"Don't say that. Maybe someday you will need to be somewhere and find someone who needs your help. You will be in the right place at the right time."

He gave her the picture back, and she put it back in the box. "They are together now, and you are with family, and that is what she was trying to do. And she is at peace, I hope. Look, there is a horned toad.

You can go chase it, but watch out for snakes."

She turned and motioned for Dona and Carter to come over to her, and Miles got her up off the ground.

"Well, you start talking."

Miles hadn't been told what was going on here. He was in for a surprise.

Dona started first. "Mama."

Oh, this was going to be good. Mama instead of Morgan. Even Miles and Carter noticed that one, so Carter took over.

"I love Dona, and I would like to marry her."

She thought Miles was going to stroke out, and then she thought he was going to kill him.

"Calm down, Miles."

"You knew about this, and you didn't warn me? She is only thirteen."

Both Dona and Carter said at the same time, "Almost fourteen."

"How long has this been going on?"

"I almost didn't make that shot at the party because it was her father I was shooting at, except he was going to kill you, and I had to."

Dona had his arm in hers and was saying to him, "I know, dear, he was a bad man."

Morgan was holding Miles's arm because he was coming unglued. "Don't touch my daughter. She is too young."

"I'll bet that is what my mother said to you, was it not?" He turned around. "Don't tell me you are condoning this."

"No, I am not, but I don't want to wake up one morning and find her gone either."

He just looked at her. That was exactly what he had planned to do with Morgan, and she knew it, so he shut up and let her handle it.

"You turn fourteen in a month, and I would like to see you wait until you are sixteen, but if you two are still adamant about this, when you are fifteen, I will let you marry. And I expect her to still be a virgin, or I will break you in two, Carter James, and you know better than to get on the wrong side of me."

He smiled. He had seen the wrong side of her, and she was right.

He wanted no part of that. "Yes, ma'am."

Dona cut in about this time. "Wait a minute. I have some conditions here. If I marry you, the day we wed, you quit the rangers, and we start ranching. I have land and will have cattle and horses of my own, and I won't worry about you coming home every night. Agreed?" Her little sister had a mind of her own. Good for her.

"Whatever you want, honey. Wherever you want, I will be there."

She looked to see where Gregory was and went to get him so they could go home. He was picking wildflowers, and she went to help him. When he thought they had enough, they put them on his parents' graves. As she walked past her grandmother's grave, she thought, *I need to talk to Martha Jean tonight before she goes back home.*

They rode home, and Greg was in front of Miles. Her lap was getting increasingly smaller, and the kids were behind her. She could hear them talking. Well, at least everything was out in the open now. Miles wasn't happy, but he couldn't control them any more than he could control how he had felt for her all those years ago.

She went in, and lunch was ready, but she went to her room first. She changed shirts, and Aunt Martha Jean followed her to her room.

"Things went well at the cemetery?"

"I hope so. I guess we will see tonight."

She started to leave, and Morgan stopped her and then closed the door and had her sit on the bed.

"Grandfather doesn't know, does he? That you saw everything that day?"

Martha Jean just looked at her. She was the only one who had ever figured it out.

"No. He assumed that your father was the one, and he never asked him, but it was me who saw everything. When you came to Dallas, I knew you were, let's say, not all right, but you hadn't been used, but this time, everything was different. I could see it in your eyes. That other man raped Mother, and then he shot her. Then he came after us in the root cellar, but she did like you do. She changed, and she killed him. I watched as the life drained out of her as Daddy held her, and your daddy tried to keep us from seeing, but I see the same pain in your eyes, and I don't know how to help."

She looked at her. "As I told Miles, I am just trying to survive and go on with my life."

"Sometimes that is all you can do. She didn't even get that." She reached over and kissed her forehead and hugged her. "Lunch is ready, and your family is waiting for you."

Morgan had the picture and the letter framed and put beside Gregory's bedside, and after that, Gregory had no more nightmares. His parents watched over him at night. They were all finally home.

Three weeks later, Justin Winters and his sister were at the ranch, and Morgan met them at the front gate. "Hot enough for you?" Stupid question. It was hotter than hell this day, and it was just two o'clock in the afternoon.

About that time, Gary Lee came around the side of the house, and Morgan introduced him to Justin's sister. She had asked him over here today just for that purpose.

"Shelbee, this is my cousin, Gary Lee Burk. He is a lawyer in town. Gary, why don't you take her inside and get her something to drink? We will be inside in a minute."

Miles was walking up from the side of the house as a rider was coming at a dead run, jumped the short fence to the yard, and came to a stop in front of Justin, Morgan, and Miles. It was Mary Jo, and she was furious about something.

"Where is he?"

Morgan asked, "Who?" though she was pretty sure she already knew.

"My eldest brother the dumb one. Who else would I be looking for?"

"What did he do this time?"

"He left the fence open again, and I have been chasing calves all morning. I am going to kill him this time."

"Mary Jo, this is Justin Winters. He helped me when I was running from Standing Bear."

"Nice to meet you, Mr. Winters." Then she spun her horse around and was gone around the house at a dead run, screaming for Gary.

Justin turned around, and Miles smiled. "Do all the women in this family look that good in boots and jeans?"

Miles was laughing. "You told me once you hoped you found a woman who you looked at the way I looked at Morgan that night at Virgie's. Well, you have that look on your face right now."

"Well, I guess we better go find her before I lose another one."

And they started to the back of the house. Morgan was already there. She was trying to keep Mary Jo from wringing Gary's neck, and Shelbee was right in the middle, protecting him.

"Mary Jo, you can't kill him. He is your brother." Morgan was trying to separate them as usual.

"He never shuts the gate. He let out six calves, and the coyotes are going to kill them, and he still leaves the damn gate open. I have been out all morning chasing calves, and he has got on his best suit and boots like he is going to church. Mama, you get out here and make your son apologize to me."

Martha Jean was coming out the door when they all heard the same thing, and they all stood still. *Rattles*.

Morgan and Mary Jo were already looking for him.

"Where are you? Just keep talking. Everybody keep still till I find him. Martha Jean, step back real easy. You are almost on top of him. He is stretched out right under the back door."

Morgan grabbed a rake, and Mary Jo got the shovel that was leaning against the house, and she walked to the door. Morgan pinned the snake, and she told everyone to move back, and she pulled him out some so she could work him. Once she had him out, she pinned him again, and Mary Jo came over, got the shovel, took off his head, picked it up, and took it away. Morgan picked up the rest of the snake by the tail and laid it over the wall and went over to where Mary Jo was digging a hole.

Justin came over to them and asked Morgan, "What are you doing?"

"Burying the snakes head deep so no one steps on it." Then he looked at the snake.

"We will get the rattles in a while. They are Mary Jo's. This time, she killed it. We keep them. They are our trophies." Then they both walked back to argue with Gary.

Justin was just smiling at them. God, there were two of them, and he wanted Mary Jo. Miles was still watching and still smiling.

It took Aunt Martha Jean twenty minutes to settle everybody down and keep Mary Jo from banning her brother from the ranch forever. He lived in town most of the time, and she wanted him there all the time.

After lunch, Justin wanted to see the new cattle, and Mary Jo was going to show them to him. Shelbee stayed to talk to Gary, and that was just fine with Justin. There was going to be a barbeque in their honor tonight, and it was going to be a big affair, so they were getting food prepared and the meat cooked

Mary Jo brought Justin back so she could get dressed for tonight, and she pulled Morgan aside and asked her about Justin. "Well, start talking. Is he married?"

Morgan just grinned. She had wanted Gary to meet Shelbee. She didn't think about Justin finding anybody, and he seemed pretty set on Mary Jo and her on him. "No. At one time, he wanted me pretty badly, but he seems to want you now."

"Good, I like what I see. I will be back in a while." The grin she gave her was just wicked. She figured she was going to be dressed to kill. Tonight was going to be fun.

Miles asked her what was going on.

"Oh, I think there are going to be fireworks around here tonight." He just smiled. He had already figured that out for himself.

Shelbee was dressed in her best store-bought dress, and she was dancing with Gary. When Mary Jo came in, she was wearing a Mexican dress, white with butterflies embroidered all over the hem, and she looked wonderful. The blouse was off the shoulder, and she had Morgan's squash blossom necklace and her silver concho belt on. Half the men in the room were already at the door, ready to ask her to dance and Morgan and Miles were just watching as Justin almost killed himself to get to her first.

"Isn't that your necklace and belt?"

Morgan looked up at her husband. "Yes, it is, but she needed a really nice piece of jewelry tonight to impress someone with. I didn't think you would mind."

"No, I don't mind. Are we going to dance, or are we just going to watch?"

"I just want to watch for a little while. This should be interesting."

"You are evil sometimes."

She just grinned back at him.

Trey and Sheri were dancing. Abigail, Sheri's little sister, was here as well. Martha Jean's youngest son Jackson was here. He didn't come around very much; he was more interested in animals than people. He had been training with the local vet, and that was what everybody expected him to be. He noticed Abigail sitting alone and asked her to dance, and then they disappeared. They weren't seen again for a while. They sat on the back porch and just talked.

Martha Jean came over to Morgan and asked her, "What happened to Abigail? I know she isn't quite right, but nobody will tell me. Why?"

Morgan just looked at the pretty blond woman and explained, "When the family was on their way out here from the east, their wagon wheel broke, and it turned over. She was pinned underneath, and her head was badly hurt. She gets awful headaches, and the doctors can't seem to figure out any cure. Their parents were killed in the accident. She has always been protected by Sheri, so she was the seamstress at the brothel. She put the pocket in the dress I wore down those stairs, and just she and I knew about it."

"Jackson has taken a liking to her. Should I put a stop to it?"

Morgan watched the two of them dance and answered her, "Some things are just meant to be, whether it's for a day or years. Leave them alone." The two of them did seem happy together.

The dance went on, and everybody was having a wonderful time.

Morgan even got to dance with Miles till she was exhausted.

When everybody was cleaning up, they couldn't find Abigail or Jackson, and they started to hunt for them. They were worried Abigail might have wandered off again like she had before. One of the doctors had told Sheri that Abigail's skull had been cracked, and he didn't know how she had survived, but she had. Sheri was still worried about her.

Morgan went down by the stream and found both of them just sitting and looking at the water. Jackson looked up at Morgan and told her, "We are getting married next weekend and moving into the little house back by the canyon. Abigail feels safe there. Is that all right with you?"

By now, Sheri and Trey were there. She told them what had been said, and Sheri nodded.

"That would be just fine. We are very happy for the both of you.

Why don't you come back to the house and tell everyone?"

As they walked past her, she turned and looked out at the canyon and the stars and thought just how very beautiful this place was, almost like God paid special attention to it.

Miles came up behind her and put his arms around her shoulders. "What are you thinking?"

"Sometimes things are just meant to be."

It seemed Abigail and Jackson had been seeing each other for a while now. He knew she had problems, and he was willing to take care of her. That was why he wanted the little house close to Morgan's house—so she would be close to family when he was working.

When they got back to the house, they heard arguing, and it seemed Shelbee and Justin were having words about something.

"Well, I am going to stay, and you can't do anything about it."

"You are my responsibility, and I can do something about it."

"You like Mary Jo, and you can ask her to marry you after one day, but he can't ask me after one day because it is too soon."

"That is different. I am a man, and I know what I am doing. You don't."

That went over like a lead cannonball. The whole room got quiet. Morgan went over to Mary Jo and asked her, "What did I miss?"

"Well, apparently, Justin wants to ask me to marry him, which, by the way, he hasn't yet, and Gary asked Shelbee to marry him, and Justin is having a hissy fit about it."

"Oh, is that all? Did you know Justin bought Virgie's house when she left Colorado?"

Mary Jo just looked at her and then said, "Well, that is going to have to go. I will not have any husband of mine owning a brothel. That is way too much temptation for any man."

Justin walked over to Mary Jo about that time and asked her, "Will you marry me?" He looked rather pleased with himself.

"Before I answer, do you own Virgie's brothel?"

"Yes. What difference does that make?"

She looked at him and said, "Sell it, and I will marry you. I won't marry a man who owns a brothel."

He was furious. Two women defied him in one night. He was fit to be tied.

Shelbee was crying, but she was headed his way, and Gary was trying to stop her when Mary Jo started walking over to Justin.

"Shelbee, come on, we are leaving right now."

Mary Jo walked over to him and took his face and kissed him, and when she was through, his knees would hardly hold him. Then she just backed away and looked at him. "You'll be back, unless you are made of stone, and you sure didn't feel like stone. As for that temper of yours, you might as well know I have one-two, and I don't back down either."

Mary Jo disappeared for a few minutes while Justin got their things gathered but was back in the main room before he left. She didn't say anything, but the look she gave him would have melted iron. Shelbee was still grinning when she went out the door.

The women were talking when Miles went to stand by them a few minutes later.

"Fifty bucks says he doesn't make it to seven days," Morgan said. Mary Jo said, grinning, "I am going with eight."

He couldn't figure out what they were talking about.

"We are taking bets on how many days it will be before they are back. Do you want to put some money on this bet?"

He couldn't pass this one up. "They will be back before five days are out, and he will be on bended knee, and the bordello will be for sale."

Miles won the bet after that kiss. That man was already hooked; he just didn't know it yet. They had already started to design dresses and were deciding where to have the weddings.

Three days later, Justin was unpacking his clothes at a hotel when he found a box with a piece of paper wrapped around a set of rattles. He sat down on the side of the bed and just looked at them. He had told Miles that if he ever looked at a woman like he had looked at Morgan that night at Virgie's, he would never let her go, so what was he doing sitting here?

The note just said, "I'll be waiting for you." No signature, nothing else.

He walked next door to his sister's room and told her they were going back. He was going back to Texas to get married, and if she wanted Gary Lee, she had every right to marry the man she wanted as well. They were on the next train back with the rattles in his pocket. They sit on his dresser to this day. He never did mind being Mary Jo's trophy.

When they got off the train on Sunday, the town was quiet except at the church. Abigail and Jackson were getting married, so they left their bags and walked to the end of the street and went inside the church. When they got inside, the service was almost over, but Morgan saw them come in and smiled at Mary Jo, and she looked at Justin. Well, it looked like her cousin was going to live in Colorado; it was a beautiful place to live in after all.

Shelbee was looking for Gary, but she hadn't gotten his attention yet because he was standing up for his brother. He could hear the whispers in the church and turned around, and then he saw Shelbee, and you had never seen a happier man except the groom.

When the service was over, Gary went to Shelbee, but Mary Jo made Justin come to her, and he got down on one knee and proposed properly to her in front of everybody. The woman he wanted was all he had ever wanted and more. He just didn't know how much more.

It was two more weeks before the next wedding could take place. Abigail had to finish Mary Jo's dress, and Shelbee had her dress sent from Colorado. They were working on Mary Jo's dress one day, and she kept looking at Morgan until she finally got up and took her outside.

"What is wrong? You have been staring at me for two days now. Out with it."

She couldn't look at her face, and then she finally started to talk.

"Everyone is saying Justin is marrying me because I am so much like you, and he couldn't have you, so I am his second choice." Then she looked at her face. "Are they right? Am I just a second choice to him?"

She looked at her funny. Sometimes she wondered herself, but he looked at Mary Jo differently. "Justin always looked at me like I was something he could own or purchase, a girl at the house. He looks at you like a woman he loves and wants to cherish. He never looked at me that way, not once. If you feel like this, maybe you two ought to take some time and be alone. You know, I was pregnant when I was in Dallas. Miles and I were together at Virgie's. I didn't expect to survive any of what happened. Maybe you should take some time and just make sure he is what you want."

Mary Jo looked at her and then asked, "Do you think I should sleep with him?"

"Maybe not that far, but if you aren't sure, don't marry him yet. McKinney women don't get divorced very often. We may bury our husbands, but we don't divorce them."

Then they both grinned at each other. "Like Aunt Sara." Their aunt's husband had died under suspicious circumstances, and knowing Sara, he was probably glad to go. She was their grandfather's youngest daughter whom no one talked about, not even her sister Martha Jean.

They walked a little farther and then went back, and there was a plan in place.

At breakfast, Justin was met by Mary Jo and was told he was coming with her for the day, so he dressed, and they left. He rode beside her for a while before his curiosity got the better of him.

"Where exactly are we going on this ride? I thought you needed to finish your dress fittings."

She looked back at him. "If today doesn't go well, there isn't going to be a wedding."

He stopped as she kept on riding until she looked back at him, and then he caught up with her. "What is going on? You haven't been happy for a few days. Now talk to me."

"Come on, we are almost to the house. It is cooler there, and we will have some privacy."

They got to the house and dismounted, and they went inside. This house was smaller than Morgan's or her grandfather's and a lot smaller than his. She took off her gloves and hat and leaned against a counter in the kitchen while he came in.

He asked again, "What's going on with you?"

"I just want to know that you want me for a wife and not just as a substitute for Morgan. I want to know it's me you kiss and make love to, not her. All I hear is how you tried to buy her from Virgie. It makes me wonder if I am just a second prize because you couldn't get what you wanted the first time."

He came over and stood in front of her. He still had his gloves on, so he slowly took them off while he talked to her. "It is all I have been able to do the past few days to keep my hands off of you. I want to touch your skin to see if it is really as soft as I think it is. I want to kiss you until you can't breathe. I just watch from the other side of the room so I don't make a fool of myself in front of everyone."

She looked into his eyes and said to him, "There is nobody here but us. We have the whole day. Show me that you want me. Just me and not Morganna."

She kissed him like she did the day he left, and they stood there for the longest time, just kissing. He pulled back away from her and unbuttoned a couple of buttons on her blouse and kissed her neck. She felt like she was on fire. She didn't even feel him pull away until she felt the cool air on her neck. He was across the kitchen, looking like a man fixing to fall off a cliff, and she didn't quite understand, but she was beginning to.

"If we don't stop now, I am not going to be able to stop, and I am sure your family won't approve of me taking your virtue today."

She started to walk toward him while she kept undoing those buttons, and then she said, "We are going to be married in two days. Unless you plan on leaving me at the altar, I don't think it is anybody's business when I lose my virginity but my husband's, do you?"

All he did was shake his head as she took his hand, and they headed to her bedroom.

When they got there, she shut and locked the door and turned around. He already had off his boots and most of his shirt. She sat on the bed to take off her boots, and he reached down to take them off. She started to pull his shirt over his back. When she was done, he pushed her down and just lay down on top of her on the bed. He put his hand inside her chemise and cupped her breast and then ran his hand down her side again. He lifted her up and got rid of the shirt and the chemise. He got up, undid her belt, pulled off her pants and underwear, and then got rid of his, and he finally realized she was everything he had ever wanted. No woman at Virgie's or Morgan had ever made him feel this way.

He stood up in front of her, and he realized she had never seen a man completely nude before, so he asked her,

"Well, what do you think, little girl? Do I pass inspection?"

She looked him over like she was looking at one of her bulls, and then she said, "I guess you will do. When are you going to stop calling me little girl?"

He just grinned and thought, *Soon, little girl, soon.* He lay down beside her and ran his hand up her leg. It was muscled from riding, but her skin was like velvet. She put her hands on his chest, and it wasn't like the women he hired. She wanted him. She pulled him to her, and he gathered her close to him, but he was so much bigger than she was. She kind of got lost under him.

"I am sorry, but I may hurt you, and there is no way around it."

"I will probably survive."

"He suckled her breasts and brought her chest up to him as he held her she was so small. He ran his hands down her legs again and then he used his finger and felt inside her he didn't want to rush he knew she was a virgin and he was going to hurt her anymore than he had to. He touched her in ways no man ever had and she was flying and she didn't understand why yet. She pulled him to her and kissed his mouth and he put his tongue inside her mouth and she went after him again. She rolled on top of him and looked down at him and smiled. She kissed his shoulder and his chest and he had never felt like this with any woman he had ever paid for she was his and really wanted just him. He pulled her back underneath him and kissed her again. He raised his head and just looked at her.

Then he grinned at her. It was time, and he knew it, but he didn't want to hurt her, so he gently entered her as he kissed her. She barely made a sound as he took what was his and only his. She jumped, and he knew he hurt her, so he stopped until she stopped tensing up and was breathing easy again.

"Are you all right now? It shouldn't hurt anymore."

He increased stroking until she was begging, and she didn't even know what for, but he did. He brought her to a climax, and then he came, and she was still clinging to him. When he could breathe again, he leaned up on his knees and looked down at her and ran his hands up her legs to her breasts as he looked at her.

"You are no longer my little girl. You are my woman, and in two days, you are my wife. Any doubts now that I want just you and only you?"

She just smiled as she pulled him back to her. "No doubts at all, but we have all day to ourselves. Come snuggle up next to me, cowboy. Virgie's house better belong to someone else soon and not to my husband. You'll never pay for another woman. You are mine."

When they came riding in later, Morgan could see there were no doubts left in either one's eyes. Mary Jo just smiled and winked at her. She was pretty sure of what had happened, but it wasn't her call. It didn't matter. It was done, and Justin wasn't going anywhere because if he hurt her, Morgan would find him and bring him back in pieces if need be. Justin looked at Morgan, and he just nodded at her. They both understood.

CHAPTER 10

The wedding took place on two different days so each bride could have their own day. Besides, there was not enough room in either house for either wedding to take place at one time. Gary Lee and Shelbee were married first. The wedding and the reception took all day and most of the night, and then they stayed at his house in town. The next morning, Justin married Mary Jo, and it was different. He was a changed man. They had wandered off each afternoon by themselves, and you couldn't have pried him from her side with a crowbar.

Morgan had never seen a man so truly in love with a woman except Miles, but there was a problem: he was also jealous, and that too was getting worse. Morgan had watched as she would dance with men she had known all her life and he would get mad. Mary Jo had to back him off more than once. The men thought it was funny because he was a newly married man. Morgan was worried about it because she had seen his possessive side and thought she had better talk to Mary Jo about it before they headed to Colorado.

The parties went well, and everybody had fun. The next morning, everybody slept late, and they had a late lunch. After lunch, Morgan was helping get things packed at Mary Jo's house, and they were talking when she brought up the jealousy thing to her.

"You do realize he was not kidding when he went after those men last night. He was really mad. He has a jealous streak, and you better watch out, or you are going to going to have to deal with it at the some time."

"I know. I just thought that after we got home and he got to know me a little better, he wouldn't be so suspicious about everybody who got close to me."

"I hope you are right, but if he ever goes after you or hits you—"

"Stop. If you are going to say you will protect me, you don't have to. It is him who will need the protecting."

Morgan just smiled. She didn't have to worry about her cousin. *She could take of herself*, she hoped. "Everybody is coming back for Christmas. Are you coming as well?"

"Of course we are. My mother would kill me if I wasn't here, and that baby should be here before then, shouldn't it?"

"It should be just before. Would you do me a favor? The commandant at the fort is a friend, and he brought his wife from Virginia to Colorado to live there. Will you keep your ears open about the tribes for me?"

Mary Jo reached over and took her hands. "You worry about his wife and children, don't you?"

"It is a hard life in the winter for women and children in those mountains, and I still wish I could have taken Little Fox with me, and now they are on the run. You stay close to the ranch unless you have an escort. Don't forget you aren't here, and you are in danger there. Indians still raid those ranches for horses and cattle. I will see your cattle are taken care of and ready to go back with you when you get back. I think we will have a good stud for you to take with you too."

"You take care of yourself, and I will see you in a couple of months. Take care of my brothers too. Watch out for Abigail. I don't know what would happen if anything was to happen to her. It would kill Jackson."

About that time, Justin came to the door and leaned inside. "You about ready, honey? We need to be going to get to the train station on time." He walked in and started to gather up boxes and carry them to the wagon.

On the second trip, Morgan asked him to help her up. As he reached down and helped her stand, she turned around and looked at him and said, "She loves you don't let your jealousy screw it up." Then she turned and walked away. He didn't think anyone had noticed, but he should have known. Morgan didn't miss anything.

Gary Lee and Shelbee went with them to Colorado to get her belongings and furniture as well to bring back with her to her new house in town. When they got back, she immediately bought out the general store from the people who owned it. They wanted to spend more time building up their own ranch and couldn't do both, so they were glad for the offer.

Winter was coming quickly, so everybody was trying to get things ready. It could drop fifty or sixty degrees in a twelve-hour period around here, so you had to have things ready beforehand. Sheds for hay and protection for the cattle were built, and the horses were brought closer to the ranch houses.

When the storm finally hit, it did so out of the blue. It was six degrees and blinding snow the next day. Everybody rounded up as much stock as they could and got them under cover and then got under cover themselves. Now all they could do was wait, so the fireplaces were well stoked, and there was plenty of food.

Later that first night, Morgan had the children down when she heard a horse coming, and she went to the door. Who should come in but an almost frozen Trey?

"What's wrong?" She got him to the fireplace so he could warm up.

"Your grandfather has a fever, and they can't get it down, and Virgie is going insane. She didn't ask me to come, but I know you are good with medicine, and that doctor is a fool. He needs help, Morgan."

She turned around, and Miles was looking at her. "Don't even try to tell me I can't go. He is my grandfather."

"I wasn't, but you aren't going on horseback. I will get the carriage. At least it will keep some of the cold off of you. It is that or you don't go at all, Morgan."

She nodded as he went one way and she went another. She was going to have to dress warm for this ride. She put on boots, skirts, a jacket, and her long coat. She looked like a bear, but she was warm.

They added a long coat of Miles's to what Trey had on to help keep him warm, and they were ready to go.

"You take care of the children, and I will be back as soon as I can, or I will send word about what is happening." She kissed him, and she started out the door.

He stopped Trey and told him, "You better take care of my wife. Do you understand me?"

Trey just nodded, and they were off. He had to help her outside; the wind almost knocked her down. It helped that it was at their back and pushing them instead of at their face as it was when Trey was coming to the ranch. She didn't know how long it took them to get to the ranch—it seemed like forever—but they finally got there. Some men took the carriage, and they went inside.

Trey was right. Virgie was going crazy. When she got inside, she shed as many clothes as she could while talking to Virgie and found out the doctor told her that Donald Roy was going to die because there was nothing else he could do for him. He had been working cattle and had come in very cold and tired yesterday and had gotten very sick with a high fever. The doctor had come and was saying there was nothing he could do. She finally got her calmed down and headed to her grandfather's room, and she was right. He was very sick.

"All right first we start boiling some water for tea. I have an Indian trick that might help."

The doctor in the room just smirked and said, "An Indian trick? I went to school for years. Don't you think I know what I am doing?"

"As far as I can see, you aren't doing anything but sitting on your well-educated butt."

"The Indians have been surviving for hundreds of years without our help or our medicines. Let's see if this might help because you are just going to let him die."

Virgie came back into the room about then, and he began to tell her he knew more about medicine than Morgan did, and then she said to him, "This young woman has survived more than you or your education could even think about, so just get out of here or watch. You might learn something, but either way, shut up."

They got the tea down him, but he was burning up, and they had to get the fever down now.

"Bring the tub in here, and start filling it with water. I want it warm to start with, and we are going to cool it slowly and hope to bring down his fever down with it."

"Have you done this before?" Virgie asked with pleading eyes. "With babies, and it worked most of the time, but we are going to need some men in here to lift him into the tub.”

When the tub was ready, they took him out of bed, and the tea seemed to be working because he was griping about Morgan seeing him in his underwear.

“Really? That’s what you are worried about? You can yell at me later.”

He was still griping, “What are you doing?” as they poured cold water into the tub, and she swished it around him.

“I am trying to save your stubborn old life, so stay put. You have a high fever, and we are trying to get it down.”

He seemed to be getting better. He was more lucid. He was fighting with them more. Now the doctor was more interested in what she was doing and how she was doing it. He even carried a pail of water in and swished it around to see what temperature she was going for.

By now, it was getting downright cold, and his teeth were chattering, but he was also lucid enough to be arguing with them. “Morgan, get me out of here right now.”

She looked at him. “You want out? You get out.” He tried, but he just didn’t have enough strength. “Now can we help you back to bed?”

He just nodded. He was tired.

The doctor and the men got him out, dried him off, redressed him, and put him back to bed but not before Morgan had him drink some more tea with herbs in it. She left Virgie and Martha Jean in the room with him after everything was settled, and he was asleep. She was sure they weren’t through, but they were for now.

The doctor came up to her and asked, “May I get some of the herbs you used for the fever? They seem to work pretty well.” He figured she would give him hell about asking, but she didn’t.

“We will talk about it tomorrow, and I will show you where to get them when it is warmer. I have some extra you can have until then. The girls have a bed for you. Go to sleep. You look tired.”

“Thank you for your help. Your herbs did work. I should have kept my mouth shut.” He turned around and headed to the back of the house to the bedroom they had set up for him.

She turned to the front of the fireplace and just stood there until someone placed a cup in front of her on the mantle. It was Trey.

"One of the maids said you like cocoa better than coffee, so I brought you a cup."

"I started liking it when we went to New Orleans. They drink it a lot there."

He pulled a rocker closer to the fire for her to sit in and a chair for himself, and they just sat there in silence for a while.

Trey looked at her and said, "He seems better."

She looked at the bedroom. "He is for now. We will have to see how the herbs work to keep down the fever. We may have to do the tub again. My aunt and Virgie are in with him now, praying."

He looked at her kind of funny and then asked her a question. "You don't pray. I have seen you in church and at weddings and funerals, but I have never seen you pray."

She looked up at him at him and said, "Neither do you."

"I didn't think anybody had ever noticed but my wife Sheri. I should have known you would have noticed. You don't miss much. Do you believe there is a god?"

"Yes. The Indians believe in a different one than ours, but I stopped praying to either one of them a long time ago."

"Why? I would think after everything you have been through, you would have greater faith in one of them."

She looked at him as she drank her cocoa and then at the fire. "I prayed we would find my father alive all those years ago, and we didn't. I prayed my mother wouldn't marry Ramon, and she did. I was praying when the Comancheros took me, and look what good that did me. I stopped praying the day White Cloud put me in front of him on that horse and said he was taking me home with him. I knew right then my life was mine to take care of and no one else was going to come help me. The only one who ever helped me was that other woman you saw that morning in the village, and I don't think she was heaven sent."

"Are you afraid of her?"

No one had ever asked her that. "Yes, I am afraid of becoming her and never coming back."

"Don't be. I don't think the Morgan part of you would ever let her stay forever, just long enough to protect you, and then she will go away."

She wondered if Standing Bear would agree with him because she wasn't so sure. They just sat there quietly until he stood up and started back to one of the bedrooms, but as he walked by her, he put his hand on her shoulder and squeezed gently. It was the first time he had ever touched her in all the time she had known him. She didn't look up or even acknowledge he touched her.

"Maybe that woman was his answer to your prayers." And then he went down the hall to his bedroom.

She just sat there and rocked in front of the fireplace and drank her cocoa. Somehow, she never thought of that woman as the answer to anyone's prayers.

Virgie came out and sat down and said to her, "He seems better. He is not so restless, and the fever is not back. I am glad Trey went to get you. He shouldn't have been out working cattle in this weather, but you can't tell that man anything. He thinks he is indestructible. I don't know if I could stand losing him. It took me so long to find a really good man."

Morgan looked at her coming back from the place she had been, thinking about what she and Trey had been talking about. "You know, I have known you since I was what, six years old, and I know you were married, but I don't know what happened to your husband. Are you a widow, or is there something else? Mother never told me."

Virgie looked down at her hands on her lap and didn't say anything for a few minutes and then said, "My husband and I were married for almost three years, and I never got pregnant. The doctors in New Orleans said there was nothing wrong, but my husband said it had to be my fault. He finally found an eighteen-year- old girl and left me for her, so I divorced him so he could marry her. She never got pregnant either, so he started hitting her. Her father found out about it when she went home one night after he hit her. When he came to get her, the girl's father shot him. He didn't kill him, but he divorced her as well. He kept coming around and saying he loved the girl, and then he disappeared. I think the girl's father killed him, but a body was never found. Louisiana is mostly a big swamp, and I think he got fed to the alligators, but he was never seen again. The girl remarried and the last I heard she had four children, so maybe neither one of us was at fault. We will never know for sure."

Morgan just smiled. Some men never learned.

"I had my plantation, and I just waited for the right man. When we ran here, I found him, but we were still running, and your grandfather couldn't see me from the grief of losing his son, your father. When we came back, I got my chance, and I don't intend to lose it."

"How old are you? Since I have met you as a child, you never seem to age. You are still as beautiful as the first time I first saw you."

"Such a question, I am forty-six."

Morgan just looked at her. "You aren't but a few years older than my mother. She would have been forty this year. You two better be careful. You could still have a baby if that doctor was right."

Virgie started choking. "Good lord, your grandfather is fifty-eight.

Don't you think we are past having children?"

Morgan just looked at her. "I don't know. Are you? Maybe you might want to think about it. I might wind up with an uncle the same age as one of my children." Then she just smiled as Virgie's face went white. She had guessed right; she wasn't past childbearing age yet.

About that time, her grandfather started calling, and both women went into the bedroom to tend to him.

Trey went back to her ranch the next day to tell Miles what was going on with her grandfather. Miles sent a letter back with him for her to stay there till the weather let up, and then he would come and get her. He also sent a letter from Mary Jo with Trey for her to read, and it was marked personal. Her grandfather was doing much better, so Trey went to get Sheri, and he brought her to the big ranch house. They didn't want her alone because she was pregnant as well.

While everybody was resting, Morgan went to her room and opened the letter Mary Jo had sent her and began to read it.

That idiot she knew he was going to screw this up. He never had a woman who actually loved him. He always had women he bought, so he thought he had to keep an iron reign on her. Well, she would be here in a couple of weeks. Maybe if she left, that would put the fear of God in him and straighten him out, or she would have to leave him.

Her due date was getting closer, and she was getting huge as well. She lay down, but she got up and walked out to the front of the house and was looking out the door to the north when Trey came up behind her.

"Is something wrong? What are you looking for?"

She just kept standing there. "I could have sworn I heard something or someone calling."

She started to turn and go back in, and she heard it again, so she just listened. Then she knew Still Water was having her baby. She didn't know how she knew, but she knew. She just stood there for a while longer till Trey made her come back inside; it was too cold to be outside.

She went by the window and stood there until she knew the baby was born and all right, and she also knew Standing Bear had a daughter. She hoped they survived the winter. It was bad up in those mountains. She said under her breath, "Good luck, Still Water," then she went and lay down in her warm room and went to sleep.

Trey took her home two days later. The children were very glad to see her, as was Miles. He had worried about her and the baby. The nursery was ready, and they figured the baby was about a month away, so no more outings for Mom.

Mary Jo showed up three days later, the day before Thanksgiving, to everyone's surprise except Morgan's. When she saw her, she was shocked. She had lost weight and she looked scared. Now Morgan was just plain mad. Miles saw the look on her face and knew something else was going on. He helped Mary Jo carry in her bolt of silk and lace and her bags, and then they got her settled. They sat down to supper, but this wasn't the same woman who had left here two months ago, and Morgan was fuming.

After supper, they got the children to bed, and the women went to the front room and they were going to talk. They shooed Miles away, but he wasn't having any of it.

"I don't know what is going on, but something sure is. Now start talking, or we will be up all night because I am not leaving."

Mary Jo put her face in her hands and started to cry.

"Has he hit you, or is he still just bullying you and intimidating the men who come near you?"

Miles looked at her. "You knew about this, and you didn't tell me? Why not?"

"I asked her not to. I wanted to see if I could get it under control. No, he has never hit me. He has raised his hand but never hit me. That is why I came early. It was just getting worse. When I said I was leaving, he told me I couldn't go, so I snuck out while he was at a meeting in Steamboat Springs. He doesn't know I am gone yet."

"He is going to know soon enough. What do you plan to do when he shows up here? Because Justin will show up here and sooner than later.

He considers you his, and that is not going to change just because you came back home."

Miles said to both women, "He was mean to some of the girls at Virgie's, and then there was what he did to you. I was worried about this from the start."

"What do you mean, what he did to you?"

Well, she might as well tell her now. It was bound to come out sometime. "He wanted me badly enough to try and blackmail Virgie, which didn't work, but he did tell Ramon where I was, and we had to start running again with two bounty hunters on our trail."

"What happened to them?"

Morgan looked up at Miles. Well, it looked like all her dirty little secrets were coming out. "I shot both of them."

Mary Jo looked at her differently all of a sudden. She had heard all the stories, but suddenly, they were real. "You really did all those things, killed all those men?"

Morgan kind of shook her head and then answered her, "Yes, I did all those things and killed all those men. How do you think I stayed alive all this time?"

Mary Jo didn't ask any more questions. She had more answers than she could handle for one night. "I think I will go to bed, and we can figure this out tomorrow. At least he won't be screaming at me tonight."

"Tomorrow night's Thanksgiving. Maybe he won't get here till after that, and there will be enough men around to keep him under control. Let's go to bed. I am tired."

The next day, everybody was cooking. The dinner was going to be at her grandfather's because he had been so sick, and he had the biggest house. Everybody was invited, hands and their families as well as all the McKinney family. The children, most of the adults, and the food had been shuttled over there today while it was warm. All that were left were Morgan, Trey, and Mary Jo. The women were baking the last of the pies. They were getting ready now. Miles had just left with the last of the children and would be waiting at the other ranch, and Trey would bring the rest of the food and the women.

They were just about ready when Justin came bursting through the door. He was screaming for Mary Jo. Trey got in his way, and he punched him. Mary Jo came out and was screaming at him to stop because he was still hitting Trey.

"Who is he? And why are you alone with him here? Where is everybody?"

Morgan was there by now, and she was getting mad. This was stupid.

"They are at Grandfather's ranch. It is Thanksgiving. And that is Trey, one of my hired hands. He was supposed to drive us, so let him go, Justin, and calm down."

"Morgan, you don't give me orders, and I will talk to my wife as I please, so get out of my way."

He kicked Trey in the ribs and shoved Morgan against the counter where the pies were and went after Mary Jo. Morgan hit the counter hard, and her hand went back to stop her fall. Her hand found a knife that they had been using to trim the pie crusts, and she wrapped her hand around it.

Trey was still on the floor, doubled over, and Justin had Mary Jo, shaking and screaming at her. Trey looked up and watched as the lady was making her appearance. All he could say was "No, Morgan—"

But she had the knife in her hand, and she just kept going, and she was going for Justin. Mary Jo saw her over his shoulder, and she just froze, then Justin turned. Too late did he realize she was coming for him? He turned Mary Jo loose, and Morgan pushed him up against a wall and had the knife at his throat, and she was going to kill him. She was pushing so hard with her left hand that his feet were almost off the floor, and the look in her eyes told him he was a dead man.

"I told you once if you hurt her, you would have to deal with me. Well, this is the other me, the one the bounty hunters are afraid of, the one Ramon saw before he died. I am going to carve you into little tiny pieces and feed you to the coyotes."

Miles had come back and walked in on this, and he didn't exactly know what to do, but Trey was talking to her, so he walked toward her slowly. Mary Jo was still frozen, just staring at the scene.

"Morgan, you can't kill him. You can't come back from that.

Remember you said you were afraid she would take over and you wouldn't be able to come back? If you kill him, she wins. Let him go, Morgan. I know he hurt you, but he won't again. Miles is here. We will take care of Mary Jo and you. You come back now." How did Trey know she was afraid of that other woman? She had never told him that.

"You hurt her or scream at her ever again, and they won't ever find your body. They say the men who rustled Grandfather's cattle were never seen again. I'll bet I can find a hole where you will never be seen again either." She flicked the knife across his cheek and cut him about an inch under his eye, but it would leave a scar.

"Something to remember me by because the next one will be across your throat and you won't survive that one."

She backed away from him and handed the knife to Trey, and then Miles came to stand by her as she doubled over in his arms. There was a puddle of water at her feet, and she looked up at him.

"My water broke. I am in labor. Help me to the bedroom."

Trey was trying to get up off the floor. Mary Jo was still staring at her as they walked by her, and Miles snapped his fingers in front of her face. Justin was looking at Mary Jo, kind of stunned.

Morgan looked at Miles, and he just said to her, "What do you want me to do?"

"Please get him out of my house. Send him to Grandfather's after my aunt and the other women." Then she doubled over again.

"Are we going to have time to get them here, honey?"

She looked at him and back at Trey and his bloody nose, and he was still trying to stand. She could hear Justin stomping in the front room, and all she could say was "I don't think so, but I don't want him in my house right now. I don't think I can stand another round of him and the lady tonight."

Trey was back in the front room with Miles as he went to Mary Jo and told her to go to Morgan. Trey was watching Justin and handed him a towel to stop the blood running down his face and grabbed one for his nose.

"She would have killed me, wouldn't she?"

"Yes, sir, she would have, and she still will if you hurt your wife again. She doesn't give idle threats. That is the only reason she is still alive."

"You would have let her do it, wouldn't you?"

Trey just looked at him and then answered, "Probably, because I was just like you a long time ago, and somebody should have shot me then for what I did to someone. It took her to straighten me out. Maybe you can learn the same lesson before you lose someone you love too."

Miles came back into the room and asked Trey if he would go and help Mary Jo with Morgan, and he left the two of them alone.

"Justin, I want you to go to the big ranch, get Morgan's aunt and cousins, tell them she is in labor, and bring them back. You can take Trey's horse and leave right now."

Justin said, "Trey can go. I want to talk to my wife. I am not going anywhere. This is not over."

Miles just looked at him. "Not over? Did you not see my wife's face? You are the only man who has ever gotten that close to that woman she becomes and walked away alive and you want to argue with me? She is in labor almost a month early because of you, and if she or my child dies, I will kill you myself. Mary Jo came home because she is afraid of you, and she wants a divorce. We will help her get one if she still wants one tomorrow, but tonight, my wife is my priority. Now get out and stay at the other ranch." Then he turned and went into his bedroom as soon as he heard Justin riding away.

"Honey, what do we need to be doing?"

"Start some water boiling, sterilize a knife, make me some tea, and find the laudanum bottle. It is on the high shelf in the kitchen. Get the fireplaces going again? I let them burn down because we were going to be gone. We need this house warm. Mary Jo can help me change and get ready. You better give Trey some of that laudanum. I think Justin may have cracked or broken some of his ribs. Can you check them please?"

Trey just looked at her. The world was coming apart around here, and she was worried about his ribs. When the men got to the kitchen, Miles started the water and then turned and asked Trey, "Pull up your shirt, and let me see those ribs."

"Really, they are fine."

Miles just looked at him. "You want to argue with her right now?

Because I sure don't."

He pulled up his shirt, and sure enough, he had a huge bruise, but it didn't look or feel like they were broken. Justin had kicked him hard. Miles looked at him.

"I got in his way when he was trying to get to Mary Jo, and then he shoved Morgan hard against the kitchen cabinet. When she tried to stop her fall, she found the knife in her hand, and you saw the rest."

"How did you know about her being afraid of that other woman?

She never even told me that."

"When her grandfather was so sick, we started talking about the morning I saw her in the Indian village. Did she never tell you I almost shot her that morning? That lady was killing the other scout, and I saw her. Colonel Martin stopped me. He didn't know the bounty was for her dead. If he had known, he would have probably killed her himself. Strange how things work out sometimes. If it hadn't been for her, I wouldn't be here with a wife and a baby on the way and happier than I have been in a long time. Why are you here? I thought you were taking the rest of the kids to the ranch."

"I heard someone riding up, and I had one of the other hands take them instead so I could see who was riding up to the house so late."

Morgan was watching Mary Jo, and she was afraid of her now, not just a little but a lot. She would hardly come near her.

When Miles came back in the room, she had him come over to her, and she whispered into his ear, "Take her out of here, and talk to her. She is terrified of me. Do something. She can't even touch me, and she is afraid to be alone with me. Trey can stay with me. Nothing is going to happen right this minute."

He leaned down, kissed her lips, gave her the tea to sip on, walked out with Mary Jo, and sent Trey back in the room.

"Looks like you are stuck with me for a while. Now why don't you finally tell me what has been on your mind since the first time I met you before it eats you alive?"

He just grinned at her. "It seems you and I don't have any secrets, do we?"

"Looks that way doesn't it. We seem to be a snake eating our own tail. We have come full circle, you and I."

"You know I wanted you out there on the trail, didn't you?"

She nodded. "What stopped you? Just the guilt you were feeling, or was there something else?"

"I kept telling myself you were like all the rest, but the more I was around you, the more I knew that was a lie. You were something special. Even those soldiers you helped could see it. I had to make myself believe you were like all the others. That was the only way I could justify what I had done to my sister."

"Was it really that bad, Trey, or have you made it that bad in your mind?"

"I was a scout for the army when they needed one. When my sister went back to Geronimo's band and they made their run to Mexico, I was one of the scouts tracking them. We found them and had them trapped, and the captain in charge decided to just starve them out. At night, I could hear the children crying, and so I decided to sneak up to the camp get Ann and her child, get them down, and take them home. I got in the camp and finally found her and her baby girl. She was so weak. She didn't even struggle when I gathered them up and started down the mountainside. When I got to my horse, I lay them down and got out some water and food when I realized the little girl was dead and had been for some time. She was a beautiful little thing, blonde, and she looked like our mother. My sister wouldn't let her go. I tried to get Ann to drink something or eat something, but she wouldn't. She said she was going to be with her daughter soon, so she just kept holding her."

He looked so broken. She didn't even know what to say.

"I didn't hear her man come up behind me. He could have killed me, but by then, I didn't care. He sat down beside Ann and just held her and their child until she stopped breathing as well. He never said a word. He had brought a blanket with him and wrapped her and the baby up, and we dug a grave for them under a tree, much like we did for your friend that night. He turned and started back up that mountain, but before he went, I unloaded all the food I had brought and gave it to him to take back up to the camp. I don't even know what his name was. I guess I never will. He walked away, and I returned home, loaded up what I needed, and left, and I never went back. Geronimo surrendered several days later, and the Apache were done. I took one more job for the army, and it was to find your camp, and that was the last job I will ever do for them."

"She loved him and her child, and this world left her with no other options but to stay there. You couldn't have done much else."

"You did. You made a place for those women out there, a home where they are safe from the outside world, where they can live and raise their children in peace. I could have at least offered her that."

"All I am doing is hiding them from the outside world, and I know that, but it will at least keep them safe. You know the woman that went to California, don't you? Christina? She is on her way back. When she got home, her family that wanted her home so badly only wanted her there so they could use her as a slave on their farm. They told her she couldn't go to town. She wasn't decent. She would have to stay on the farm and work. That was all she was good for. I suspect they wanted to pimp her out. The sex trade is alive and well in San Francisco, and a white woman would command a high price. I had sent her with enough money to get back if things didn't work out. She will be on the stagecoach the day after tomorrow. I suspected things weren't as she was told, so Christina ran. You can't fix everything sometimes you just hide it and hope it works."

"At least you tried, and they are living in peace and are thriving here. That is more than most people would have done."

"Most people haven't lived the life I have. I have seen that world from both sides. Christina will at least have a chance at a life here and sometime that is all you can do." She doubled over in pain again. "This baby is early, isn't it?"

She nodded as she waited out the labor pain. "Several weeks, but it should be fine. Those little shows that the lady put on and Justin pushing me around didn't help matters any."

"Tell me what to do."

"In the cedar chest over there are clean blankets and braided sheets to tie on the end of the bed for me to pull on when I need to. Get them out."

He got them out and was tying them to the end of the bed when Miles came back in the room. Miles had heard most of the story standing outside the door, but he had just stayed quiet so he would tell it all to Morgan. They started to get things ready because the labor pains were coming faster, and help was at least two hours away if not more.

Mary Jo sat down beside her and held her hand while the men went about carrying firewood into this room and stoking the other room's fireplaces until the whole house was warm. Morgan was just watching her until she finally asked her, "Are you still afraid of me?"

Mary Jo looked at her and then finally admitted to her, "I thought they were making it up, how you changed and about all the men you killed. I didn't understand until I saw her tonight just what you had to do to stay alive for all those years. Miles tried to explain, but I don't think he really knows what you had to do."

"I am not sure he really wants to know it all. Some things are better kept secrets, like your mother watching her mother die."

Mary Jo just looked at her. "No, it was your father who saw it all."

Morgan just shook her head. "And your mother has kept that secret her whole life to protect Grandfather. We all keep secrets to protect the ones we love. Mine just have a lot of blood soaked on them."

"I am sorry. I was just thinking about me and Justin."

"He won't be back tonight. He was told to stay at Grandfather's ranch, and if he does come back, there will be more men with the others, so you will be safe."

They took turns sitting with her as the labor pains got closer, and they waited. Several hours later, a carriage arrived at almost a dead run with Virgie, Martha Jean, and her grandfather. He was the only one who could manage those roads in the dark at those speeds and not kill them. They all came in at a run, and her grandfather had the start of a black eye.

"What happened? As if I didn't know. Is he still alive?" Morgan just looked at her grandfather.

"So far, but I told him if he showed up here tonight, I would hang him, and I damn well mean it. He told me he had an argument with Mary Jo and pushed you, and out came the lady. I know she doesn't come out unless something bad is happening. So he finally confessed Mary Jo came home to divorce him, and he beat up Trey, and you got in the way. He said he pushed you against a counter, and the lady threatened to kill him with a knife, and Trey talked her down, which I would have liked to have seen. I didn't know anybody could talk that lady down. Then he said you went into labor, and we came running. We told the men to keep him there. Then he got in my face and tried to tell me what he was and wasn't going to do. I won that argument."

Virgie was talking by now. "How is she, Miles?"

"I think this baby is close. Everything is ready for you in there. We will start some coffee out here."

Virgie went into the bedroom and started taking off her coat and looked down at Morgan as she started to cry. She hadn't let anyone else see how worried she was about the baby until now.

Virgie turned and shut the door and went over to Morgan and took her hand. "It is going to be all right. This baby is not that early, and we are all here now. Calm down." She picked her up and put her arms around her and just rocked her like she would have her own child. Truth is she probably was as close to her child as she would ever know.

Another labor pain hit, and she laid her back down and told her, "This baby doesn't want to wait. It is going to be coming soon."

Morgan looked up at her and asked of her, "Please don't let this baby die too. I don't think I could stand to lose another one."

"No, *ma petite*, not this time. This time, you will have a healthy boy or a sweet little girl. What would you like?"

After this pain was over, she told her. "A little girl, and I already have a name picked out for her."

"Oh, and what is it?"

Another pain hit her, and she couldn't answer.

Virgie called for Martha Jean to come help her, and they were busy for the next hour, but then the men heard a cry from the room, and they started breathing again.

Virgie came out with a bundle wrapped in pink. She was small, but she was crying, and she was healthy. "Well, Daddy, you have a girl. She is little but in good shape. I don't know her name, but your wife wants you and Trey to come to the room and hear it."

Both men looked at each other, and Virgie handed Miles his daughter. They both headed to the bedroom and found his worn-out wife lying in bed. Miles looked at his daughter and then his wife.

"Close the door. This conversation is just among the three of us." Trey turned and closed the door and then turned back around as Miles started to talk. "Virgie said you wanted to talk to both of us. What is it you want us to tell us, darlin'?"

"I would like to name our daughter Justine."

"All right. That is fine with me."

"Justine Ann, if it is all right with the two of you, and it will be just among the three of us why we named her that." She thought Trey was going to cry, and Miles wasn't much better. "You two decide right here, right now, because if you don't like it, we won't do it, and no one else will ever know."

Miles looked at Trey and said, "I think it is a wonderful name for a new life and a way to start over, don't you?"

Trey finally looked at her. "Are you sure this is what you want to do?"

Morgan took her new daughter and then told him, "It won't bring her back, but maybe when you hear her name called now, it won't be such a devastating pain. She will be alive here in this world. Like I said, do what you can where you can. Maybe someday you can even tell Sheri what happened, but if you can't, that is up to you."

"Yes, I think it is a wonderful idea. Thank you. I will leave the two of you alone so you can enjoy your new daughter."

"Trey, we are going to need godparents. Are you and Sheri interested?"

He did cry then as he nodded and left the room.

"Do you think it will help him get over his sister by doing all that?"

"I don't know, but you have to start somewhere, and a name is as good a place as anywhere."

By now, her daughter wanted her mother to feed her. She wasn't interested in what her parents were talking about. She was hungry.

Miles was rocking his new daughter while Morgan slept, and he was just watching her when she awoke later that night. Martha Jean had tried to put the baby in the cradle, but he just couldn't let her go, so he just sat there and rocked her.

When Morgan woke up, she was just watching them, and he looked so content. She asked him, "Are you pleased, even though you wanted a boy?"

He looked up at her and smiled and answered her, "I don't care either way, boy or girls, just as long as you are both all right, and she is perfect. You already had a name picked out for a girl. What had you picked out for a boy? Or am I not supposed to ask?"

"Grayson Miles after Gray Dove. I thought you would like that, so maybe next time."

He was smiling again. "Do you have any idea how much I love you, especially right now, holding our baby girl?"

Their daughter was waking up and wanting to be fed again, so he brought her over to her mother.

"Before I feed her, call Martha Jean in here, and have her help me get into another gown that I can breastfeed easier in. This one doesn't open from the front."

He called her aunt into the room to help her up off the bed and help her change while he held the baby, and while she was changing her, they both saw the bruise across her back. She had a long black bruise from one side of her lower back to the other where she had hit the counter. Justin had shoved her hard. He knew she was pregnant, and he still hurt her. No wonder the other lady had showed up. Her aunt just looked at him and then finished dressing Morgan and got her back to the bed.

When she was in bed, she could see they were both mad, and she asked them, "How bad is it?"

Her aunt answered, "You have a bruise all the way across your back. Is this what Mary Jo is running from? Is he hurting her like this?"

She just looked at her aunt. "She swears he isn't hitting her, but I don't want him around her until we can talk to her alone, so keep him at Grandpa's. She is afraid of him for some reason, and we will find out tomorrow."

She took the baby and fed her, and then she and Miles lay down and went to sleep with the baby in the cradle next to them. He pulled her close to him and thanked God everybody was alive and well. Tomorrow was another day, and they could deal with everything else then.

Hours later, when the baby woke up, she got up and took her to the rocker and was nursing her. Miles awoke to her softly talking to her.

Justine had her small hand wrapped around her mother's thumb, and Morgan was saying, "I was so afraid I was hurting you when we were coming down the mountainside, but I had to hurry. We were in danger. We had a friend helping us though, and I am going to have to thank him someday. Right now, Mama is just glad you are all right and here in my arms with your family. Tomorrow, you will get to meet your brother and sisters. They are going to love you."

He wondered who she was talking about, but before he could ask, she looked up at him and asked, "You know, I don't know anything about your life before you and I met. Do you have family somewhere I don't know about?"

He smiled at her and leaned his head up on his arm and started talking. "You just don't want to explain that comment about the man who helped you on that mountain, do you? So now you are going to distract me, aren't you?"

She just smiled at him.

"My family is all gone. My parents were farmers until cholera killed them one summer. We lived in Louisiana, and I was with my uncle, trapping, and we didn't get it. We were way back in the hills. When we got back home, nearly everybody was dead. The only way they finally stopped it was to burn everything down, and then the rain washed everything clean. My uncle and I just loaded up and left with our traps and started over. I spent two years with him, learning trap lines and trading with the Indians, and we were doing pretty well until he got bitten by a big rattler, trying to take a beaver out of a trap. It got him in the arm, and it got him good. We got to a Comanche camp, and they tried to help, but you know there isn't much to do. One of the medicine men saved his arm, but he chopped his lower arm off to do it."

"Sometimes that is the only way if you want to live. At least now I know why you are so terrified of snakes." Morgan told him.

"I know, but my uncle resented him for it and me for letting him cut it off. One night, he was just gone, and I haven't seen him since. I did meet a pretty Indian woman in the camp though, Gray Dove, and before I left the camp, I had traded half my pelts for her."

He was smiling, and Morgan watched as he remembered the wife he had lost and wondered what she had looked like. Virgie said she was a beautiful woman with long black hair and smoky brown eyes.

"We went back to the land in Louisiana. I built a new house, and we started ranching. I took what money I had made from trapping and sold all my traps, and we were doing pretty well. I worked for Virgie, helping her with her place, getting her cotton planted for extra money. She didn't care if I was married to an Indian woman." No, Virgie wouldn't have cared one way or the other who he was married to.

"The people in town called me squawman and worse, as you can well imagine. They shunned her, so we didn't go to town. If we went anywhere, we went to Virgie's. We had a pretty good stock of horses and a few cattle and some land when the war broke out. We didn't want to be involved with it either way, so we just kept our heads down. That was until Quantrill and his raiders needed some fresh horses, and some men in town told him about the squawman outside of town. When they hit the ranch, Gray Dove was outside on the porch, and she didn't stand a chance. I grabbed my rifle and killed two men before they shot me. They ran off the horses and left when they saw Virgie and her men coming. One of the men was an older man, and I hope it was Gregory's grandfather. At least he won't be coming for him. The house was on fire, and I would have sat there and held her and just let it burn down around us, all three of us."

He looked up at her. "She was finally pregnant. We had tried for years, and now she was going to have a baby. Now I understand why you were so devastated by that miscarriage in Dallas. It was a living thing, even if it wasn't born yet, and Ramon killed it."

She just nodded. He finally understood.

Morgan had the baby on her shoulder, and after she burped, Miles said, "She is sound asleep. Mama, why don't you put her back in her bed and come back to yours and get some more sleep? You look worn out."

She laid her daughter down and crawled into bed beside him, and he pulled the covers over her. He accidentally brushed the bruise on her back as he covered her up. She jumped, and he told her, "You stay away from him tomorrow. There are enough men around here to take care of this. Let us take care of you this time, all right?"

She just nodded, and everybody went to sleep.

CHAPTER 11

The next morning, as she awoke, she could hear riders and yelling, and she knew Justin was here. The war was on.

Miles was already up and dressing. She could hear someone coming down the hallway and knocking on her door. The door opened a little, and Martha Jean poked her head in a little.

"He is here, and the men are going to kill him if someone doesn't calm them down and right now."

She grabbed her robe and ran past her and said, "Take care of the baby for a few minutes, and I will be right back."

She walked down the hall and past Mary Jo. She grabbed her arm, and they walked into the front room together. She walked toward Justin, and then she punched him in the stomach and said to him, "Shut the hell up. You are scaring my baby, and I am sick and tired of listening to your big mouth. You don't have anything to say anyway."

The rest of the men got real quiet after that and just let her talk. Martha Jean had walked into the room and was carrying the baby on her shoulder. Morgan hurt. She was tired, and she was in no mood for all this, so she got to the point.

"I don't know what has been happening at your house since you left here, but your wife is scared to death of you, and that is going to stop right now. You saw what can happen to you last night. Well, look around. I am not alone in my feelings for how the women in my family get treated around here. This is how this is going to work. You are leaving my house, and Mary Jo is staying here. When she is better in a few days, we will discuss this again, so go to town and get a room. We don't want you on our land. If anybody sees you on any McKinney land, you will be shot on sight. Are we clear?"

He stood up and stared at her and then the men around her and then at Mary Jo standing beside her, and he asked her, "Is this really what you want? Are you really afraid of me?"

Mary Jo looked at him, and she couldn't believe he could even ask her that. "I run from you, you attack Trey and hurt Morgan, half the men in this room are ready to kill you, and you still can't see what you are doing to me. I don't know if you will ever understand. Please go now."

He turned to leave. His bags were still by the door. "She is still my wife."

Morgan looked at him. "Maybe not for very long. Get out of here, and don't come back until you are asked."

The men in the room helped him out and made sure he was off the ranch land while Mary Jo and her mother got Morgan back to bed. She didn't need to be fighting battles yet.

It wasn't long before she heard riders and wagons. The family was coming to see the baby and find out what was going on with Justin. The women went to Morgan's room first, and the men went to Morgan's grandfather and then to Trey. He looked like a horse had kicked him, and they didn't have to even ask who did it. Gary Lee arrived with Shelbee, and the whole room got quiet. She looked around and went straight to Morgan's room, and Mary Jo was there. She asked the other women if they would please leave.

When she was out of the room, all she said was "Are you all right?" She was looking at Mary Jo.

She nodded and then said to her sister-in-law, "It was Morgan he hurt, and she went after him, and if Trey hadn't stopped Morgan, we would be burying him this morning or, God forbid, her or that baby."

"I was afraid to leave you with him. He just can't control his jealousy, and I was afraid it was going to get the better of him. Are you going to divorce him? Is that why you came home?"

Mary Jo sat down on the bed and just held her head in her hands. "I don't know what to do. I love him, but I can't take this. He is always watching me and screams at every man who gets close to me and accuses me of having affairs behind his back. At least here, I have a little peace." By now, she was in tears.

Then in walked Miles. "Justin is at the fence line, and he wants to talk to Mary Jo. What do you want me to do? Let him come back on the ranch?”

She thought for a minute and then told him, “Have him come around back to the porch, and we will meet him there.”

“Are you sure, darlin’?”

She nodded. She would have all the men in the house to back her up if things got out of control.

Mary Jo and Shelbee were both looking at her, then Shelby said, “Do you have a plan to make him a calm human being? Because nothing I have ever done has worked.”

“Let’s see what he has to say and if he has any remorse. If he doesn’t you will have to leave him, and we will protect you from him. Meanwhile, I will start looking for a really nasty lawyer.”

Shelbee was looking at her and then said, “You know, you are scary sometimes.”

Mary Jo just looked at her, and after last night, she had no idea just how scary and deadly her cousin could be. She hoped she never saw her that mad again.

As they walked to the back of the house, she told the men to stay back and just watch unless he started to get out of hand, and then she would signal Miles. He rode up and dismounted and tied up his horse to the hitching post. He could still see bullet holes in the walls of the house and fence from where the bounty hunters had tried to get to her. Morgan came out first, then his sister and then Mary Jo followed.

He started toward her, and Morgan said, “Stay put, Justin. She doesn’t want you close to her right now. We are going to sit down and talk.”

“I am tired of all this, Mary Jo. Go pack your bags. You have embarrassed me enough. We are leaving, so go get ready.”

Morgan walked toward him and asked him, “Or what, Justin? You going to throw her over your shoulder and drag her out of here? She isn’t one of your whores, and she isn’t a piece of meat. She doesn’t have to go with you if she doesn’t want to.”

About this time, Shelbee started to talk. “I never thought I would ever say this, but you are acting just like our daddy. What are you going to do? Push her until she kills herself like Mama did?"

Justin stopped in his tracks. "How dare you say that to me? Mama was unhinged, and that was why she killed herself."

"That is bull, and you know it as well as I do. She worked herself to death trying to please Daddy and couldn't while he had his whores and his bottle, and that last night at her birthday dinner when he finally showed up, he was drunk and abusive to her. She sat there and took it, and then she told him she was going to have another baby, and he laughed at her and then asked who the father was. I have never seen her face so calm. She knew he was going to say that very thing, even though you could smell the perfume on him, and it wasn't Mother's. She got up from the table and went to her room as he ate supper, and in a little while, we heard the shot, and he found her at her desk. He climbed into a bottle after that, and you raised me after he died, but he might as well have killed her, and that is what you are doing to your wife now."

He just looked at Mary Jo and then said to her, "I am going back to town. I will talk to you in a couple of days." And then he walked away, got on his horse, and left the ranch.

"Well, at least you don't have children to fight over. Maybe that will make this a little easier, and he will come around."

Then they looked at Mary Jo's face, and they both knew she was pregnant and Justin didn't know. Morgan just said, "In Texas, a rich husband has a lot of rights. If there is a child involved, I will start looking for a mean lawyer." And they went back inside the house.

The men inside had heard it all and were as scared for her as the women were, especially Gary Lee. He was a lawyer and knew how much trouble they were in.

Justin sent a letter to Mary Jo the next day, and after she read it, she dropped it on the floor and went to her room. Morgan picked it up, and she and Shelbee read it together.

Mary Jo,

You can stay here and have your little temper tantrum, but you are not going to make a fool of me anymore. I am going to go to the governor's ball. You were supposed to go with me, but I will tell them you are indisposed. When you get tired of playing this game, I guess you can come home or not. We will see. I won't wait forever. Don't think I will have an empty bed either just because you are playing the wounded bird.

Justin

"Well, he was never subtle, and he always goes for the soft spot. That is why when we left on that train, I knew when I got to Colorado, I would pack my stuff and come straight back to Gary Lee with or without his permission. I had finally found what I was looking for, a family and a good man, and I wasn't going to let it get away. I am just sorry Mary Jo got caught in his web. We need to keep an eye on her just in case until she feels better."

Morgan thought the same thing. She was going to stay with her mother at the little ranch house, and she should be fine there for now. "Did your mother leave a note to your father?"

Shelbee looked at her funny. "No. She left one to me, a nine-year-old girl, and no one knows about it. I never told anyone. She had put it in my room before she shot herself. She told me to find a man not like my father, someone who would love me and never let anyone treat me like he had treated her. The only man who ever treated me like he did was Justin, and I got out from under his thumb as soon as I could. I thought Mary Jo was strong enough to handle him, but I was wrong."

"Looks like we both were."

They just kept walking to the kitchen. They were both strong women. They would figure out how to take care of this situation somehow.

Days turned into weeks, and Sheri had a baby boy. The cattle had to be branded and calves separated, and there were a lot of new men around the ranches. Trey was running crews, and Sheri was at Morgan's ranch house so Morgan could help run a crew as well. Sheri helped wet-nurse Morgan's baby when she wasn't around.

Mary Jo was getting bigger and staying at Morgan's house as well so someone could keep an eye on her. She was very depressed. Justin hadn't even written a letter to her except to send clippings about the governor's ball showing him escorting another woman on his arm. His sister and Morgan were ready to strangle him.

He didn't bother to show up until a couple of months later and surprised Morgan at the door. Morgan let him in.

"Where is she, Morgan? I want to talk to her right now."

She was in the kitchen at the table with corn piled high in front of her so he couldn't tell she was pregnant. Morgan led him into the kitchen after she told Mary Jo he was there, and Morgan stood at the doorway.

"Well, Jo, you are playing the busy housewife at somebody's house, just not mine. Are you ready to come home yet, or are you still playing the martyr because we had a fight? It looks like you have put on some weight, so you aren't grieving too much."

She looked at him like he had slapped her, and Morgan thought if this was what he was like when he was trying to be nice, what was he like when he was nasty?

"That is all you have to say to me? No apology? Not sorry about the picture you sent to me? Nothing, just 'come home'? Nothing has changed. I am still something you own and nothing more. You can't even say you love me anymore."

He crossed his arms across his chest and told her, "Jo, I married you, so what has love got to do with it? You are mine, and if I divorce you, I will see to it you get nothing."

"Is that all you are worried about? That I might take something away from you? I never wanted any of your land or money in the first place. I married you because I loved you."

"Then get up from that table and pack your bags, and let's leave. This is your last chance to be with me. I won't give you another one." Under the table, she put her hand on her belly and felt her child and knew she couldn't raise a baby with this man, so she looked up at him and said, "No, Justin. Go home and file for divorce. I want the man who made love to me before we got married in my mother's house that day, and if I can't have him, I don't want anyone else."

She watched for a reaction, and there was none. He turned and walked out the door, and Morgan watched as all the blood drained out of her face. Morgan ran behind the table and caught her before she fell on the floor. He had finally broken her, and now he was gone.

Miles carried her to bed, and Morgan told him, "We watch her till this baby is born, and we put a watch on this house. I don't want him popping in here unannounced again." She had a feeling this was about to get bad, and she was right.

He showed up in town a few weeks later, and she wouldn't let him on the ranch lands, so he went to see Shelbee at her house with some papers. "I have the divorce papers, and I want to present the papers to her myself, Shelbee, so I guess you have to escort me out there."

Shelbee had already sent word ahead so they would be prepared, and Gary Lee was going with her. They had everything set up when they got there. When they went inside, he was met with icy coldness. Mary Jo was standing behind a wingback chair. If they could pull this off without him knowing she was pregnant for just a little while longer, he would have no claim on this child.

He came stomping in and said to her, "Mary Jo, here are the papers I filed in Colorado under desertion, and it should be easy enough to finish. Here, just sign them and then file them, and we are done. I just wanted to present the papers to you myself."

Mary Jo stood behind the chair as she told him, "I will have Gary Lee look at them, and then they will be filed, and we are done. Are you staying in town, or are you leaving?"

He looked at her and kind of smirked and then said, "I am staying at the hotel till this is finished. I want to be sure it is filed and I am free of you."

She inhaled deeply and was trying not to cry. This was killing her, but she didn't want him to see how badly he was hurting her. He would like that too much. "Just have someone bring me the papers when they are done, and I will be on my way back to Colorado and done with this family except you, Shelbee."

His sister looked at him. He was going to be done with her as well.

He just didn't know it yet.

After he was gone, they sat down and read the papers. He had cut her out of everything he owned. She would have nothing, but from the way it was worded, he wanted nothing of hers.

Gary looked at her and said, "He has cut his own throat. He has cut off all parental rights he might have had to that child. Are you good with that? Because once you sign this, it is done."

"Hand me a pen, and let's do this and then get them filed. This baby is not far off, and I don't want him anywhere near it or me again." She signed the papers, and Gary Lee took them.

He and Shelbee started back to town, and as they were headed back, she looked over at him and said, "I am sorry to bring so much trouble into your life with my brother. He has hurt your sister so much."

He looked at her and smiled. "It was worth all of it to get you in my life. I never thought I would be so happy until I met you. My world is complete."

"Really? Are you sure? I thought maybe adding one more might add a little spice to the mix. That house is so big and quiet."

She looked at him sideways, and when it finally hit him, what she was saying, he lit up like a Christmas tree.

"Are you sure? I thought maybe we couldn't after so long."

She looked at him lovingly and just said, "Maybe I was not motivated enough or there was too much drama from my brother going on. Who knows? But we are expecting now. Are you good with that?"

"Oh yes, ma'am. I will show you just how happy when we get home."

"Sounds very interesting, but file those papers first, and I want to be the one who delivers them to my dear brother. I have a few things to say to him when he finally gets them."

"He is not going to like it, is he? You are going to show him your mother's letters aren't you?"

"Yes. It is finally time he saw what a monster our father really was and what he has turned into, and I want to be the one who shows him."

After getting everyone to bed, Miles and Morgan were finally alone. He was kissing her and nuzzling her neck when she took over. The little demon came out to play, and she was on top, and he was having a most enjoyable time. The two of them were always so good together. She knew just the right places to touch, and he knew just the right time to take her over the top and with her hair hanging in his face and her hand sliding up his chest to his face, she had him flying again. Then he would roll her over, and she was under him. He would stroke and stroke, and sometimes he would stop just to make her ask him for more. Then she would take her hand and reach down and find him, and then he was the one begging, but lately, they had to be quieter because of the baby. They had woke her up last time.

He finally took them over the top, and when he finished, they were both breathing hard but quietly as she whispered in his ear, "I love you, Miles, just as much as the first time, and I always will."

He held her even closer until they heard moaning coming from another room. "Something is wrong."

She scrambled out from under him and got on a gown and robe and went looking. Miles went to the kids' rooms while she went to Mary Jo's room, and she found her sitting on the side of the bed, doubled over. "Are you all right?"

"I guess it was just a long day. My back is hurting, and I can't find a comfortable place to lie down." She tried to stand and couldn't. She doubled over, so she just sat back down.

"I think you are trying to go into labor. Just lie here and rest, and I will rub your back."

Miles walked by the door, and she told him, "You might want to get some help here. We may need them."

"The baby can't come yet, not till those papers are filed so he can't get my child."

Morgan already knew that, but if this baby was coming, there wasn't much they could do about it. "Just relax, and maybe we can slow things down and buy some time. I will send Miles in the morning and see about getting things done quickly."

"You know what is so scary? I still love him and wish he wanted this baby, but I know we would not survive in that house any more than his own mother could."

Morgan understood and just sat there and rubbed her back and tried to make her more comfortable. *Please, little one, give us a couple of more days or just one more day.*

In the morning, Miles was at Gary's house first thing and told them what was going on. He found out that Gary had filed the paperwork yesterday and would go see the judge today and see if he could get a rush put on it so it could be done sooner.

When he left, he saw Justin talking to a pretty woman at the general store. He just rode past him, and Justin looked at him strangely. Gary wasn't too far behind, going to the judge's office, and he watched as he stayed there for several hours. It seemed they wanted those papers done as soon as he did, and now he wondered why.

When Gary came out of the judge's office, the papers were almost ready. He was to pick them up before six tonight, but Shelbee had been called out to the ranch, and she had been gone for several hours. Those papers had to be finalized before that baby was born, so he went back to the judge's office and waited.

Shelbee had been at the ranch since morning. The baby was coming. The labor pains were slow and far apart, so they were keeping her calm and quiet. Shelbee knew they had to wait for those papers till the end of the day, so everybody waited and just kept Mary Jo company. They talked and congratulated Shelbee about her baby and just tried to keep everybody's mind off those papers. Finally, they heard a horse ride up, and it was Gary Lee, and in his hands were the legal documents. Mary Jo was finally free, but all she wanted to do was cry.

Morgan and Shelbee got everybody out of the room and then just let her cry. They both looked at her and said, "The hard part's done, darlin'. Now you can have a baby." Then everybody came back in. The contractions started, and that baby was on the way.

Seven hours later, she had a baby girl with dark hair who looked a lot like Shelbee and couldn't have been anybody's baby but Justin's, and he was never going to see her. Mary Jo just held her and rocked and cried. This was not how she had wanted this day to turn out, and now it was done. She was so tired, so after she fed the baby, they finally got her to bed and to sleep. It was the best sleep she had had in a while.

Shelbee began to gather up her things and got ready to leave.

"What's the hurry? You can stay and have supper with us."

"No, I have some things to do before morning."

Morgan watched her get ready to leave. She asked her cousin, "What is she going to do, Gary?"

"She is taking the papers to her brother in the morning, and I think there is going to be a family meeting like they haven't ever had. I think she wants to break her brother like he broke Mary Jo. She has the stuff to do it with, and she has been waiting a long time to go after him with it. She wants to hurt him, and she is going to for her and Mary Jo. She has waited a long time."

Morgan just wished she could hear that conversation and smiled to herself.

The next morning, Shelbee was at Justin's hotel room door early, and he told her to come in. He was shaving. He was just dressed in pants, and his shirt was hanging over the end of the headboard. It was obvious he had a woman in here last night.

She took his shirt and dropped it on the back of a chair, and he commented, "I didn't have it pressed, so you could wrinkle it on the chair."

"Does it seem like I give a damn about your shirt being wrinkled? I have come to bring you your divorce papers. I asked to be the one who delivered them to you because I had some other papers I wanted to give to you as well."

He looked at her as if she was boring him and then turned and cleaned the blade of his razor on a towel on the sink. "I guess this is going to be the big lecture about how I treated Jo so badly, and now when I visit you, it is going to be uncomfortable. Really, don't you think I can stay out of the way of the McKinneys when I come see you?"

"Won't really be a problem because I don't want to ever see you again? I don't want my child around that venomous mouth of yours any more than I would have wanted it to be around Daddy. I brought your divorce papers, and I also brought Mother's suicide letter that she left it in my room the night she died. She also left some letters Daddy had written her before and after they married. I brought them too. You should read them. You will see the resemblance to you. Maybe then you will understand why she wouldn't bring another child into his world with our monster of a father."

He had stopped shaving somewhere along the way and had cut his face, and it was bleeding.

She was getting up off the bed and started out the door, but before she left, she said, "Oh, by the way, this morning, Mary Jo had a little girl who looks just like Mama. She named her Hazel after Mama, but you made sure from the way you wrote the divorce papers you won't have contact with her, so thank you for that. We had to make sure they were filed before she was born so you couldn't touch that baby, so it worked out well. Now you can climb into a bottle with whatever woman you want and live in that big house alone without anybody bothering you. It should be a perfect world for you because the only woman who ever truly loved you, you had to break and make her life a living hell. Goodbye, big brother."

He just stood there, looking in the mirror as she walked out of his life and took his world with him. He had a daughter he was never going to be able to see, and he had done it to himself. He put the razor down, wiped his face off, sat on the bed, took the letter his mother had written to his sister, and started reading, and before he was through, he thought he was going to be sick. It described him down to the bone. He had treated Jo just like his father had treated his mother, and now it was too late.

He started opening other letters from his father to his mother from when he first met her till later in their marriage and realized the progression was the same, only Jo had just gotten out sooner. Then he got to thinking about the last two times he had seen her sitting behind the table and then behind the chair when he couldn't see she was pregnant. He had outwitted himself, and now Jo and his daughter were gone, as well as his sister.

He started thinking about what he was going to do, and the first thing he did was reach for the whisky bottle on the dresser. He had a woman in here last night and had sent her away; he hadn't had a woman since Jo left him. She was the only one he wanted, so why couldn't he just tell her that instead of yelling at her?

When he got up the next morning, he had a giant hangover, but he also had a plan. He cleaned up and bought a train ticket and was on the noon train. He didn't go far though, just to the next stop about eighty miles down the road, and then he got off. He went to the general store and bought a tent, blankets, lanterns, matches, food, and anything else he thought he might need to live out on the range for a while, including a pair of good binoculars. He bought a good horse and a pack animal to haul what he had bought, and he was off, back to Amarillo. He was going to see his daughter if he had to live in that canyon above Morgan's ranch till he figured something out. He had screwed this up. Now he was going to try and figure out how to fix it.

Martha Jean had asked Morgan about a new wrangler who Mary Jean seemed interested in. They seemed to disappear at the same time each day, and she didn't know where. She had asked Morgan if she would check on her since she had been at Morgan's ranch so much, taking care of Jo. Morgan told her she would check on her today, anything to get out of the house for a while. She had thought Jo would be better when the baby got here, but it seemed to be worse, and they didn't know what happened to Justin. She really wanted to just pinch his head off. Maybe a ride would help.

When she got to the other ranch house, she didn't see any horses, and she wasn't riding her Appaloosa, so she put her horse into the corral and went inside. The table had a bottle and some glasses on it, so she opened the bottle and smelled what was inside and then smiled. She then walked to the bedroom. The bed had been slept in and hadn't been made, so someone had been here last night, and Mary Jean was supposed to have been at her grandfather's. Morgan went back to the front room and sat down in the chair by the fireplace and just waited. She figured someone would be here soon.

She didn't have to wait long. She heard a man's footsteps walking in, and he went to the bottle on the table and poured a glass and started to drink when she said, "I see you still prefer tequila, Raphael?"

The glass was halfway to his mouth when he turned. "Hello, Morgan. What brings you here?"

About that time, Mary Jean came running in and threw herself around him. He started to pull her off him as he was trying to show her they weren't alone. When she realized Morgan was there, she got very quiet. "Does she know?"

"Know what? That you two are sleeping together, or is there something else I should know about?"

Miles walked in about that time, and then things got very interesting. "Morgan, your aunt sent me to see if everything was all right. What is going on?"

"Miles, this was the man on the balcony. He was one of the Comancheros looking for the guns in Dallas. He seems to have taken a liking to Mary Jean. By the way, he hunted me down on that mountain top and helped me escape from Standing Bear. If it hadn't been for him leading him away from me up there, Standing Bear would have caught me."

Miles walked over to Raphael and shook his hand and said, "How do I ever thank you? None of us could find her even with the army's help."

"He had much better contacts, and he speaks Comanche."

"We still have a couple of problems, don't we? What were you talking about, Mary Jean? Were you planning on going somewhere?"

She couldn't look at her face. "Are you pregnant?"

She just nodded.

"And you were going to leave with Raphael?"

"We figured we would just go and then no one would be the wiser."

Morgan rolled her eyes. "After all the hell going on around here, half the state and all the Texas rangers would be looking for you and I don't think that Raphael would think that would be such a good idea."

Raphael looked down at her and then commented, "I would just as soon find a way that wouldn't get me hanged."

"Do you still have any ties to the Comancheros at all, or does anyone know your last name?"

"No, I could change my last name, and the gunrunning was my brother's business. They are mostly dead or disbanded."

"What were your grandparents' names?"

"Priz, they were farmers in Mexico."

"Well, as long as they didn't sell guns to the Indians, I think

Raphael Priz sounds wonderful. So what are your plans for my niece now, Raphael? And remember, I can still shoot you."

He just smiled at her. "I was thinking a wedding rather quickly and then settling down nearby."

"That sounds like an excellent plan. She will introduce you to the family tonight, and a wedding will be in a week or two. I will get you a new suit. Don't plan on going anywhere, or I will come after you, and we don't want that, do we, Raphael?"

It looked like everything was settled, so Miles and Morgan headed back to the ranch. Miles finally asked her,

"Do I want to know what all happened up on that mountain or not?"

"Probably not, it was all I could do to stay alive most of the time. He helped me get down, and there were times I just wanted to stop and say enough, and I would have just lain down and frozen to death. That was the reason I didn't take Little Fox with me. It was all I could do to get me and the baby down alive."

Miles looked at her and realized she had almost given up at some point and something kept pushing her down.

Mary Jo and the baby were doing fine, but she still wasn't smiling. She was still lost, and Morgan couldn't figure out how to make it better. Her mother was trying to take her mind off Justin, but she wasn't having any better luck than Morgan was.

Mary Jean had introduced her new boyfriend at dinner last night and told them about the wedding plans, and everybody converged on them to ask about where Raphael had come from and about his family. Morgan watched as Jo got up and quietly left the table and went outside with the baby to the back porch, so she followed her.

They just sat out there, and she finally asked her, "When does it get better? Or will I always feel this lost? I thought when the baby got here, it would be better. It isn't. It is worse now. I want him to see her and be proud of her."

Morgan didn't know what to tell her. She just wanted to strangle him for treating her so bad, but she still loved the fool. So they just sat there and watched the stars.

The next few days were much the same—babies and children—

except Morgan couldn't get rid of the feeling she was being watched, and she kept looking up at the hills behind the house. There wasn't any reason for anyone to be watching the house, but she still had that feeling she always got when someone was around.

Justin saw her looking up at the hills one afternoon, and he could have sworn she was looking straight at him. He picked up his camp and moved it.

He hadn't been gone an hour when Morgan got curious, and she came looking. Sure enough, she found his camp. He had cleaned up everything, but she could tell someone had been there and recently. She looked around some more. She didn't find him, but she knew someone was up there. He was much more careful after that.

He had watched Jo and the baby a couple of times on the back porch, and he had seen his daughter. Then at night, he reread the letters his father had written and the letter his mother wrote on the last night of her life. Maybe sitting out here was what he had needed all along. He watched as Morgan took care of Jo and the baby. He had never taken that kind of care of her or Shelbee. Morgan made sure everyone was taken care of, and there was a new man down there he was sure he had seen somewhere before, and it wasn't here.

He was watching today. Jo was taking the baby down to the creek behind the house, and she had a blanket with her. She went down by a big cottonwood and laid down the blanket, laid down the baby, and sat down beside her. He could finally see his little girl's face. She did look like his mother. She was beautiful. He got on his horse and rode down the gully so he could get a little closer. She couldn't see him, so he could get a closer look.

He was watching from the back of his horse when he saw movement on the right of Jo, and she didn't see it. She wasn't paying attention. She was crying. He hadn't seen her smile in so long. It was a coiled rattler, and it was a big one. The only way to help her was to make his presence known and now. He kicked the horse and started down the gully and pulled the shotgun out of the scabbard and was coming off the horse as he got close to her.

She saw him and the snake at the same time. The rattler was already too close and ready to strike, and she grabbed the baby and pulled her to her and turned. If it struck, it would hit her in the back, so Justin shot and cut the snake in half.

Morgan heard the shot, saw Justin by Jo with the gun, assumed the worst, and hit the ground running. Miles was at the barn and did the same.

By the time they were close, Justin was throwing the snake away with the end of the gun, and then he was on the ground, holding Jo and the baby. "Are you all right? Is she all right?"

She just looked at him, kind of stunned, and then said, "Where did you come from, and why are you here?"

By then, Morgan and Miles were there and were wondering the same thing.

"Ever since Shelbee brought me the papers and told me about her, I have been hiding in the hills and watching you and the baby and thinking about what I did to you. I don't know if you can ever forgive me, but I couldn't let you get hurt, so I had to let myself be seen."

They all just stood there. They didn't know what to say.

Morgan went over, stepped on the snakes head, cut off the rattles, handed them to him, and told him, "They are yours, but I still don't trust you." Then she stood back and let Jo talk to him for a minute, but she didn't go too far. Neither did Miles.

"Should we leave them alone?"

She stood just where she was. She wasn't going any farther. "Justin, I don't know what you want from me. You treat me like trash and divorce me, and then you watch me from the hills? I want a man who wants a wife, not a slave, or a man who is not so jealous that I can't even talk to another man."

"I am trying to understand. I have been reading my father's letters to my mother, and I don't know how she stood him for so long. Maybe you could let me see you for a while each day and try again so I could see you and the baby. Would you at least let me try?"

Jo looked back at Morgan, and Morgan begrudgingly nodded because she knew how miserable she was. Jo was smiling for the first time in such a long time. Maybe it was worth it.

"I have a camp up in the hills. I will stay there tonight and tomorrow and then I will move back to town into the hotel. Maybe I can come out here for a while each day if that is all right?"

Morgan nodded. She started back to the house. If she had looked at the sky, she would have told him to move to town now.

Supper was cooking when she and her aunt started looking at the sky. They both walked around the house and then started to gather up the candles and the lanterns. Mary Jean was riding in by then, and the men were letting the horses out.

She yelled at one of the men to saddle Thunder, and he looked at her strangely. She told him to bring him up to the house.

Miles had walked out by then and asked her, "What is going on? It is just a thunderstorm."

She looked at him and pointed to some clouds. "See those clouds that look like round balls? Those aren't good clouds. There is a reason this is called Tornado Alley around here, and those clouds are why. This storm is coming in backward, and that isn't good either. We are in for some really bad weather, so we are getting the kids ready for the cellar. We have one for more than just pickles."

"Where do you think you are going in this weather?"

Her aunt was handing her the saddlebags, and they were full of something.

"Where do you think? He is up there on top of a hill. He doesn't know what is coming, and he will get killed. I am going to get him down from there. At the bottom of the canyon is a cave, and we will get there and spend the night, so I won't be back till morning."

About that time, Mary Jo came out of her room, and she was in a panic. "Morgan, he doesn't know about these storms. He will get hurt." You could already hear the lightning cracking in the distance and the thunder beginning to roll.

"I know, honey. I am going to go get him, and we will go to the cave. Just take care of Justine for me, and go to the cellar. I have to go while I still have light."

She kissed Miles, grabbed the saddlebags, pulled on her slicker, and went out the door. She got up on Thunder, and off they went at a dead run. She had a pretty good idea where he was, so she headed straight there, and sure enough, she wasn't far off.

When she got to his camp, he had a fire going and was cooking supper. "Put out that fire and saddle your horse, and do it now. We are running out of light, and we need to get out of here now."

He didn't even ask questions of this woman. He just did as she said.

She got down and helped him get the fire out as he saddled the horse. He started to gather up things, and she told him, "Just things you can't afford to lose, and be quick." So he just grabbed the letters. Before he got up in the saddle, she handed him a slicker, and he put it on. They started down the trail, and then the clouds closed over them.

"Hand me your reins, and just hang on. My horse can get us down this trail."

He did as he was told because he couldn't see in front of him, and he didn't know how she was. It took a while, but they soon were in a cave at the bottom of a ravine, and she told him to look for some wood before it started raining so they could have a fire. He started dragging in everything he could find inside the cave, and she had lit a lantern she had brought. She had the horses inside, and then it was like the heavens opened, and the winds were horrific. She got a fire going like nothing was going on, and then she took care of the horses as he watched the storm. He would have been in serious trouble on that hill. The lightning alone was hitting the ground and lighting up trees.

"You shouldn't stand so close to the opening. The lightning could still hit you there. Move back in some. You will be safer. And get closer to the fire. I brought you some food. It is in the saddlebags. Hand them to me."

"Why did you come after me? You could have left me up there, and it would have solved all your problems."

She didn't answer him. She just kept unloading the saddlebags, but he kept pressing.

"Why, Morgan? You aren't generally this forgiving."

"Because she still loves you—God knows why—and she is miserable. Nothing is helping, and I fear for her. But I promise you, if you screw up again, she won't have to divorce you. Next time, she will be a widow. Do we understand each other, Justin?"

She turned around and looked at him, and he just nodded, then she turned back around and was putting out some jars of food that her aunt had packed for her. He walked up behind her, and when she stood up and turned around, he kissed her.

She looked at him and then asked him, "What was that for?"

He looked at her in her Western boots and jeans; she looked a lot like she had the night at Virgie's when he had first seen her. "I always wondered what it would be like to kiss you, and Mary Jo has always wondered if it was you I wanted and if I just substituted her instead."

"Well, what do you think? Which one is it you want?"

"Well, it really wasn't a real kiss, so I won't ever really know, will I?"

As he started to turn around, she grabbed his face and kissed him, and it was a real kiss. There was no doubting she meant it. "No fireworks for me. How about you, Justin? There is only one man that makes my world round, and he is the only one I have ever wanted."

He smiled at her, and then he told her, "You are the strangest woman I have ever met, but you are right. You don't make me feel like Jo does when you kiss me. No one does."

"Then stop acting like a jackass and take care of her like you love her and that baby."

"You would have killed me that night, wouldn't you?"

She was standing at the front of the cave and watching the weather, and she looked at him and told him, "You are the only one who has ever seen that woman up close and not wound up dead, so yes."

He just stood beside her and then asked her, "What are you looking for?"

"Watch the lightning. When it lights up the clouds, look for long tails. Those are tornadoes. The house ought to be all right. Everybody ought to be in the fruit cellar if it is too bad. It generally goes over the top of the canyon, but your camp will be gone in the morning."

"You saved my life. It would have killed me."

"The wind or the lightning would have yes. You were in the wrong place for this storm. I should have paid more attention this afternoon and had you come down to the barn. By the time I figured out this storm was going to be a bad one, I had to make a mad dash to find you."

"Did Jo send you?"

"Of course she did, you idiot. Why else would I be out here in this weather? I probably would have let you stay out there. You could have found some rocks to hide in."

He looked at the little grin on her face. She probably would have too.

"Come on, let's eat. We are going to be here all night."

They sat by the campfire and had what her aunt had packed in mason jars and biscuits wrapped in dishcloths then lay on the saddle blankets and saddles to sleep.

In the morning, they were awakened by Miles and Raphael on horseback at the front of the cave, looking for them.

"Good morning, darlin'. Is everything all right at the ranch?"

Miles just smiled at her, as did Raphael. "Everything's fine. The storm made a mess but nothing major. We found what was left of his camp. He had better have gotten anything important because it was swept clean. You got him out of there just in time from what we saw. The trees are ripped up. A little twister or straight-line winds went through there."

He looked at her. He wouldn't have survived last night. He wondered if she regretted that or not, but he didn't ask. He had a second chance. He had better use it wisely.

"Well, let's get out of here. I smell like my horse, and I am hungry." Raphael had already dismounted to saddle her horse as she gathered up their things on the ground. Miles was helping her so they could leave. "What are you going to do with him?"

"Justin, you can go to town and get a room at the hotel and see Mary Jo for a couple of hours a day until this is settled. Agreed? We will go to the ranch and have breakfast first so she can see you are all right."

He nodded to whatever she wanted as long as he could see Jo and the baby until he made this right.

When they got to the ranch, Jo was waiting at the door with Hazel in her arms, and she looked better than she had in months. Morgan had to say if this man was who she wanted, she was going to whip him into shape or beat him into shape until he was a decent man.

They went into breakfast, and she went to her bedroom and took a quick bath. She really did smell like her horse after sleeping on her horse blanket all night. After changing clothes, she was met in the hallway by Mary Jo, and she told her the plan to have him stay in town and come out a few hours a day until they were all satisfied he could behave himself and not hurt her.

CHAPTER 12

The next day, Mary Jo looked better than she had in months, and Morgan had a plan on what to do to straighten Justin up, but she didn't know if it would work or not. They were also planning a wedding as well, so the women were working on that in the house, and Morgan and the men were still trying to get the horses and cattle separated and ready for sale or into the pastures they belonged in.

When Justin came out, he and Mary Jo sat on the back porch for a while with the baby and just talked as Morgan watched, and then she rode up and told him, "All right, Justin, you are going to work with me in the corral. We will see if you can take orders from a woman without losing your temper." She knew he didn't like it, but she wasn't going to just let him take Jo home until she felt she was safe, and she didn't yet.

Justin looked at her and asked, "Where do you want me, and what do you want me to do?"

"Grab a horse and start working those steers into the pens so we can move them to the pastures."

She was already in the corral and working cattle where she wanted into the pasture when she saw one of the young bulls she thought she had already sorted out had gotten back in. He had backed Justin into a corner, and he was getting mad and yelling at one of her men.

"Justin, just give me a minute, and I will get him out of here and get him back into the pasture."

About that time, Justin took his whip and lashed out at the young bull, and he panicked and started through the fence, and he was going to get himself killed or hurt somebody else. Morgan got him maneuvered around so Raphael could get the bull out of the corral and to the pasture. Justin was still yelling and was off his horse, going after one of her men. Morgan stopped, got down, walked by the horse trough, grabbed a pail, filled it with water, walked over to Justin, and dumped it on his head.

He turned around and was going to say something when she stopped him. "You have about one minute to cool off and think about what you are going to say before I toss you off this ranch. You took a whip to that bull and scared him after I told you not to. Now do you have anything to say to me?"

He just stared at her for a minute as the men waited for an explosion, but none came, and then he smiled. "No ma'am it won't happen again. Shall we get back to work?"

Miles was watching from the barn. He had his hand on his pistol.

Well, one down and a long way to go.

The rest of the afternoon went reasonably well, and he kept his temper under control—barely. He had supper with them and then went back to town.

Morgan was exhausted. It was more tiring just trying to make him be nice than fighting with him.

"Is it worth it, honey?" Miles asked as he helped her undress.

Then he was kissing her shoulder.

"It would be a lot easier and a lot more fun if I could make him do what you are doing. This trying to keep him in line is exhausting, and I don't know if he is going to stay that way when and if she goes home with him."

"She was watching all day long what you were doing and how you were doing it. I don't think she will let him cow her again like she did before."

"I kissed him in the cave that night when we were in the storm."

He turned around in his arms and looked at her. "Why would you do that? Did he force you?"

She just looked at him and shrugged. "No. He had kissed me, and it surprised me, and then he told me that Jo had always wondered if she was his second choice, so I kissed him and asked him what he thought."

"And what did he think?"

"She wasn't his second choice, and now he knew, and I told him you had always been the only man I had ever wanted, so he should start treating Jo like she was what he wanted."

"That isn't all, is it, Morgan? You threatened him, didn't you?"

She looked at him and started to unbutton his shirt and just smiled at him, and he knew Justin wouldn't survive a second time if he hurt Mary Jo. "Why don't you get back to the kissing me part while the baby is asleep? Things were just getting interesting."

They did get quite interesting, even though they got a little noisy, but Justine was sleeping much better lately, even through a little noise. Miles had Morgan soaring and over the top before they got too noisy and woke her up, and then they were both giggling to each other.

"You know, I think it is time that Justine got her own room next door, don't you? So we can have some privacy of our own."

Morgan was still grinning at him and finally said, "I think we need a door put through that wall, don't you? Tomorrow, I will have a carpenter start drawings for some modifications on this room. Now I have to feed your daughter who you woke up."

"Me? I don't think it was just me who woke her up. You had something to do with it too."

She just went and picked up the baby and went to the rocker, and he watched as she fed his precious little girl. If Justin wasn't so stupid, he could have all this, but it might take a shovel to his head to make him realize it.

The next day went better. She didn't have to put a pail of water on his head but almost did. When she called it a day, they both stomped away, and she got on her horse and rode away. He went inside and had supper with Jo and the baby and then went to town, and Miles went looking for Morgan.

She was at the top of the canyon, just sitting there, looking out at the view, and trying to calm down. He sat down beside her and waited for her to talk to him. He didn't have to wait long.

"Any better today?" he asked as he looked straight ahead into the canyon.

"Some, but he is the most stubborn man I have ever met, and that is saying something."

He smiled and kept his mouth shut. She was one to talk. They were two of a kind. She just couldn't see that because it was right in front of her, but she didn't hurt the people she loved. He did.

"Do you think you can fix him, or is he a lost cause?"

She looked at him sideways. "Either I am going to fix him, or we are going to kill each other because she loves him. Don't you see how much better she is in just the few days since he has been back?"

He had seen the difference—everyone had—but they didn't have to deal with him. She did. Morgan didn't know that there was always someone watching them with a gun on him just in case he got out of hand.

The wedding between Raphael and Mary Jean was this Sunday, and Justin had been invited, so he was going to meet them at the church, but that left two more days she had to deal with him on the ranch. They had to have the cattle and horses taken care of before the snow got here, and they were running out of time. The next two days went pretty smoothly. He didn't come out till late. He had to be at the telegraph office and send some instructions to his ranch manager so his ranch was taken care of as well.

Sunday came, and the wedding was going well. Mary Jo and Abigail were standing up for Mary Jean, and Morgan was taking care of both of their babies. Abigail had a little boy named Mathew, who was three months old, but when she had him, her headaches had become so bad; the doctor had told her she shouldn't get pregnant again. Whatever was wrong in her head was getting worse, and even a trip to a Dallas doctor hadn't given them any answers.

Jackson and Gary Lee stood up for Raphael. It was a family wedding, but this wasn't a small wedding, so the church was full.

Before the wedding was over, Abigail began to look pale. Morgan motioned to Mary Jo, and she looked beside her and grabbed her arm and held her up until the ceremony was over, and then they got her to a pew and sat her down. After they sat her down, she was brushing their hands away and making nothing of it, and she was saying it was just hot up on the podium. Both of the other women looked at each other, and they knew she was lying.

When Mary Jo walked away, she looked over at Morgan and took her little boy and asked her, "Morgan, I don't think I have much time left, and you are going to have to take care of Jackson and my baby boy Mathew. Will you promise me that you will do that? You have always been my friend, and I don't think my family is going to keep it together, even though they have known this was coming for a long time. You have to promise me."

"I will do whatever needs to be done when it needs to be done. You can count on me."

She just sighed like a load had been lifted off her shoulders, and they went back to watching the wedding. Morgan watched her as she held her baby boy. She loved him so much.

Jackson came over and checked on both of them. "Are you all right, honey? I saw you sit down. Do you have a headache?"

She looked up at him with such love in her eyes. Morgan just sat there and kept her mouth shut. "No, honey, just got a little too hot up there, so I sat down to take care of the baby. Go congratulate your sister. Are they going on a honeymoon?"

"Not till the cattle are all in and taken care of in a few weeks, and then they are going to go somewhere. Don't know where yet."

That afternoon, while everyone was in town and they were dressed up, Morgan had the photographer take every family's picture, even Justin and Mary Jo. She got some balking from some of the men, but she was pretty sure it was going to be the last time that some of them would all be together, and she wanted pictures.

Justin asked her later, "What, are you afraid you will kill me and my child will need a picture of me to remember me by?" He said it half kidding.

It wasn't him. She was worried Mathew wouldn't see his mother growing up.

The next week went by, and Justin was turning into almost a decent man. She hadn't had to dunk him but twice. The men watched them like a couple of the young bulls sparring and kicking up dust, just waiting to charge, but they generally both backed down. They had everything moved and all the cattle and horses settled and in pastures when it snowed—and boy, did it snow—and the wind howled.

Justin got caught at the ranch and had to stay the night. He stayed in the same room with Mary Jo, and Morgan just about came unglued, but Miles told her it was Mary Jo's idea, and she had to let her decide sooner or later.

The next day, Morgan still wasn't happy, but she couldn't say much. He had been pretty good. They walked outside into the snow, and the men were walking to the barn when Mary Jean picked up a handful of snow and started to throw it at Raphael, but Morgan stopped her and grabbed a handful of her own. Then she looked at Justin walking away and threw it at him and creamed him in the back of the head.

He looked back at her and said, "What the hell was that for, woman?"

She looked at him and held her hands out. "Really? You have never had a snowball fight? Where have you been living? On the far side of the moon?"

He looked around at the other men who were smiling at him. "You mean I can throw back at her as hard as I want and hit her?"

Raphael answered for all of them because their wives were out there now. "Oh yes, sir, we all can."

Morgan held up her hand and said, "Wait just a minute. There are a few rules. No rocks or ice in the snowballs, Gary Lee."

"That wasn't me. That was Mary Jean."

"Really? I always thought it was you." She looked back to see her cousin at the door shrugging and smiling.

Then her aunt came out. "Go to the end of the house away from the windows so you don't break the glass, and you have to quit when breakfast is ready."

Then Morgan said, "Guys on that side of the wall, and girls on this side. Now go."

They all went running, but Justin got Morgan on the side of the head before she made it to the drift at the side of the house. It seemed she was his main target, and he was hers. They took out all the frustration they had on each other all those days with snowballs.

When her aunt finally called them in, they were all frozen, and the women had to stand in front of the fireplace in the bedrooms before they could feed their babies because the babies wouldn't let them touch them.

They were so cold.

That night, Justin was again staying because the drifts were just too high to get to town. Miles and Morgan were in the main room when Mary Jo and Justin came in and sat down with them. Justin started the conversation.

"You already know what I am going to ask, so what do you think, Morgan? You are the one she is going to ask for permission."

Morgan looked at him. Today, they had fought with snowballs. He hadn't lost his temper, and he had acted like he was having fun. Jo had told her later she had never seen him that way.

"I don't know what to tell you. I am not sure I trust you, but we can't do this forever. You are divorced, and I remember every word you put on that paper, and she should too. You will have to remarry if you want to go back with him, and if you do, I want a telegraph from you once a week so I know you are all right, and if I don't get one, I will send someone after you. I will send Raphael or Miles, but I will send someone to check on you. I promised him you wouldn't need a divorce twice. The next time, you would be a widow. Am I understood, Jo?"

She looked at her, kind of shocked, and then she nodded. All this was to protect her, and she wouldn't do it again. If she couldn't protect herself from him, Morgan would permanently.

"If you want, we can have the preacher come out here and do the ceremony so the whole town doesn't have to know your business, but you are going to have to talk to your sister and ask her forgiveness. I don't know if you can fix that relationship yet. It may take some more time."

Justin just nodded. His sister hadn't said a word to him since the day she had been to his hotel room, not even at the wedding.

"Shelbee will either forgive or she won't. That is her decision. One thing at a time she has held this resentment for you a long time."

They went back to their room, and Miles looked at her. She still didn't trust him. "What is wrong, honey?"

She looked at him, and then she finally told him what had been said at the church. He stopped rocking and took her hand. "You knew this was coming. She just put it into words. Now we have to prepare for it."

"I know, but I don't know how to tell Mary Jo or even if I should tell her before she goes."

They sat there a while and watched the fire until she said, "I think I will just keep this between us and let them see if they can work out their problems without worrying about Jackson and Abigail until we have to."

Miles just nodded. So she was going to keep it all to herself and bear the guilt if need be and try and give them a start.

The next morning, they started packing and getting ready to head back to Colorado. Preparations were made to have the preacher out to the house when the weather was better, and a small group of family was to be present, including Jackson and Abigail. Within a week, they were off back to Colorado, but before they went, Morgan took Mary Jo aside and talked to her.

"At the fort, there is a Commander Williams who helped me and Miles when Standing Bear had me. He has continued his stay at the fort and has brought his wife out here to live with him. Could you please keep an ear out for the Comanche's coming down off the mountains for me? I know Standing Bear will never come off that mountain alive, but Still Water might if things get bad enough. There is a General Custer trying to run the Sioux to the ground and make a name for himself, and it is going to get a lot of people killed. I am going to send money with you because I have seen how Indian agents treat Indians at the forts. If you can help them, use it. If you hear anything about her, get in touch with me, and I will help her."

Mary Jo looked at her and asked her, "You would help them after what was done to you?"

"They kept me alive when most Indians would have killed me or worse, and you don't want to know worse. She helped me get away from him because she loved him, and they are dying up there, and I know it."

"I will get in touch with the commander and his wife and see what I can find out. I left an envelope with some money for Abigail for the dress. She finished it while you were trying to make Justin a new man. If things work out, I am going to wear it to the governor's ball this year. She was shaking so badly by the time she finished it, I don't know how she did **finish it.**"

"Is it all right?"

"If it isn't, I will have someone else correct it. You watch out for her. You know she doesn't have much longer." So Jo knew after all.

Morgan just nodded, and they hugged, and Morgan told her, "She knows, and it is taken care of."

They walked out of the bedroom and met the men by the door, and out they went to the train station.

She got a telegraph the first couple of weeks, and everything was going well. Then she got a letter from Jo, and there had been an incident.

Dear Morgan,

Well, he finally lost it, but you would have been proud of me. I didn't let him scream at me and get away with it. I pushed him into the horse trough in front of his men. He came out soaking wet, and his men didn't say a word. They just started walking backward, and I starting talking. I told him to calm down or I would start packing. Then I started to walk to the house.

All of a sudden, I got a snowball in the back. I looked back, and he was smiling at me. Before long, the hands and all of us were having a snowball fight, but I stopped it because Justin was soaking wet. He told the hands to finish what we were doing, and we went inside, and I got him into a hot bath. Afterward, I was drying him off and tried a couple of those tricks you told me about, and now my dear husband thinks we should solve all our disputes with snowball fights and a hot bath. You are going to have to tell me where you learned those little tricks.

I got in touch with Commander Williams and met his wife Rachel, and you are going to love her. She is a stick of dynamite wrapped in a small package. She is beautiful, and she is as concerned about the Indians as are we. The Indian agent is letting them starve. He was selling off all their provisions. I provided cattle for them, and the commander saw to it they got them with a military escort. I was told Standing Bear is very ill, but Still Water and the children are all right for now.

She showed the letter to Miles and Martha Jean, and Mary Jo's mother was very happy.

"Do you think she is lying to you? Would she tell you the truth?"

Morgan looked at her aunt. "She went through a lot of trouble to tell me about the Indians and about Richard and Rachel, and she is just talking. I don't think she would do that if she was in trouble. She would word her letter differently."

Her aunt looked at her. "You talked about this, didn't you, if something was wrong? Some word or phrase?"

"Yes, and she hasn't used it. I told her to go to Richard and his wife at the fort if she felt threatened, and I contacted him and told him what was going on so he knew and told him to protect her if she needed help until Miles could come get her."

Her aunt just looked at her and then smiled. "You didn't let her go back unprotected, did you?"

"Of course I would never have let her go if I didn't have a plan in place. Do I suddenly look stupid?"

Her aunt took her in her arms and just hugged her and then walked away.

Miles watched and smiled. He had known about the letter to the commandant and his wife. She had everything ready before Jo left to go back to Colorado, and he knew they had a code if she got in trouble. She had left nothing to chance. Now it was all up to Justin. He thought everything was taken care of, and they were just waiting to see what was going to happen with the Comanches on that mountain. He was wrong.

It was time for Gregory's birthday or what they thought was his birthday; he didn't know. They had taken the date on the picture and made a guess of when they thought she would have been due and set a date from letters Glen had sent his brother and come up with October 25. It was as close as they could figure, and that was a few days away.

They were going to town this morning. She had a present ordered for him, and it should be here, and Mama Ruby and Ivy were coming with her. Rosa was at the house, cooking, and she needed some supplies, so they headed to the general store first, and Raphael was with her. Miles and a couple of the men went ahead of her to the stables. They had bought it from Arnold last year when he wanted to retire, and he went to check on it.

Ruby and Ivy were in the wagon with Gregory, and they went in the general store as she tied up her horse, and Raphael followed her in. They headed to the back.

"Ruby you start getting your supplies while I look in back room at that other item."

Ruby knew what she was looking at. She had ordered a small saddle for Greg's birthday. She had one specially made in Dallas for him—all the ones around here were too big—and she had a colt picked out for Greg that she had been training just for him to ride.

She and Raphael went in the back as two men came in the front, and one of them started to give Ivy some trouble.

"Well, look here. I had a gal like this one back in Georgia before the war, and she was all mine, and if she talked back, I could teach her a few manners on a whipping post. Not like today where we have to be so nice."

They were both laughing. It was the first time in a long time that Ruby was actually scared. These men were hardcore Confederates, and she had Gregory with her as well as Ivy.

She backed away and pushed Gregory behind the counter, and then she called for Morgan. "Miss Morgan, we need you out here."

"Oh, who are you calling for? Is your lady going to protect you?"

Morgan walked to the door first and was going out when the other man said, "Oh, *Chiquita*, come on out and play with me. We will have some fun."

She thought she might be sick, but she shut the door just enough so they couldn't see Raphael behind her. She turned her head and said quietly to him, "Raphael, go out the back door, go get Miles and the other men, and tell them I need help. Then get on a horse and get back to the ranch. Don't come back to town, and make sure no one sees you."

"What is wrong? I am not leaving you alone."

"That man talking is one of the men who were with your brother the day I was taken from the ranch in Dallas, and he might recognize you. Now do what I say and get out of here now." Then she opened the door and walked out of it and closed it behind her. As she heard the back door shut, Raphael was gone and going for help.

As she walked out, she recognized the man instantly. He didn't seem to recognize her, or he hadn't yet.

The woman walking out of the back room wasn't what they were expecting. She was in jeans and Indian boots, and she was wearing a pistol—it was tied down—and she had a knife in her boot.

"Get away from my women and my son." She motioned the women into the back room, and Ruby got both of them into the back room as the Mexican man was beginning to realize he might know this woman.

"I know you from somewhere, don't I?"

She just looked at him and smiled. She needed to stall for some time. Besides, she wanted to know why these men were here. "Maybe from somewhere. Why are you men here, it doesn't seem like you would have any business in this part of the world."

"Our boss is looking for a family named McKinney. It seems his sister was married to a man named McKinney, and she had a son with him, and now he is looking for the kid."

Now she really did feel sick. Gregory's family had come looking for him, and now they were here. Well, they weren't going to get him, but one thing at a time. She could see by the look on the other man's face he was beginning to figure out who she was, and he was reaching for his gun.

"That would be a stupid idea. I never did know your name, but I remember that voice and your face as long as I live." She had already pulled the leather strap off the top of her pistol and had her hand on it and was ready to pull it if she needed to.

"You are the girl from the ranch in Dallas who we sold to White Cloud, the one that got Juan killed."

"You blame me for getting him killed? You kidnap me and short a Comanche war chief, and it is my fault you get half the state of Texas and the rangers on top of you? What did you think was going to happen?"

The other man looked at her. "Who are you?"

"Then I was Morganna McKinney Calderon. Now I am Morganna McKinney Douglas. Either way, you are in a lot of trouble, and the little boy you are looking for is now my son. Who is your boss?"

"Shawn Williams. He is across the street."

Both men looked at each other. They didn't care anymore who she was. They needed to get out of here, but it was too late. When they turned to leave, there were several men standing at the door, waiting, and one was a sheriff. They had been watching and listening, especially Miles and he had his gun drawn. She just looked at them, smiling, and the Mexican man knew he was dead. She would have him hanged for what he had done, so he drew on her.

He should have taken his chances with a judge. It wouldn't have mattered either way. Most of her men had heard about her skills but had never seen them. They did today. He never even got his gun out of the holster, and then he was dead on the floor. Well, Raphael was safe at least. The sheriff took the other man while she started across the street. She wanted to talk to Gregory's uncle.

When she got to the hotel, she asked the desk clerk which room he was in, and he told her number 10. She started up the stairs. Miles was behind her.

"Stay down here for a bit till I see what is going on with this man. Have the men help Ruby at the store. I forgot about her, and she has got Greg."

She went upstairs and went to room 10 and knocked on the door.

Someone yelled at her, "What the hell do you want? It is too early in the morning."

So she backed up and kicked the door open. After all, she had just killed a man. She wasn't in the best mood, and this man was pissing her off. She hadn't even met him yet.

He turned and looked at her, and there was a woman next to him in bed. She had seen her before; she worked for the hotel. Morgan didn't care. Work was work, and there wasn't much for a woman out here.

"Honey, you need to leave. He and I need to talk." She was terrified and scrambling.

"Take your time. I am not going to hurt you."

So she dressed and was going to leave when Morgan told the man in bed, "Pay the lady."

The woman looked surprised, and when he paid her—and Morgan didn't think it was enough—she said, "She is a pretty lady. I think she deserves more than that."

Then he threw her a twenty-dollar gold piece. "Much better. You have good day, honey."

The woman nodded to her as she left. It was probably more money than she made in a month.

After she left, Morgan sat down in a chair across the room, and the man sat up in the bed and asked her, "Who are you, and why are you here?"

"A couple of your men told me you were looking for a McKinney, and I am one. You were also looking for someone who knew Donald Glen. He was my uncle. What do you want?"

He was looking at her more closely now. "They say one of the McKinney women is raising my nephew. Is it you?"

"Yes, it is. Why did you want to know after all this time?"

"He is family. I want to take him back home with me."

"You don't have a home anymore. Didn't you ride with Quantrill and his band? There are still people who would hang you if they could get their hands on you, and we both know it. He is my family as well. He was my uncle's son, and now he is mine, and I will kill you before I will let you take him from me."

He leaned on his elbow and looked at her and kind of smirked. "Do you think you are good enough to do that?"

"Oh, I don't know. I killed one of your men a while ago. Shall we ask him?"

That got him very interested in her all of a sudden. "Why did you kill one of my men?"

"He was with a band of Comancheros that kidnapped me several years ago, and then he pulled a gun on me. Wrong move to make this early in the morning."

"I have seen him draw. He was fast. You're the Calderon girl? I thought the Indians killed you."

She just raised her eyebrows. "A lot of people think that, they are wrong. What was the name of the man who brought your sister down here, looking for her husband's family?"

"His name was Kevin Stewart. They were supposed to be married, and then she married your uncle, and it infuriated my father."

She just looked at the man lying in bed. He looked so much like the picture of his sister.

"He brought her here, all right, but not to find our family. He just brought her here to torture her. No one in the town they lived in even knew there was a child living with them. He beat her to death with a hammer and tried to kill Gregory as well, and then he buried both of them. Greg got out of his grave and went after Kevin, who was busy hanging himself, or he would have finished the job, I am sure. Gregory piled rocks on his mother's grave and then walked three days to a way station, where I found him half-starved and wearing rags. I took him with me, and he has been mine ever since and always will be. We have a deal. I didn't find out until later who he was when I met Glen's commanding officer."

"I don't even know where she is buried."

Morgan didn't know whether she should tell him or not, but she would have wanted to know. "She is buried at my ranch. I had her dug up and moved there, and she is buried beside Glen so they would be close to Greg. He hardly knew her in life, but Sandra died trying to protect him. She will at least be where he can honor her in death."

He had no right to Sandra's child. He knew that now. This woman would raise him with a home and a life that Sandra would have wanted him to have and died trying to give him. "Will you at least let me see him? You don't have to tell him who I am. Just let me see him, and then I will take my men and leave."

She looked at him and nodded then stood up to leave, but there was one more question she wanted answered.

"Your father is dead, right?" He nodded.

"Where and how?"

"We were close to New Orleans and needed a change of horses, and a man told us about a squawman and his wife on a small ranch outside of town. We raided the ranch and killed the woman, and the man came running around the side of the house, and he shot my father twice before one of our men shot him. I saw him get to his wife and pull her into his arms while the house burned. My father died several hours later. We couldn't stop the bleeding. He was a stupid man who would willingly marry a Comanche woman."

"You really should be careful how you talk around me. I was saved by a Comanche war chief after that raid in Dallas. I think more of that Comanche chief than the men who shot an unarmed Comanche woman on her own porch, so if I were you, I would keep my mouth shut around here. My family lost people to Quantrill's butchers."

He started to defend himself and then thought better of it. His men had been nothing better than butchers, and that was why his sister ran. "You are the woman they talk about who killed all those bounty hunters after they raided that Indian village, aren't you? And you killed Calderon to get back your inheritance?"

She nodded.

He had heard all the stories, but he never thought he would ever meet the woman they talked about. Well, at least Sandra's child would be safe even from him.

"I will meet you downstairs. We are trying to get ready for Greg's birthday."

"How did you figure out the date?"

She looked at him funny. "We guessed nobody knew for sure. Do you know the actual date?"

"I was there when she delivered him. It is October 30."

Well, they hadn't been off a lot. Well, next year, they would get it on the right day. "Thank you. She didn't leave anything with the date on it."

He smiled. At least he knew something she didn't know. Sandra would have liked her son to a least have the right birthday.

She left the room, and he was dressing, and he pulled out the little box he had carried all this way. It was Sandra's, and he wanted to give it to Gregory, and today was the day because he would probably never see him again. She was right. There were people who hunted them. Quantrill's men were hated, and people still wanted them on dead both sides.

When he was dressed, he went downstairs and met her on the sidewalk with her husband. Morgan watched, and Miles didn't recognize him. If they could just get through the next few minutes, he would be gone, and they could get back to their lives.

Mama Ruby was coming from across the street with Greg, and he took off and was running to her. "Mama, we heard shooting, and somebody shot a man in the general store while we were in the back. Are you all right?"

She smiled at him and lifted him up and held him on her hip as he put his arms around her neck. He never saw her as the monster lady. She was just his mama.

"There is a little saddle in the back room. Mama, is it for me? Is that my birthday present?"

"You spoiled the surprise, you little stinkweed. What am I going to do with you? I can't ever keep a secret from you."

"It is beautiful, Mama. Is it for that foal you have been training? Is he going to be mine?"

She kissed him on the cheek and then told him, "Yes, he is for you but not quite yet. You have to act surprised tonight when I give you that saddle, all right?"

He nodded and smiled at her.

"I want you to meet someone. He knew your mother. His name is Shawn."

Then she turned, and Shawn looked at Gregory, and he looked like his sister. He was such a happy little boy.

He reached out his hand and shook his nephew's hand and said to him, "It looks like you are happy here, young man. I must say you look a lot like your mother."

"How did you know my mother?"

Morgan looked at him with a warning glance.

"We grew up in the same town and were friends. When I started to head this way, my sister had something of your mother's and asked me to see if I could find any of the McKinney family and give this to you. It was hers. She left it behind when she left with Kevin."

Gregory almost yanked his hand out of Shawn's and then shivered. Gregory reached out and took it from Shawn, and Morgan helped him hold it. It was small music box, so she put him down on the sidewalk, and he held it. "How does it work, Mama?"

She turned it over and wound it up, and then when he opened it, it played a tune, and Gregory smiled as he listened. He pulled out a small cameo necklace, a ring that matched, and a wedding ring. Morgan had always wondered what had happened to Sandra's. She didn't have it on when they had dug her up. She must have hidden it from her father or Kevin. Well, now Gregory had it.

"This was my mama's jewelry?"

Shawn just nodded as the little boy cried, and Morgan picked him back up. "Now you have something of your real mama's to put up for safekeeping to give to your wife or children."

He just looked at Morgan strangely. "You are my real mama too. You saved me."

Shawn didn't miss any of this. His nephew was safe here and loved by this woman and her family. That was a statement for her courage. Morgan was his mother now, and as far as he was concerned, none of his other family would ever know where Gregory was. It was their secret.

"This man has to be leaving now, so say goodbye."

Gregory shook his hand and gathered up the little music box and went with Ruby, and they got in the wagon and started down the street.

"Do you need money or my help with anything to raise him?"

She looked back at him. "All I need from your family is your absence. I don't ever want him to know who his grandfather or you were, and neither did his mother, so don't come back. I am having your other man released from jail, so get out of town, and the sheriff doesn't know who you are. He will next time. I will see to burying the other man."

"How many men have you put in that cemetery?"

She didn't even answer. She walked back inside the hotel. She wanted to talk to the desk clerk.

Miles answered his question after she left. "There are seven graves out there with dead bounty hunters in them. She doesn't know I recognized you from that day in Louisiana, but I did. Your father was the one who shot my wife, wasn't he?"

Shawn just stood there and didn't say anything he knew.

"She obviously has made some sort of arrangement with you to go away and not let Greg know his family is a bunch of murdering bastards, but if I ever see your face again, you will pay for killing my wife." He walked past him and into the hotel.

Shawn hadn't even known that her husband was the man on the porch. He thought they had killed him. He gathered his men, and they started to leave. He would get the rest of his things in a bit, and they would be gone and never come back to this part of the world. They were running out of world to run to.

Morgan went up to the hotel clerk and asked him, "Who was the woman in the room with that man out front a while ago? She looked familiar."

He grinned a dirty grin and then said, "Oh, the whore? Her name is Ellen Griffith."

Morgan looked at him. She thought she recognized that girl, and she wasn't much more than a girl. "I don't like that word. Don't call her that again. Where is she now?"

"She is probably dressing in the back room. I let her change in there."

"How generous of you," Morgan said sarcastically.

"Listen, lady, I could make the whores change in the outhouse. They don't give me that much of their cut."

Morgan just kind of turned her head, and Miles smiled. This man was fixing to get it, so he just stood back and watched.

"I told you I don't like that word, and you get part of their cut? Just how many of the ladies are you running in here? And does the management know about it?"

"Of course they don't. Then they would want a cut as well. They just pay my wage and stay out of my way, and I don't give a damn what you think about what I call these women."

"Who does sign your paycheck? Now I am interested."

"An M. Douglas, so you will have to find out for yourselves who owns this place."

She just looked at him. Miles sat down. This was getting good. "You didn't ask my name or my husband's. Don't you want to know who is getting you fired?"

He had a kind of sick look on his face, especially when he looked at Miles.

"Who are you? I have only heard you called Morgan."

"I am Mrs. Morganna Douglas, and he is my husband Miles, so either way, your paycheck is signed M. Douglas, but you won't have to worry about that anymore because you are fired. Get out now."

He started scurrying away from her as she turned, and she told Miles, "I am going to the back room. I want to talk to that girl. She and her husband had a ranch out south of us, and I want to know why she is turning tricks in this hotel. Do you think you can hold down the fort for a bit while I talk to her?"

He nodded while she walked to the back.

She found Ellen dressing in the back room while another woman held a small child. There were a couple of other women in the room as well. She knew why they were there. This wasn't the first time she had seen women who kept men entertained. She just didn't like the word "whore" and never had.

"It's Ellen, isn't it? May I speak to you for a minute?"

She started to cry, and then she grabbed the baby. "Please. Thank you for the extra money upstairs, but don't throw us out. I need the money to try and make the mortgage payment for this month, and the other women need the money as well to feed their children."

She looked around at the other women and realized the other women were wearing dresses that were in tatters. The man at the desk was taking a large cut and leaving them with nothing.

"Are you going to call the sheriff on us? We already pay the clerk as much as we can."

"I am not worried about that now. I am worried about what is going on here. Don't you have a ranch and a husband?"

"He disappeared several weeks ago, working cattle, and the sheriff said he abandoned me. The bank is ready to foreclose on my ranch, so I went to doing this to make ends meet."

"The bank didn't offer to buy you out or extend your loan? Did the sheriff not even look for your husband when he disappeared? What about you other women? How did you end up here?"

One woman's husband died in an accident and left her with two little children, and the bank foreclosed on their farm. The other woman's husband did abandon her for another woman, or so it seemed, and she was left with a small house that the bank again foreclosed on.

"Did they not offer to buy them from you? That would have given you some money to at least have gone back home on."

"You don't understand. We don't have anywhere to go. We all have no family to go back to, so the banker had us between a rock and a hard place. He didn't have to offer us anything. He just had to wait for our notes to come due and then kick us out."

She sat there and thought for a minute, and then she called Miles in the back room. She gave him a brief explanation of what was going on, and he was shocked at what was going on. She pulled him aside and talked to him for a minute, and then he nodded. They both sat down on the bed.

"Ellen, do you want to sell your ranch? We will give you a fair price for it. We need the land for my cousin and her husband. As for the rest of you, we just fired the clerk of this hotel, and we need a new one as well as someone to clean the rooms and run this place. Would you women be interested in living here and running this place with a wage?"

"Don't you have to contact the owners and ask permission first?"

"We are the owners."

The women looked at each other and nodded.

"Ellen, you come with us now to the bank, and let's get this started on the ranch before he can foreclose on you. Tomorrow, we will take some men out to your ranch, and we will search it and find your husband if he is there."

She nodded. They all knew if they found him after all this time, they were just recovering a body. She could at least lay him to rest.

As they walked to the bank, she passed Ruby, and she told her what was going on and to take the children back to the ranch with the guards and that they would be along soon. They passed the sheriff along the way, and she stopped and asked him why no one had looked for Ellen's husband when he went missing, and he told her husband's went missing all the time. The sheriff was generally more diligent than this. Who was giving orders around here lately?

When she got inside, she asked to see the president of the bank and was told he was busy.

"We will wait until he is not if it takes all day."

He finally came out of his office. After all, the Douglas's were his biggest clients.

"How may I help you today, Morgan? Is there a problem?"

"I want to buy Ellen's ranch."

"Well, I don't know about that. It may already be in foreclosure."

"Well, you better have the papers to prove it, or I will have a lawyer in here in the morning to fight it and the other foreclosures of the other women at the hotel you threw off their land. I am going to have a federal judge up here by next week looking into your banking practices anyway."

He was turning white, and she was enjoying this. She was

wondering what it took to buy a bank and run it.

"As I said, I want to buy Ellen's ranch. Draw up the papers now because tomorrow, we are starting a search for her husband. You and I know he didn't abandon her. He is on that ranch somewhere, and we are going to find him. He had better not have any bullet holes in him, or I will see someone hang for it."

She didn't know a man could get that white and still stay on his feet, but he did, and they started the paperwork.

"When we get done with that, I want to know why those other women weren't offered a buyout price for their land. They were just thrown off of it. Have the paperwork ready for Gary Lee to oversee in the morning. We will be back."

"Why do you even care? Those women are nothing but whores now."

She turned, and if looks could kill, he would have been dead. "Those women were forced to make a living any way they could because of you, and I am going to find out why. They are living and running my hotel now, and if I ever hear you call them that name again, I will have a piece of you, and I get to pick the piece. Before this is done, I may own this bank as well, so start scrambling."

After they left the bank, Miles was looking at her, and he asked her, "Were you serious about buying the bank?"

"Why not? At least we could see this doesn't happen anymore, and we own half the town anyway. Besides, who better to run a bank than accountants? And James and Francis would be great. The last time I wrote to Francis, she hated Dallas and was talking about coming up here anyway but didn't think we had enough business. Between them and Gary Lee, we could own a bank, couldn't we?"

He just kind of nodded sideways. Might as well. Like she said, they owned everything else or almost all of it.

"You might want to put a couple of our men outside of the bank to watch it and make sure that the banker doesn't decide to make a run to Mexico with all the bank funds tonight with the sheriff in tow."

"I thought you liked the sheriff—or you used to."

"Something is going on, and I don't know what yet."

He nodded and left the guards in town until they found out what was going on.

As they walked back, Shawn and his men were getting ready to go. As Morgan saw one of the men with a rifle in his hand with an Indian cover on it, she started toward him. When she got close to him, she stood in front of him, and then she asked him, "Where did you get that gun, and what do you want for it?"

The man looked at her and kind of laughed at her. "You wouldn't be able to handle a gun like this, woman, so get out of my way."

She didn't, and now she was getting mad. "How much for the gun, and where did you get it?"

Shawn was walking toward her as well as Miles because he could see she was getting mad, and she hadn't done that in a long time.

Shawn told the man, "Tell her what she wants to know now."

He watched her face. She was changing. Miles was holding her arm and talking into her ear.

"I won it in a poker game in Colorado from a soldier. He thought he had a winning hand. He said they took it from a Comanche war chief, and the cover was made by his white captive daughter. He was a captain at a Colorado fort, and he didn't like the woman. He didn't want her to get the gun back, and she had been looking for it. Why do you want it so bad?"

Miles already knew, and Morgan was getting madder by the second. "Morgan, calm down. We will buy it from him."

She just looked at Miles. "One way or the other, I will have it back, Miles. It is mine, and that mealy-mouthed captain had it all along."

Shawn asked Miles, "What does she mean hers?"

"White Cloud was my adopted father. He saved me from the Comancheros. Why do you think I killed that man in the store today? It was because he kidnapped me. And the cover on that rifle, I made for the chief, and if you don't think I can use that gun, ask the dead men on that hill up there. Or ask the sheriff coming this way. I will have it one way or another."

Miles asked the man, "How much did you pay for it?"

"Sixty dollars was the winning pot."

Miles pulled out a hundred-dollar bill and handed it to the man, and Morgan took the gun, and then she turned to Shawn and said, "A lot of Confederate men are going to Mexico to fight with Juarez against the French. Maybe you can find some peace down there. You are never going to find any here. Now go before too many people start asking questions about you."

She pulled a picture of Gregory out of her wallet and handed it to him. "If you ever do find a place, write me with a post office box, and I will send you a picture of him, but don't ever come back. I don't want Greg to ever see your face in the paper hanging from a tree and find out you were with Quantrill's men. Your sister ran trying to get him away from that."

Shawn got on his horse and rode away with his men, and he never looked back, but the man she got the gun from did. He was still angry. If he knew how good she was with that gun or what she was going to find out in the next couple of days, he would have ridden faster.

As she calmed down, they went into the hotel and told the women what was going on with the bank. She told Ellen they would have men there in the morning to start hunting for her husband. If she wanted to go, they would bring an extra wagon to gather her things.

She asked the other women what had happened to their things and found out they were stored in the stables or the bank had put them somewhere to sell later. She told them she would find out where their things were tomorrow and try to get them back. She told the women to go to the general store and get whatever they needed for themselves and their children and put it on her account, especially some new dresses. After all, they needed to look good running the hotel. And no more turning tricks; it wasn't necessary anymore.

They headed home. They still had a birthday party to get ready for. When they got to the ranch, it was lit up and everything was ready, cake and presents and all. Morgan changed, and Mama Ruby as well as Raphael asked what had happened. When she got them aside, she told them everything. She told Raphael to tell the men about it in the morning. She wanted about ten men and two wagons to help Ellen load her things and to find her husband's body, and she was sure they were looking for a body.

She wanted Gary Lee to supervise the bank and a couple of men to stand guard over him as she was pretty sure it was going to get ugly before the day was over. He was also going to talk to the judge in the morning and see if he would join him at the bank while they were at the ranch. Raphael and Mary Jean were going with them. Mary Jean wanted to see the ranch, especially since Morgan had bought it. Raphael and Mary Jean might want to buy it from them. It was close and had good water and a good well. She could hardly wait, even though this wasn't the best of circumstances. She could at least help Ellen load up her stuff and be there if they found her husband's body.

The party went well, and Gregory got everything he wanted and even acted surprised when presented with his new saddle.

When Morgan put him to bed that night, he asked her, "That man today really knew my mother?"

She looked at him and wondered if she should tell him the truth and then decided no. There was too much he wouldn't ever understand about his family. "Yes, he did, and he told me something else. He was there when you were born. He knew your real birthday.

We weren't off much. It is October 30, so next year; we will have it on the right day."

"It doesn't really matter just as long as I am here with everybody.

Do you think they know I am all right and happy?"

She reached down and kissed him. "Oh, I think they have always known. I think that is why I found you. They sent me. How else would I have been in just the right place at the right time unless they had sent me there? Now you go to sleep, Two Bits."

"You haven't called me that in a long time."

"No, I haven't. Happy birthday, my little love."

He just hugged her neck and rolled over, and she covered him up, and she looked out the window to the cemetery and thought to herself, *I will take care of him just like he is my own. Rest in peace.*

She went to her room and snuggled in beside Miles, and he pulled her close to him. They had a door and a room added, so Justine had her own room now. Well, it had been a long day, but she turned over, and she looked at him and said, "We are so lucky we have so much family to watch over us and we are never alone. What would I do without you beside me?"

"I hope you are not going to have to find out anytime soon, but even if I am gone, you are never alone again. You still have our children, and I wouldn't mind adding to that count if you agree."

She smiled at him and ran her hand down his chest, and out came that little devil smile he liked that only he ever saw or had ever seen.

"Really? You don't think this house is full enough as it is?" Her hand moved lower, and her smile became more wicked. He sucked in his breath as she found what she was looking for, and then he said with what breath he had left as he pushed her underneath him and went inside her, "We will add on to the house."

He found her mouth, and they forgot about the house. They could build another house if they wanted to. It didn't really matter. They both wanted more children, and they both wanted each other, so they just enjoyed the moment.

He took his time so they wouldn't wake the baby now, and they had time, so he stroked and brought her almost there and stopped, and she looked up at him and asked, "What are you waiting for? Finish it. You are killing me."

He looked down at her and said, "Oh, I was just wondering if we really needed to buy a bank."

She looked at him like she wanted to kill him until she realized he was just giving her a hard time. Well, she could play that game too. So she flipped him over, and now she was on top, and then she started to play. As she moved her hips, she started to talk, and she was driving him mad. "Well, let's see. We could give out loans and help when things get bad, and we would be in control."

That was as far as she got when he flipped her back and continued stroking. "Sorry, stupid idea. I thought I was being silly. Instead, I was being stupid. Won't ever happen again."

He took her over the top, and she came in delightful convulsions. She could feel him inside her as well. She just held on to him as he finished and was pulling away. "Stay for just a second more. It is the only time we are like one person. Give me just a second more."

He held her to him. He felt the same way. Maybe that was how Standing Bear had felt for just a second—one person. That was what he wanted back. Well, he was never going to have it again. He rolled off her, and they went to sleep, and she hoped tomorrow went well, but she was sure it wasn't going to end well for Ellen. She had lost her love her one more second and Morgan was going to find out why.

They had two wagons and ten men when they started out just after sunrise, and they headed to town. They had several blankets and boxes for loading her things into, as well as a tarp for a body. When they got to town, they found the banker was in jail. It seemed he had tried to make a run for it during the night, and Miles's men had stopped him. The sheriff had arrested him and put him in jail. He had a large suitcase with him and in it a large amount of money and deeds to several ranches and farms.

Gary Lee was looking over them now, and the judge was on the way to look at them as well. It seemed it wasn't that hard to own a bank. They just needed someone competent to run it, so Morgan and Miles asked Gary if he was interested in the job. He told him they could contact his friends in Dallas and see if they would be interested in coming up here and helping him with the bookkeeping. James was thinking it over.

Morgan went over to the hotel and got Ellen and put her in a wagon with Mary Jean, who was going as well. Everyone was afraid this was not going to be a good day for this lady. They headed out to the ranch. It was about an hour's ride, so the women talked to each other while they rode. Morgan was on her Appaloosa Thunder, and she was carrying her Sharps rifle in her scabbard.

Raphael asked Miles, "Why?"

"If this man is dead, someone killed him, and we don't know why. She is just prepared. Watch your backs, all of you." Raphael noticed Miles was also carrying his Winchester.

As they got closer to the ranch, Miles noticed a horse in the corral. He turned around in the saddle and asked Ellen, "Is anybody supposed to be out here besides us today?"

She shook her head.

Miles told Ellen and Mary Jean to stay with the wagon till they could check it out, and then he turned to Morgan and started to say something, and she just said, "Save your breath. I am coming. Let's go. This was my idea from the start. Get moving. Just be careful. Four of you men, stay here with them."

They walked up slowly to the house. Raphael opened the gate, and they went through the fence. They were on the blind side of the house where there were no windows. Miles split the men, half in front and half out back.

Miles and Morgan went up front and carefully went to the front door. When she started to open it, Miles heard something and pulled her back, and the door exploded from a shotgun blast. Then they heard a door open at the back and some fighting, and then her men brought a man around the front. It was the man from yesterday whom she bought the Sharps from. He had just tried to kill her.

"Damn, I was hoping I got you. That captain said you were a bitch, and he was right."

Morgan just looked at him. "You have no idea how right he was. Now how are you involved in this? Did you kill her husband? Where is he?"

He just looked at her. "Why should I tell you anything? It is just going to get me hanged anyway, but I am going to tell them all about who your son's family is, and that ought to get the town talking. I am going to keep my mouth shut till it matters."

She just looked at him. He had her, and he knew it, and there wasn't anything she could do about it right now. She turned around and walked away from him, and another shot rang out. She started to duck, but the man beside her fell, a hole right in the middle of his chest. She turned and looked up on the hill and saw a rifle glint and a flash of blond hair. No one else saw as he disappeared, and Miles grabbed her and threw her to the ground. It was Shawn, Gregory's uncle. He was protecting Gregory from this man and his mouth and his own family from ever finding him.

Raphael asked, "Who was that?"

Miles answered, "Don't know. Maybe one of his men getting even about something before they left, but it seems they are gone now. Let's load him up and see what's in the house that he was after."

As the men loaded the body up, Morgan walked to the other side of the house where she couldn't be seen and waited. He stood up, and she took off her hat and waved it side to side. Then he did the same, and then he turned and left. Miles had been watching as well as soon as she walked away. Shawn did what he knew she couldn't do to protect Gregory as one last gift.

Miles never said a word about what he saw that day. Shawn didn't know it, but before Morgan would let him ruin Gregory's reputation, he would have had an accident. Miles knew his wife too well. She would have protected her son or Miles would have.

They went into the house as the men brought the women up to the ranch house. Inside was a map partially folded. He was trying to get it and some other papers out of here before they got here. As they spread the map out, they figured out what all this was about.

"Look at the marking on the map, Miles. He had bought property from Hereford to Canyon to Amarillo. All along the watershed. He was trying to get all the water rights. If he had dammed anywhere along the way, we would have had to pay for our water. He would have been a millionaire. So what are a few murders along the way? Look here. There is a canyon south of here marked, and there is nothing there. Why would he mark that?"

She looked at Miles, and he said, "Maybe something else is there. Let's try looking for his body there first."

They gathered up the paperwork and helped the ladies get started and left several men with them, especially since they had been shot at. They put the body in the barn and started out to the spot marked on the map. It took about an hour, but when they got there, it didn't take them long to find what they were looking for.

He had been covered in snow, but the snow was melting now, and the critters were getting to him. Trey and Raphael went down the side of the incline using ropes and brought his frozen body back up. When they got him back up, some of the other men didn't want her to see the body. They didn't know she had seen much worse, so she moved them aside and cut open his shirt. She could see the bullet that hit him went in the back and left a little hole, but when she turned him over, it had come out through very large hole. That man had used the Sharps to kill him, and he had never even known. He was dead before he hit the ground. But where was his horse? Either that other man killed him, sold him, or someone else had the horse. She was going to see that Ellen got him back.

"Wrap him in the tarp. I don't want her to see him like this."

"She will have to identify him, Morgan. None of us knew him well enough to say it is him."

She thought a minute and then told them, "Wrap all his body so she can't see that. Just leave his head so she can identify him. She doesn't need to see all the rest."

"Someone is going to have to tell her what happened."

"Telling someone and seeing it is two different things. Just do as I tell you."

They did. They wrapped the body and left his head so they could just pull the tarp back so she could see it.

They headed back to the ranch house, and Morgan held back and rode up next to Raphael so she could talk to him. "Well, what do you think of this place? Do you think it is something you and Mary Jean would like?"

"You mean with the dead bodies and the men getting shot in front of you? Morgan, has anybody ever told you that you are one strange lady?"

She leaned her head to the side and said, "Almost daily. So what do you think?"

"I am glad you are on my side. I love it. We will have to see what Mary Jean says, but I think we want it."

Morgan just smiled, and Raphael was grinning. Miles was a lucky man.

When they got back to the ranch, Morgan wasn't looking forward to this part of the day, but it had to be done. When they got there, Ellen was waiting on the porch, and as they got close, she came down to the wagon.

"Is my husband in there?"

Morgan got off her horse and stood beside her. "We think so, honey, but we didn't know him well enough to be sure. When you are ready, we will let you look."

She nodded, and Morgan just pulled back the tarp a little to let her just see his face, and then she put it back down after Ellen nodded. Then she and one of the men helped hold her up and then sat her down on the porch.

"What happened to him? Was it an accident?" She looked up at Morgan as Morgan looked at the men.

"No, that man from this morning shot him for your ranch and the water rights as near as we can tell, and you are not the only ones. The other ladies land as well."

"All this just for water? They ruined our lives for water?" How do you explain? It was just plain greed.

She began to cry, and Morgan just held her. That was enough for today. *Now we bury the dead and sort out what is left.*

They gathered up what they had, and as they brought out the dead man, Morgan asked, "Is this your husband's horse?"

She shook her head.

There were no horses or cattle left on this ranch. Where had that horse gone, or who had ridden it off this ranch? She wondered who else was involved in this mess.

When she got back to town, she was met at the bank by Gary. She got down, and Miles sent the men on ahead. He told Trey to take care of the body and not to let Ellen see any more and tell the undertaker to send the bill to him.

Gary was having a fit, as was the judge. "Morgan, this is as big a mess as Dallas. I have already sent a telegraph to James and asked him to come. He was embezzling big time."

"Do we have any money left, or are we broke?"

"He was smart enough not to touch too much of your money, but he got into the girls' accounts and a lot of little accounts. The judge has already put a judgment against his house, and the sale of it will help replace a lot of the money, but people around here are not going to be able to make mortgage payments or even pay for groceries. He has left some of them with next to nothing."

"Groceries, we can take care of right now. Start a line of credit for anyone who needs it at the general store. After all family owns it I will take care of that. Can we do anything about the mortgages?"

"You said something about buying the bank were you serious? If you were, you could offer extensions until we get this mess straightened out and his house sold and the money replaced?"

Morgan looked at Miles. "What do you think?"

"Will it bankrupt us? We may need to expand our house."

She smiled at him. "No, you will still have plenty of money. The girls will be short for a few months that is all."

"We can cover anything they need until this is straightened out. What about the banker? Will he stay in jail?"

The judge spoke up and said, "He isn't going anywhere except to the federal prison."

Morgan looked at Miles. "Well, looks like we just bought ourselves a bank, one in trouble no less."

CHAPTER 13

James and Francis moved to Amarillo and bought the banker's house. Seemed they had made enough money in Dallas straightening out that fiasco that they could afford it. The banker had been spending lavishly with the banks money, and they got the house and all the furnishing for a song. Now they worked for the town and the bank, and they had plenty of clients, as did Gary. He and Shelbee had a new baby boy as well, she had started to talk to her brother through letters and they seemed to be mending their relationship. Justin seemed to have turned over a new leaf, and he and Mary Jo were very happy. Shelbee hadn't seen him face to face yet but time would tell.

Then one morning, Morgan got a telegram from Mary Jo, one she wasn't expecting.

Morgan, he is dead. Standing Bear is dead. STOP
Little Deer sent word with some women who he sent down the mountain. STOP
She won't come down. She won't leave. They are starving. STOP
Justin sending meat up with scouts for remaining women and children. STOP
What do I do now? Mary Jo. STOP

She sat at the table, rereading it until Miles came in and sat down beside her, and then he took it out of her hands, and he read it as well.

He looked at her. "You can't go up there. You promised Gregory you wouldn't. You promised, and he wouldn't forgive you if you broke this one."

"I know, but she will stay up there and starve unless someone goes and drags her down. I know her, and she will do just that. She will let him die before she lets me have Little Fox."

"Why would she put her children at risk?"

"Because she doesn't see any other way out except a reservation, and they are hellholes at best. She would rather see the children dead."

"What other option is there, Morgan?"

She turned and looked at him, and he already knew. Why did he even have to ask? He already knew the answer.

"There is here. She could come here. He isn't alive. He is no longer a threat, and she never was a threat. They could come here and live."

"How are you going to get her down?"

About that time, they heard a baby crying. She turned, and Raphael and Trey were at the door. They had been listening to their conversation as well. They all turned, and Jackson was riding up the road. He had Mathew in his arms, and he was screaming. He was hungry, and Morgan got chills.

She went running out the door and grabbed the baby and asked Jackson, "Where is Abigail?"

"She is sleeping. She won't wake up, so I covered her up good and brought the baby up here so someone could feed him."

Trey and Raphael both got on their horses and were gone while Miles helped Jackson in the house. He seemed to be in some kind of trance. Morgan took the baby to the fireplace and warmed him while she fed him and then went to the window. When she got him calmed down, she looked down at the house and watched as both men came out of the house crying. They looked up at the house, and they knew she could see them, and they shook their heads and waved their hats. Abigail had finally lost her battle. No more headaches. Now Morgan would keep her promise.

Trey went to tell Sheri her sister was dead, and Raphael came back to the house. Morgan took him aside as she held Mathew.

"She is just lying in bed. She is barely cold. She must have just died. He covered her up, got the baby, got on a horse, and came up here."

"Go get Aunt Martha Jean and Mary Jean. They will help Sheri take care of her and see how they want the funeral handled."

"What about that?" He pointed to the telegram.

"I don't know yet, but I am going to have to send a telegraph to Mary Jo. She is Jackson's sister, but she won't have time to get here. Just go take care of what has to be done right now. I will talk to Aunt Martha Jean when she gets here."

The next two days were a blur. The weather was not cooperating. It was freezing cold. They even had trouble digging a grave. There was no way that Mary Jo could get here in time. It was at least a four- or five-day trip. The adults gathered around the casket and said farewell. They didn't even let the children come, and two of the women had to stay for the babies. The wind was screaming, and it began to snow, but Morgan just wouldn't leave. Finally, Miles picked her up and put her in the surrey, and they were the last to leave. She didn't talk all the way home, and Miles was beginning to worry about her.

When she got home, there was a letter from Mary Jo, so she sat down to read it. She already had an idea what it said.

Morgan,

Please tell me what to do. Justin just came back from the camp, and even he couldn't believe how bad it was. The women who came down off the mountain were little more than skeletons, but he said when he got up there, it was worse. They gave them food, and he plans on taking more to them, but they can't last much longer. He says there are tepees full of bodies of women and children. Little Deer is staying, trying to talk Still Water into coming down but with little success. She says there is nowhere to go. Tell me how to make her come down. We don't know about Little Fox. She won't let anybody inside her tepee.

Mary Jo

"You might as well read it to them and tell them your idea. I will go and get Still Water if you will tell me how I am supposed to get her off that mountain when nobody else has been able to."

"Just like you did with me today. You pick her up and put her on a horse and bring her down and tell her you are bringing her and the children to me. If she won't come, you find Little Fox and bring him home to me."

The whole room got quiet.

"How many do I bring home with me Morgan?"

"According to this, there aren't many left, a few women and children and Little Deer and maybe less than that when you get there, and if you don't want to do it, I will. I will not leave Little Fox up there to die. He is mine." She was getting mad now with Abigail's death and this letter. She felt helpless, and she wanted to do something.

"You promised Gregory you wouldn't go."

"I promised to keep Abigail's family together after she was gone, but I won't let everyone die on that mountain either. Somebody has to help them."

Raphael said, "I will go with you. I speak Comanche, and Trey was a scout for the army. He could help us."

Sheri began to say no to Trey, "You can't leave me now. You don't know what it is like to lose a sister."

Morgan looked at him as if to say, "You still haven't told her."

"Sheri, come with me. I need to talk to you in private."

They went back to the back room, and when they came back in the front room, Sheri looked stunned. She had always thought Trey was so cold and aloof, and now she knew why he was broken, and maybe this would help. She looked at Morgan. She had known all along and never told her, and Abigail had trusted her too. Maybe this was the right thing for him to do.

They started out the next morning after Morgan sent a telegraph to Mary Jo, telling them they were coming. She told her to try to keep them alive until they got there and to have some wagons waiting to bring them home in. The telegraph operator commented about her bringing more Indians home to her land. He didn't think it was right. She reminded him she had extended his loan this month, didn't she? He shut up.

It was a long, cold ride. The weather was getting worse as they got higher in the mountains, but Justin was waiting for them at the station.

He had horses and pack animals loaded with food, warm coats, blankets, and anything else he thought they might need. He was going with them. It was a two-day trip up the mountain. Halfway up, they would have to stop and rest and camp then make the other half of the trip the next day.

Miles asked, "How are Still Water and her children doing?"

Justin looked at him. "I don't know. I have never seen the woman or her children. I have just seen Little Deer. He speaks a little English. She won't come out. I have no idea if she is even still alive, but if she wasn't, I think Little Deer would take his family down. I think he only stays because of her. I really think he was hoping Morgan would come when Standing Bear died. How are you going to get her to go with you?"

"Morgan said to pick her up, put her on a horse, and tell her I am taking her home to Morgan."

"Is that what you are doing?"

"Yes."

"What about the rest of them?"

"All of them if they want to come."

"Let's get some rest. It is still a long trip tomorrow, and I have got to see you get this woman on a horse."

They broke camp early in the morning and were on their way. They could smell the camp long before they got to it. The smell of death was everywhere.

Justin just looked at Miles. "We are almost there. There are tepees full of bodies."

When they arrived at the camp, Little Deer was the first out, and he looked at Miles first and said, "You are Running Knife's man, aren't you?"

Miles just nodded.

"I remember you from the camp. She didn't come?"

"She promised our son she would never set foot out of Texas again, so I came."

"She won't leave with you."

"She will. You all will. We are going home to Morgan. Start packing your things. We are going to Texas."

"We are going to your home, Running Knife's home, in Texas? All of us?"

"All who want to come? We would like you to come live with us. We will make a home for you, not a reservation, a home. Where is she?"

He pointed to a tepee, and Miles started toward it with Raphael close behind as Little Deer and Trey started getting the others gathered up and moving. Trey and Little Deer went from one tepee to the next and got the packing started, but some could barely move. If Justin hadn't been bringing food, they would have all been dead by now.

There was one last tepee, and Little Deer said there was no one left alive in that one. It was of some white women who had been captured and left when the braves who captured them were killed, and they had all died, so they just left them in the tepee. Trey went to check anyway. He didn't know why. He just did.

The smell was awful. He pulled back the opening and saw a woman and her dead child in the corner and another dead woman. He started to leave when he noticed movement, and a small blond- haired, blue-eyed little girl came out from behind the dead woman's back. She couldn't have been more than three years old, and she was filthy and starving. He went over and picked her up, and she went to him and just looked at him, never saying a word. He checked the tepee, but there was no one else. She was all that was alive. He took her out into the sunlight, and she covered her eyes. She hadn't been outside in days. Her mother had kept her hidden, probably afraid they would kill her.

Little Deer saw him with the little girl. He hadn't realized she was in there. He went to take her from Trey, and Trey told him, "She is mine now. I will take care of her," and he never let her go again. He had found his Ann, finally.

As he was walking back to the others, Raphael saw that he was smiling. He had never seen this man smile in the whole time he had known him. It was like he had been reborn. He would have to find out the whole story later from Miles. It must be a good one.

He and Miles opened Standing Bear's tepee, and a little boy was there trying to protect Still Water and his little sister. Miles just went inside a little and got down on one knee, and Little Deer was going to talk for him when Still Water said, "You are Miles, Morgan's husband, aren't you?"

He looked at her and smiled and said, "How did you know who I was?"

She never moved. He didn't know if she could; she was so thin and weak. "I remembered you a little and she described you and your blue eyes. You couldn't be anyone else. She didn't come with you?"

"She promised our son she would never leave Texas again when she got back, so I came to get you, and I am going to. She told me if I have to hogtie you and put you on a horse in front of me, you are coming home to her, and that is that."

"What about all the others here? I can't leave them I promised Standing Bear." The tears started to slowly fall down her face.

"Anyone who wants to come can come with us. Morgan is getting a building ready until we can get permanent places ready for all of you. There are wagons waiting at the bottom of the mountain. Justin is the husband of Morgan's cousin, and he is the one who has been bringing food to you. She sent her with word to supply your people when she came back after she married him. She made sure you weren't starving up here. She was worried about you, and she knew you wouldn't ask for help."

"How did she know about Standing Bear?"

"Little Deer sent word down with some of the other women. He knew someone was talking to her about what was going on up here, and she sent me to come get you. If I don't bring you down, she will break her promise and come get you herself, and there will be hell to pay. Now you don't want that, do you?"

He just smiled at her, and she smiled back. He was trying to flatter her into coming.

A little boy walked out of the shadows, and he recognized him instantly with those blue eyes and the necklace with the silver half-moon Concho on it.

Raphael asked him, "This is Little Fox, the boy she sent us after?"

She said something to the little boy, and he went over to the side of the tepee and pulled up a hide and then brought something to Miles. It was a knife and a medicine bag—they were both Morgan's —and he handed them to him. Miles nodded and took the knife and looked at Still Water.

"He wore the medicine bag till the day he died."

He put the knife in his boot, but he undid the knot in the medicine bag and tied it around the little boy's neck and then had Raphael tell him it was his now. The little boy just looked at it and then at Still Water, and she nodded, and the little boy smiled. He didn't quite understand what was going on, but he had always watched his father wear that bag, and now it was his, and that was all he understood.

"What else do you want out of here? We are going to be leaving soon so we can camp halfway down the mountain before the sun sets."

She just looked at him. "There is nothing left but memories and most of them we are going too. They are with Morgan. Can you help me stand?"

He did more than that. As she wrapped the baby, he picked her up and carried her out and into the sunlight and toward a waiting horse.

"Can you ride with the baby, or do I need to ride behind you?"

"I am fine, but Little Fox can't ride alone."

Miles already had that taken care of. He had wrapped the boy in a clean blanket and sat him on his horse and then helped the others get everyone on a horse, and then he was going to get up behind Little Fox. He had almost forgotten Morgan's final instructions, and then he looked at the men.

They all got down, even Trey, and it was all he could do to leave that little girl, but he did. They each reached into the fire, lit a torch, went from one tepee to another, lit them, got back on their horses, and watched.

"Morgan told you to do that, didn't she?"

"No. Running Knife said to burn it to the ground. It was the end of the Comanche nation on this mountain, and it deserved a proper funeral."

Raphael translated, and they watched for a minute. Then they all turned and started down the mountain. The Comanche were done. The Sioux weren't through yet, but General Custer was going to bring their world to a crashing finish soon as well as his own.

Several hours later, they stopped. Everyone was tired, and they needed to get the children fed and rested for tomorrow. The men they had left down here had food and water waiting for them. The women washed their children, and Justin had brought clean clothes for them and clean dresses for the women. The men had made cornbread and a large pot of venison stew; it was thin enough for the children to eat as well. Not fancy, but these people had been eating Lord-knows-what, and they were thankful for anything.

When everybody was full and lay down for the night, Miles had made sure everyone was warm and had enough blankets. Still Water was close to him. He didn't want her going back up that mountain. He finally settled down for the night.

It was a little while later when he felt someone crawl onto his blanket with him, and it took a second to realize it was Little Fox. He looked over at Still Water, and she had seen what he had done, and Miles just kind of nodded, *Is it all right?* And she nodded. He had missed his father so badly, and it seemed, since today and the medicine bag, he had taken Miles as his own. Miles just pulled him closer and covered him up, and they went to sleep. After all, Morgan had been responsible for saving the boy's life and raising him for a while. He guessed he was partially his.

The little boy turned over and asked him something in Comanche, and Raphael had to translate.

"He wants to know, 'Are you taking us home to Running Knife?'"

Miles looked down at the little boy and answered him, "Yes, we are going home to Running Knife. Is that all right?"

The little boy just shook his head and then said, "Standing Bear said she would come for me." And then he went to sleep.

They loaded up in the morning, and Still Water was looking a little better. At least she could walk better. They fed them breakfast, and then they started down the rest of the mountain. Miles wanted to be down before the sunset so they could be at Justin's ranch and spend the night there. They could rest a day there and then start the journey home from the ranch. It all went well, and they did make the ranch, and Mary Jo was waiting for them with plenty of food and baths for everyone. She must have hired every maid in town to get everything done. She also had more clothes for children and more for the women. She couldn't wait to meet Still Water, and she had a telegram from Morgan. She wanted one sent back to her as soon as they were safe.

Little Deer had commented to Raphael that it must run in the family because Mary Jo reminded him of Morgan. He asked him if his wife was like the two of them.

He looked at him and told him, "My wife is her twin, so yes, they are very much alike, but I wouldn't trade her for anything because the whole family is like that, but Morgan is unlike any woman I have ever known."

They ate and rested for all of the next day, and they were beginning to look like people again instead of walking dead. Miles had sent a telegram to Morgan about their trip and that Trey had found the little girl and that she had better talk to Sheri about it because he wasn't giving this child up. He wasn't calling her Ann, but he might as well be, so he asked for her to talk to Sheri and explain what was going on before they got there. He also told her Little Fox had kind of adopted him as a father, and he didn't quite know what to do about that, so he was going with it. He wasn't sure Still Water was all right with it, so he thought there was something else going on.

When they left, Mary Jo took Justin aside and asked him if there was anything else they could do for the Indians on the reservations. He told her that most of the people around here didn't want him doing what he had already done for them. He told her they were going to the governor's ball in a week, and he would talk to the governor about it then.

She looked up at her husband and asked him, "What if you can't get any satisfaction from him about it?"

"Well, I guess I could always run for governor." He said it half-kidding until he looked down at his wife's face.

"You would make a good governor, even if it was for a small state like Colorado."

He looked at her, and she wasn't kidding.

"You could get something done around here because this governor isn't doing much for the Indians right now, and you could."

The next day, they, Miles, and his men started to Texas, and it was still a long way to get there, but they took their time. They avoided as many big towns as they could and stayed outside towns at night because they weren't welcome. It took seven days to get to the ranch, and it was almost dark when they began to come in. Trey and Raphael got there first, and the wagons were coming in behind. Trey had a pretty little girl in front of him, and Sheri met him outside and took the little girl from him when he rode up.

Trey got down off the saddle, and he told her, "I don't know her name. She won't talk, but I thought we might keep her. She doesn't have anybody else."

Morgan and Sheri had already talked. She had told her everything, and she had already decided to do whatever Trey wanted to make him happy. She hadn't ever really seen him happy, and right now, he was smiling.

Miles rode in front of the wagons with Little Fox in the saddle in front of him, and he launched himself out of the saddle into Morgan's arms, and she caught him. He remembered her after all. She got down on her knees and just held him. Miles had telegraphed her he was alive. He was Still Water's son, but Standing Bear had always wanted him to be Morgan's, and she always felt like he was supposed to be her son. She leaned back and looked at him, and he was so skinny. Then he reached for the medicine bag around his neck and started to take it off and give it to her.

She stopped him and told him. "No, now it is yours. I will teach you how to find the herbs for it and teach you how to be a medicine man." He still had on the necklace she had made for him before she left. And then she hugged him again. She didn't know how they were going to handle this situation, but they would figure it out. He was here and alive.

Gregory was walking toward them, and she took his hand and introduced him to Little Fox and then took both boys' hands and asked Little Fox, "Where is Still Water?"

He pointed to the wagon coming up the drive, so she took the boys' hands, and they walked back to the wagon and went to the back of it, and out came Still Water with her baby girl. Morgan reached for the little girl, and Still Water was reluctant to let her hold her, and Morgan knew they had a problem. She was jealous of her and Little Fox, so she backed away, and Miles helped her out.

She just looked around, and she asked her, "Where are we to stay? In the barn?"

"No, you are to stay in my home. You let me stay in yours." She smiled at her.

"You really didn't have a choice, did you?"

"Shall we stand out here and fight, or would you rather go inside and fight? It is warmer in there."

She finally got a smile out of Still Water. Everybody was just watching them. They didn't understand they were enemies before this. Being friends was still new to them.

"Warmer would be better, and then the children could play while we fight."

Morgan nodded. "And we could feed them as well."

"Even better."

So they walked inside with the children while they talked in Comanche, and no one knew if they were fighting or not, so they just stood there and stared at them.

Little Deer walked up beside the men and asked, "Where do you want the rest of us to go for the night?"

Miles turned and looked at them, kind of dumbfounded, and led them to the back of the house, where Morgan had set up makeshift housing for them in the new barn. It was warm and cozy with a place for fires and bedding until tomorrow when she had more permanent housing set up.

When they got inside, Mathew was screaming again, ever since his mother died no one seemed to make him happy. He was always crying. No amount of feeding, rocking or walking would make him happy. Only Jackson could calm him, and when he was at work, they were all trying to take care of him with little luck.

Morgan got everyone settled, and then she was taking her turn at walking when Still Water came in and asked what was wrong. Morgan tried to explain, but the baby was screaming. Still Water took him and started walking him, and he began to calm down. Then she began to chant to him, and he got quiet. She finally sat down in the rocker, and he fell asleep as she rocked him and chanted. Morgan understood what she was saying, but no one else did. She was saying a prayer for the dead.

Jackson came rushing in because he knew the women were having trouble with his son, only to see an Indian woman rocking his sleeping child for the first time in weeks. He just walked over to Still Water and sat down beside her and watched her and his son. He seemed to be getting some kind of peace from what she was doing too. Before long, he was asleep with his head by the fireplace.

Morgan covered him with a blanket and let him sleep for a while as well. Morgan smiled as Still Water rocked and chanted, and both of them slept for the first time in days. Morgan told everybody else to go to bed. She would take care of this. As she found Gregory and Little Fox in the same room, they had already fallen asleep on his bed.

She found out the next day that the name of Still Water's little girl was Blue Cloud, and she was lovely. She looked like her mother, and she was so quiet, but Mathew wasn't, and he didn't want anyone but Still Water to touch him. Jackson finally asked her if she would be his wet nurse. Still Water agreed. It wasn't any more trouble to take care of him and Blue Cloud, and it made her feel useful around here and made her feel like she belonged.

They still had a problem with Little Fox. He went to Morgan more than he did to Still Water, and it still made her mad. Standing Bear had always made a point of making Morgan the one he went to at the village, and Still Water had never been his mother figure, even when he died. Now that they were here with Miles in the mix, it was even worse. He wanted Miles for a father, and he was shutting her out even more.

She had housing for the other Indians with the women she had brought before, and everyone was getting settled. The only problem she had was when they tried to butcher one of her Hereford bulls, and that caused quite a stir. When she got everybody calmed down, she explained those funny-looking cattle were special, and she would make sure there were some longhorns available for them to butcher. After that, they seemed to be finding a permanent home at the end of the canyon.

Jackson was depending on Still Water more and more for Mathew, and he seemed to be becoming very fond of her. She was a very pretty woman and always had been. Jackson was lonely, and so was she, and now she was safe. He didn't care that she was Indian. He had been living around Indians for years. It seemed they were falling in love.

The only problem was Little Fox didn't want to live with them. He had another family in mind. Jackson's mother Martha Jean was getting to where she needed help at the other ranch since Raphael and Mary Jean moved to their new ranch, and Jackson and Still Water decided to move in with her and help out. The only problem was it was not within walking distance from Morgan's ranch, and Little Fox hated that.

It was Easter Sunday, and they were all at lunch at her house, and Jackson was talking to Morgan about Little Fox. "Morgan, he is miserable with us, and we don't know what to do. He won't listen to his mother. He tells her you are his mother. His father says so. He has left the house several times to come here."

"So let him come here and live with me. Standing Bear wanted me to raise him. Let me. You are not that far away. Soon, I will have a horse for him, and he can come and see her. She has her baby and yours, and you two are talking about marriage. Let me have him. Talk to her about it."

"She loves him, and she has raised him most of his life."

He was called to the barn to look at a mare that was in foal, and Still Water was getting ready to leave when Little Fox started to go to Gregory's room, and she yanked his arm and knocked him down. Morgan saw what she did, as well as most of the women in the room, and then she hit him in the back of the head and called him a name in Comanche. The other women didn't understand, but Morgan did, and she was on her feet and went after her. She was talking in Comanche, and they couldn't understand, but there was no denying they were ready to kill each other. Raphael came into the room and started to translate to Miles.

"What did she say to the boy?"

"She called him a half-breed and no child of hers." By now, they were screaming in English.

"If you don't want him so badly, let me have him."

"No, don't you know that I know that the only reason you sent somebody after us is so you could get him?"

"I sent somebody after you all. I could have sent someone after just him and left everyone else up there to starve, but I didn't. Why did you marry Standing Bear anyway? You have never wanted Little Fox."

"It was the only way I could get him after his wife died. He needed a wet nurse, and then he wanted me until you came along. His first wife was white. He had captured her from a ranch, but she was such a puny little thing. She barely made it through childbirth. But you are a different story. You never give up. I was hoping you would take him with you when you left and you would both die on the way down the mountain and I would be done with you both."

"So that is it? You won't let me have him just so you can torment me?"

Still Water smiled, and Morgan went after her. She grabbed her by the neck and pushed her up against the wall, much like she had done Justin. The women and Raphael and Miles were trying to get her off her when Jackson came back in.

Jackson said, "Morgan, what is going on? She is no match for you. Get off of her."

"She doesn't even want Little Fox. I do. Figure it out. He is mine. Standing Bear wanted it that way, and she is hurting him. Fix it, Jackson, or I will."

"I will see to this. We need to go. This storm is getting worse. I will talk to you later." He looked at Still Water and then at Little Fox, and they walked out the door. Little Fox wouldn't even look up at him, and his mother Martha Jean was furious. He hadn't heard what had happened but his mother had.

Once outside, he got Still Water and his mother in the surrey and asked her, "Is she telling me the truth? Did you hurt him?"

She wouldn't look at him. She looked straight ahead. He got in beside her, and they went home. He would ask his mother when they got home, and he wasn't going to like the answers he was going to get or the story he heard.

Miles came to her and told her, "You have to calm down. Martha Jean can tell Jackson what she said, and then he will understand he belongs with you."

"All right I will give it a day or two, and then we will go at this again when I don't want to kill her in front of him."

He shook his head and walked away, and they started to clean up the dinner dishes. Nothing else was said until a day later.

A winter storm, a late one, showed up. They sometimes do on the panhandle, and sometimes they are monsters. This one was. It had started to snow. The wind was howling, and the snow was already drifting.

Suddenly, there was pounding on the door. It was Jackson.

"You were right. She admitted to hitting him and just keeping him to make you mad."

"He is gone. We can't find him anywhere. He said he wanted to live with you. Standing Bear told him to go home, and then we couldn't find him. We have looked everywhere."

Morgan was already grabbing coats as Gregory was behind her, crying. As she began to pull on her coat, something fell out of the inside of the coat. She reached down, and it was a silver half-moon Concho.

Miles just looked at her. "Where did that come from? You have had that coat on a hundred times since you came back."

She just looked at him and shook her head. "Maybe somebody is trying to tell me something."

"Mama, he will freeze out there."

She turned around and got down on one knee. "You look at me. I will find him and bring him home. I won't let him freeze any more than I would let you freeze. You look after your sister, and I will be back. Mama Ruby, see that one of the women feeds Justine. I have got to go. Jackson, you and Miles start back to your house, and I will go south. If anyone finds him, fire two shots and then get inside somewhere. Does your old house have any food left in it? If he gets lost, he might be going there."

"Yes, and there is some firewood as well."

"Good. If I find him, don't come looking for us. Just get to safety, and I will too. When this storm quits, we will meet up. Let's go."

They headed to the barn and got horses and headed out in different directions. The snow was blowing so hard, you couldn't see in front of your face. She had her hat tied down with a scarf and had that covering her face. There were drifts everywhere. If he had fallen or lain down, she would never find him.

Little Fox had pants and a coat on when he left and had started to Morgan's house. Still Water wouldn't listen to him, but he wanted to live with Morgan and always had. He kept walking, but he was getting so cold and couldn't see anymore, and he didn't know if he was going in the right direction. He thought if he just sat down for a few minutes and rested, then he could start again, but he thought he saw his father pointing at something, so he kept walking, and then he heard someone screaming his name.

Suddenly, out of the snow came a horse. It was Morgan's spotted horse. She grabbed his arm, pulled him up in front of her, and put him inside her coat. His face was in her chest, and she was warm. She wrapped her coat around him, and they were running. He just closed his eyes and lay against her warm skin. He heard two shots, but he didn't care. He was warm.

She was headed to his old house. When she got there, she put her horse in the little barn. She laid him down and wrapped him in her coat. She quickly unsaddled her horse, took off his bridle, threw down some hay, enough for a couple of days, grabbed Little Fox, shut the doors, and went inside. She laid him down in front of the fireplace and grabbed some wood and started a fire. While she was still dressed, she went back outside and brought all the wood there was inside and then shut the doors.

She dragged the mattress from one of the beds to the fireplace and pushed it close, and then she took off almost all her clothes except her chemise and underwear and hung them by the fireplace. She then undressed Little Fox, put him on the mattress with her, put him as close to her as possible, pulled every blanket and quilt she could find left in the house on top of them, and started to rub his skin. He hadn't said a word since she had grabbed him, and she started praying, swearing anything to anybody. She was even asking Standing Bear for help.

"Damn it, you sent him out in the cold looking for me. Are you trying to kill him? Well, now I have him, and I am not giving him up again, so help me save him, you idiot."

She rubbed and rubbed until he began to warm up, and then he looked up at her, and she was crying.

He reached up and touched her face. "Are you mad at me?"

He was talking to her, and she could barely breathe; she was so happy. "Of course I am. You scared me to death. What in the world were you thinking going out in this weather?"

He was crying as he said. "I heard you calling me, saying, 'Come home,' so I started walking, but I got lost in the snow. Standing Bear kept pointing, so I kept walking, and then you were there, and you saved me. Will you take me home with you now?"

So Standing Bear was there. If he wasn't already dead, she would kill him. "When the snow stops, we will go home, and you will stay there with me and the rest of the family. I think that is what your father wanted."

He snuggled against her and went to sleep. And she said into the darkness around her, "All right, you win. He is mine, one way or another Standing Bear, you can rest now. It is settled. No one will take him from me ever again."

It was another day before they could get to them, so they ate canned peaches and whatever they could find left in the pantry, but they had enough wood to stay warm. When they got back to the ranch, Jackson and Still Water had a talk with Morgan, and she told them what Little Fox had told her about why he had left—his father had told him to. Jackson wasn't convinced, but Still Water was, so she finally let go. Little Fox stayed to live with Morgan, and it was done. It didn't really matter what anybody else thought. She wasn't giving him up again, and she told Still Water that when they were alone. The look in Morgan's eyes settled the matter once and for all.

"Well, the boys can share for a while, but Justine is getting bigger, and Dona is planning on a summer wedding. I still think we need to start expanding this house. It is too small."

Miles looked at her. "Who else are you moving in here? We do need a little privacy. There is Mama Ruby and Ivy and . . . ?"

"Would you shut up, Miles? You were the one who wanted another child. Remember that night when we weren't being so quiet? Well, about summer this year, you might just have another son. I think we talked about naming one Grayson."

"Boys are nice, but girls aren't bad either. Guess we better get to expanding before you do."

"Well, thanks for reminding me."

He pushed her into their bedroom, and maybe he could coax out that little devil smile he so loved while Justine was still asleep. They could add on another wing for all he cared.

"Well, what are you waiting for? An engraved invitation?" She was already grinning.

Miles stopped and looked down the hall and he saw two Sharps rifles over the fireplace. One was Logan McKinney's and the other was White Clouds with the leather beaded scabbard on it. She had avenged both men she had called father. Now maybe she could live her own life and the scary woman could finally leave her in peace.